SO-ATO-095

The Speaker's Compact Handbook

Jo Sprague
San Jose State University

Douglas Stuart

THOMSON
—*—
WADSWORTH

Australia • Canada • Mexico • Singapore • Spain
United Kingdom • United States

THOMSON
WADSWORTH

Publisher: Holly J. Allen
Editor: Annie Mitchell
Senior Development Editor: Renée Deljon
Assistant Editor: Aarti Jayaraman
Editorial Assistant: Trina Enriquez
Senior Technology Project Manager: Jeanette Wiseman
Senior Marketing Manager: Kimberly Russell
Marketing Assistant: Andrew Keay
Advertising Project Manager: Shemika Britt
Project Manager, Editorial Production: Mary Noel
Art Director: Maria Epes
Print Buyer: Judy Inouye
Permissions Editor: Chelsea Junget
Production Service: Vicki Moran, Publishing Support Services
Copy Editor: Diane Ersepke
Text and Cover Designer: Lisa Devenish
Compositor: Stratford Publishing Services, Inc.
Printer: Transcontinental Printing/Louiseville

Printed in Canada
1 2 3 4 5 6 7 09 08 07 06 05

For more information about our products, contact us at
Thomson Learning Academic Resource Center
1-800-423-0563
For permission to use material from this text or product, submit a request online at http://www.thomsonrights.com.
Any additional questions about permissions can be submitted by e-mail to thomsonrights@thomson.com.

Thomson Higher Education
10 Davis Drive
Belmont, CA 94002-3098   USA

Asia (including India)
Thomson Learning
5 Shenton Way
#01-01 UIC Building
Singapore 068808

Canada
Thomson Nelson
1120 Birchmount Road
Toronto, Ontario M1K 5G4
Canada

Australia/New Zealand
Thomson Learning Australia
102 Dodds Street
Southbank, Victoria 3006
Australia

UK/Europe/Middle East/Africa
Thomson Learning
High Holborn House
50–51 Bedford Road
London WC1R 4LR
United Kingdom

Library of Congress Control Number: 2004116704
ISBN: 0-495-00006-X

6. Getting Your Ideas Across / 112

    22. Developing Informative Strategies / 113

    23. Developing Persuasive Strategies / 116

    24. Presenting Your Reasoning / 124

    25. Using Motivational Appeals / 130

    26. Establishing Credibility / 134

    27. Designing Presentation Aids / 137

7. Crafting Your Speech / 148

    28. Selecting Your Mode of Delivery / 149

    29. Using Language Effectively / 152

    30. Capturing Attention and Interest / 159

    31. Creating Effective Introductions and Conclusions / 161

    32. Linking Speech Components / 170

    33. Practicing Your Speech / 175

8. Presenting Your Speech / 183

    34. Achieving Effective Vocal Delivery / 184

    35. Achieving Effective Physical Delivery / 190

    36. Using Your Presentation Aids / 193

    37. Answering Questions / 196

Appendix A / 199

Appendix B / 210

Appendix C / 213

Index / 218

Using This Book

The Speaker's Compact Handbook provides a concise, usable, and portable resource for speakers. It's not coincidental that it shares these characteristics with its sister text, *The Speaker's Handbook*, the first handbook of its kind and now in its seventh edition. Even more concise and portable than our full handbook, *The Speaker's Compact Handbook* is appropriate for certain kinds of academic public speaking classes, the student who has to give an individual or group presentation in a class from any department, the beginning speaker who needs individual guidance in preparing for a particular kind of speaking situation, and the professional who wants a quick refresher on some basics while also picking up numerous pointers on topics such as the effective use of presentation software.

Why a *Handbook*

A handbook differs from a textbook in a few important ways.

- First, handbooks are brief: They present a distilled version of the most useful advice gleaned from centuries of academic research and decades of practical experience.

- Second, handbooks are reference books. They are not intended to be read from cover to cover, but are designed to help you locate what you need when you need it.

- Third, handbooks are *handy*. Quite literally, this compact edition fits in your hand. It's easy to keep on your desk or in your briefcase, coat pocket, or purse without adding weight or bulk.

Starting Out in This Book

To make the most efficient use of the *Speaker's Compact Handbook*, we recommend that you take a few minutes now to look it over. You will see that the inside front cover and first page give an overview of part and chapter titles and that the last page and inside back cover of the book give a more in-depth picture of the content of each chapter. Explore these chapters in any order that works for you (see the section How to Put Together a Speech, below, for the quickest approach to getting started on a speech); but here are two basic suggestions to help you begin using this book as effectively as possible.

1. *Take time to establish a foundation.* In the first four chapters (Part 1—Approaching Public Speaking), we pulled together those topics that give you ways of thinking about and beginning the task of preparing a speech. We suggest that you read these chapters before delving deeper into the book.

2. *Be prepared to always consider the context in which you will be speaking.* Before you go about selecting sections of the book to guide you, it is essential that you understand the expectations of your particular situation, be it the classroom, the workplace or the public arena. We suggest that you look at chapters 5 through 9 (Part 2, Tailoring Your Speech to Its Context), where you'll find sections that discuss which elements of speaking are most relevant in each of four general contexts.

How to Put Together a Speech

There are three important charts in this book that provide an easy reference to the basics of speech planning, creation, and organization.

- **The Five Steps of Public Speaking**, Figure 1-1, page 9. This figure lays out the elements that go into just about every speech and provides cross references to the chapters that deal with each element.

- **Speech Planning and Practice**, Figure 10-1, page 47. This timetable graphically demonstrates the relationships of the elements described in Figure 1-1 and shows where tasks overlap and ways for progressing through them.

- **Speech Structure Chart**, Figure 32-1, page 174. This chart shows the relationship of a speech's main points, subpoints, supporting materials, transitions, introductions and conclusions and how they flow together in a standard speech.

Other Features to Help You

Emphasis and Review Tools

- **Key points**. Throughout the text you will find Key Point boxes. These brief discussions highlight related ideas or information to consider or present helpful hints about, or a review of, the subject under discussion.

- **Checklists**. The checklists, which also appear in boxes throughout the text, provide a summary of steps that must be taken in a process, or a list of questions that must be asked to help define a situation or find a solution to a problem.

Appendixes

At the end of the book you'll find three supplemental sections for further reference:

- Appendix A, **Sample Speech and Outlines**. This appendix contains an example of a persuasive speech and the outline created during its development, as well as an example of an outline used to develop an informative speech.

- Appendix B, **Citation Guidelines**. Using the wrong word, mispronouncing it, or using bad grammar can distract your audience from your message. This appendix lists some common errors to watch out for.

- Appendix C, **Common Pronunciation and Usage Errors**. This appendix contains a sampling of citations for 13 types of print and nonprint sources. The samples model how you cite sources using APA and MLA style in a list of references or works cited, or a bibliography.

Remember, a handbook is a reference text, a resource that tells you how to do what you need to do when you're getting ready to do it, or are in the middle of doing it. This handbook, like all other handbooks, is therefore intended to be a lifelong tool. We hope you use it throughout your own life whenever you need or want to speak in public, and that it contributes to the success of your presentations.

Acknowledgments

For their helpful suggestions that influenced several important decisions during this book's development, we owe thanks to these dedicated public speaking teachers:

Mark Banks, *Slippery Rock University*

Mary Haslerud Opp, *University of North Dakota*

Mark Hovind, *Clayton College and State University*

Approaching Public Speaking

CHAPTER 1. Understanding Public Speaking

Understand that public speaking is the act of creating meaning with your listeners, and approach your role as a speaker by consciously combining communicative resources you already have at hand.

CHAPTER 2. Listening

Develop your skills as a listener to enhance your own speaking and to meet your obligations as an audience member.

CHAPTER 3. Speaking Ethically

Commit yourself to a set of ethical principles that will guide you as a public speaker.

CHAPTER 4. Overcoming Fear of Speaking

Understand, analyze, and accept your fear of speaking. Combine thorough preparation with relaxation and visualization techniques to increase your confidence.

CHAPTER 1

Understanding Public Speaking

Giving a speech is never a simple act. There are dozens—or perhaps hundreds—of decisions to make. This daunting task becomes more manageable, though, if you approach it with a few basic principles and theoretical frameworks to guide you.

1a. Why speak?

Chances are, if you are reading these words, you will soon have the opportunity to give a public speech. Many people approach the idea of public speaking with an attitude that falls somewhere between mild apprehension and sheer panic. As widespread and real as such fears are, we suggest that there is one thing worse than being called upon to give a public speech when you *don't* want to give one—that is not being *able* to give a public speech when you *do* want to. The latter situation plays out in scenarios like these:

- You attend a public meeting on an issue crucial to you and your family but are so intimidated by the articulate speakers on the opposing side that you never speak up.

- You sit in class, knowing the answer to a question that is asked but lacking the confidence to raise your hand.

- You attend a business meeting in which colleagues are discussing a problem. You think you have some insights that could be part of the solution, but you can't formulate your thoughts clearly enough to present them.

- You would like to take on a leadership role in a work group or social group, but the position involves giving speeches, and you are paralyzed with fear at the thought.

- You are being interviewed for a job you really want and think you are qualified for, but you cannot seem to answer the questions without rambling and stumbling over words.

The individuals involved feel powerless and miss out on the attention and credit they deserve. More seriously, all of us miss out when voices are left out of the conversation because people lack the skill or confidence to participate in public events. Additionally, a democratic society is structured around the free exchange of ideas so that people can listen to each other's views and select the best courses of collective action; organizations depend on participants to pool their expertise through communication; and our social connections and family bonds are cemented through storytelling and the sharing of personal feelings. There is great joy and power in finding our voices in the public sphere.

> **KEY POINT** **Professional Benefits** A quick glance at job descriptions on the web reveals regular and frequent use of phrases like "excellent oral and written skills," "strong ability to motivate others," and "excellent interpersonal and communication skills." The skills you develop as a public speaker will help you get a job: the candidate who gives answers that are concise, who can express ideas and desires in memorable ways, and who remains calm in a stressful situation will make the better impression. Once you get the job, you can use these communication skills to shape your career environment so that you gain personal satisfaction while being an effective and valued professional resource.

As with any other skill (such as dancing, programming, or tree surgery), with public speaking there are principles to be mastered, there is a need for concentration and practice, and there are benefits to working with a skilled teacher and supportive colearners. That's why so many colleges and universities require or strongly recommend courses in public speaking. Why thousands of people voluntarily join groups like Toastmasters International. Why corporations and public agencies spend millions of dollars on presentation training.

1b. Understand what it means to be a speaker

For many people, the mental image that forms when they hear the words *public speaking* features them standing behind a lectern, on a podium or stage, in front of listeners in an auditorium. This image covers only one type of speaking; public speaking is really a lot more. You are a speaker when you stand behind the lectern at an awards banquet, or when you approach the floor microphone at a planning commission meeting, or when you sit at a table with three other members of your work group and present your proposal for tackling some problem. You are a speaker in class, you are a speaker at work, and you are a speaker among friends and family. And in any one of these settings, you are a different speaker from the speaker you'd be in another.

However, not all oral communication in a group setting is public speaking. Perhaps the distinguishing characteristic of public speaking is that it is an event when a contract is reached among a group of people such that one person, the speaker, is given consent to direct the event.

Though listeners contribute to the creation of meaning, you should understand that as speaker you are an originator and inventor, and that you bring something uniquely "you" to shape the transaction.

1c. Approach public speaking as meaning-centered communication

Even in a practical handbook, it is worth examining your own assumptions about the nature of communication and how meaning is created. Working from a view that is too narrow or mechanical will hinder your effectiveness as a public speaker.

1 Communication as more than information transmission

Viewing communication as the clear transmission of information from a sender to a receiver tends to direct your thinking toward discrete, sender-controlled steps. "Giving a speech" becomes a matter of selecting ideas, packaging them, shipping them efficiently, and verifying their receipt. For most purposes, speakers are better served by embracing a more collaborative and complex model of communication.

2 Communication as the joint creation of meaning

Think about a group of filmmakers at work, or a software design team. At any given time, one individual may be putting forth ideas while the others listen and react. The end product is a composite that emerges from the interaction and did not exist in any one person's mind at the outset. The shift in emphasis from messages (speaker controlled) to meanings (jointly created) has important implications.

Meaning is social This statement refers to the idea that no individual, either sender or receiver, can control the "true meaning" of a statement. For example, a speaker who has violated a social norm cannot get off the hook by saying, "I did not intend that remark to be offensive, so it wasn't."

Meaning is contextual Similarly, few disputes about meaning are settled by pulling out a dictionary. That is, words or messages alone cannot tell us the "true meaning" of the communication. Why? Because words take their meanings not just from a dictionary but from all that surrounds them—their context—as they are uttered. A message can be repeated verbatim, but its meaning will not be identical if the context has changed: when and where a statement was made, who was present, what happened previously, and what tone of voice and expression accompanied the utterance.

Meaning is contingent This idea implies, in turn, that no sentence or act frozen in time has acquired its "true meaning." The meaning has to be interpreted within a chain of events. A speech may begin with an anecdote that initially seems to reflect the speaker's view but is later revealed as exemplifying what the speaker opposes.

Meaning becomes clear as it unfolds in the interplay between speaker and listeners. Often, we do not know what something meant until we reflect on an entire encounter.

Meaning is negotiated by discourse communities In cases in which the "true meaning" of a message is contested, examining the words themselves or the speaker's intentions or the listeners' response has been shown to be inadequate. Therefore, meanings are worked out over time by larger groups whose members already agree on some things and who work toward agreement on others.

1d. Draw on familiar communicative resources

When you enter into the contract that designates you as a speaker, you are not required to master a new skill. Rather, your challenge is to adapt several communication skills that you already have in your repertoire: conversation, writing, and performance.

1 Conversation skills

In everyday conversations, you do certain things that make you effective. You are probably relaxed and spontaneous, responsive to the situation, and naturally expressive of your changing feelings. You do not worry about your exact words because the event is highly interactive, with meaning clarified in the give-and-take. A lot of apprehension about public speaking can be dissipated if you carry this aspect of the conversational model into the speaking event.

One of the highest compliments a speaker can receive is to be called "conversational." The skills drawn from conversation that are useful to a public speaker include speaking in a comfortable and confident manner, listening to and considering the perspective of others, and adapting constantly to feedback.

2 Writing skills

The written word enables you to distance yourself from your ideas and to freeze them on paper. This distancing allows you to craft and tinker—to experiment with alternative forms and play them out in your imagination.

In writing, you pay close attention to word choices and organization to produce a carefully crafted message. You have the time to enjoy wordplay, to explore nuance, and to find elegant phrasing that makes the message memorable.

Writing can create the distance you need to view your ideas objectively, test them for logical coherence, and see how well they fit together. In writing, you can weave in multiple voices of authorities along with your own.

From writing, then, a speaker draws on the attention to language, the order of ideas, and the internal unity of the speech. Good writing requires time to rework and polish your words to achieve the most economical and forceful way to convey your message.

3   Performance skills

Most people would say they are not performers because they have not starred in a TV show, a rock concert, or even a company talent show. But this is a narrow definition of *performance*. Actually, we are all performers—whenever we *do* something, rather than merely think about it. In this handbook, when we talk about your performance skills, we mean the ways you have learned to use certain physical qualities—tone of voice, gestures, movement—to create a focal point for a group.

To downplay the performative aspects of public speech is to deny the essential power that makes a speech more than conversation, more than an outline or a transcript. *Performance* refers not to display or phoniness but to the enactment of an event between speaker and listeners that transcends the message or exchange of information. This transcendence is what makes people say, "You had to be there."

Performance skills useful to the speaker include the ability to pay attention to the entire effect, the knowledge of how to use setting and timing, and the capacity to turn a collection of individuals into a cohesive group. Performers know how to make use of all the senses. They tie together visual effects, lighting, sound, music, humor, and drama. They have a superb sense of timing and understand how to direct emotional buildup toward the right moment for climax. Speakers can make use of these skills by learning to visualize the desired impact and carefully planning details that contribute to that overall effect.

4   Combine and balance these domains

A speaker needs to draw some behaviors from all three of these domains: conversation, writing, and performance. Though the ratios may vary, it is just as bad to overuse one or more of these elements as it is to neglect them. An effective speaker seeks the right balance.

CHECKLIST

Balancing Resources

Conversation

❑ Underreliance leads to stiffness, excessive formality, distance, lack of spontaneity.

❑ Overreliance leads to uneconomical use of time and language, blunders, disorganization, the tendency to go off on tangents and lose focus.

Writing

❏ Underreliance leads to imprecise word choice, repetition, scattered organization.

❏ Overreliance leads to unnatural use of language and a "canned" sound, inability to adapt to an audience, an almost inevitable tendency to read or memorize the text.

Performance

❏ Underreliance leads to monotony, low emotional impact, reduced energy level.

❏ Overreliance leads to distraction from the message, unnatural or melodramatic persona, audience passivity, questions of sincerity.

1e. Understand the role of consciousness in skill learning

We learn complex skills differently than we learn simple facts. A complex skill like public speaking involves the combination of a number of intellectual and physical operations. Most of these operations are already in your repertoire. What you may not know is how to combine these skills to make an effective public speech.

KEY POINT **The Four Stages of Skill Learning** There are four stages in learning a skill:

1. unconscious incompetence (ui)
2. conscious incompetence (ci)
3. conscious competence (cc)
4. unconscious competence (uc)

As we move through the stages, we progress from not being aware that we are making errors in some area or that we need to learn a particular skill (ui), to realizing that there's room for improvement (ci), to having worked toward improvement and being vigilant when we use the skill (cc), to, finally, having integrated the learned skills to the extent that competence comes naturally, and we no longer need to devote conscious attention to it (uc).

A great deal of your communication behavior is unconscious. You do not think about how you move your lips to make sounds or why you speak one way with your friends and another with your boss. These may be areas of unconscious competence. At the same time, you may not be aware that you mispronounce "escape," or twirl your hair when you are nervous. These are examples of unconscious incompetence. When do your communication behaviors receive your conscious attention? Usually when you are learning new skills or when you run into difficulties in communicating. As soon as a skill is mastered or a communication problem is solved, your behavior becomes unconscious again.

1f. Beware of common misconceptions

There are many approaches to teaching public speaking and much folk wisdom about how people become effective speakers. Mastery of speaking will come more quickly if you can avoid being affected by misinformation and oversimplifications.

- *Misconception 1: Good speakers are born, not made.* Regardless of appearances, no one is born an effective speaker any more than one is born a good tennis player or an accomplished violinist. Inborn predispositions and early learning mean that some people will learn faster and go further. However, virtually anyone can learn to give a clear, effective public speech.

- *Misconception 2: Good speaking should be easy right away.* Many speakers think, "I know how to talk, so I must know how to give a speech." When they recognize this fallacy after a speech that fails badly, they become discouraged. In addition, the discouragement may be compounded by Misconception 3.

- *Misconception 3: Speaking will always be difficult.* Sometimes people forget that, although learning a skill requires effort and attention, performing the skill becomes much simpler, and almost automatic, once you reach a certain level of mastery. When you get discouraged with a speech outline that just won't come together or with phrasing that just won't flow, remember: It *will* get easier.

- *Misconception 4: There are simple formulas.* Communicating with an audience is an incredibly complex and sophisticated act. Every public speaking event is unique. No one can give an all-purpose recipe for preparing or delivering a speech. The quickest way to do something is not always the best way. In the area of public speaking, we have some basis for agreeing on the fundamentals. Certain basic principles date back over two thousand years to Aristotle's *Rhetoric* and continue to be refined through social science research. We have confidence in these principles. The advice in this handbook is based not on what is easiest or fastest but on what has proved to be the soundest. With these sound public speaking techniques, you will be more flexible and effective than if you had nothing but some all-purpose recipe.

> KEY POINT   **More Than Prescriptions** Although the chapters of this handbook are written as prescriptions, you will not find simple dos and don'ts to apply automatically to every situation. The fundamentals of speaking are stated simply, but the application and combination of these principles depend on your good judgment in each speaking situation.

1g. Follow five steps for speech preparation

Preparing a speech is complex and can be daunting. We offer this streamlined list (see Figure 1-1) of the bare essentials that go into preparing any speech, even the most basic one. These ideas and references will guide you as you get started. Later you will add variations to these steps, master different speech formats or types of speeches, and incorporate sophisticated strategies.

For simplicity the five steps are laid out in a linear fashion, but in fact they are recursive. This means that a speaker is always revisiting earlier steps in the *Think–Investigate–Compose–Practice–Present* cycle to ensure analytical and developmental completeness, and to facilitate polishing of the message. For a major speech you might return to refine your analysis after some research. Or,

THINK Initial decisions and analysis	Prepare plan 10 Select and narrow topic 11 Consider occasion 11 Clarify purpose 11 Determine mode of delivery 28 Frame thesis statement 11 Analyze topic 11 Analyze audience 12 Counter anxiety 4
INVESTIGATE Research for resources and materials	Locate resources 13 Investigate articles, books, and websites 14 Conduct interviews 15 Keep research notes 16
COMPOSE Development of speech materials	Develop rough working outline 17 Develop full-sentence outline 20 Add supporting materials 16 Add attention factors 30 Prepare introduction, conclusion, and transitions 31 Prepare presentation aids 27 Prepare speech notes 33
PRACTICE Preparation for oral performance	Give the speech aloud 33 Practice with presentation aids 36 Work on vocal delivery 34 Work on physical delivery 35 Get feedback 33
PRESENT The culmination of all your work	Relax, enjoy, connect with your audience, and debrief to learn something for next time.

FIGURE 1-1   The Five Steps of Public Speaking (with chapter references)

when putting the speech together you may discover the need for further research. In any speech, even a simple one, we certainly hope you don't stop thinking *after* Step One: Think!

These essential steps are developed in more elaborated form in Figure 10-1, which shows how they overlap in time and how important *oral* activity is at every step of the process.

CHAPTER 2
Listening

Listening is a crucial communication skill; you will find it listed as an essential component for most careers, and designated as a key factor in why relationships fail or succeed. Listening is not something experienced passively; it is a complex set of actions that requires explicit attention and practice.

Effective speaking and listening go hand in hand. Listening in a close and thoughtful way to public speakers gives you rich information about what works and what doesn't. You will be more appreciative of good speaking when you hear it. You will also be more critical of speaking that fails to measure up to the standards you set for yourself. Improving your habits and attitudes as a listener will directly enhance your effectiveness throughout the steps of preparing and delivering a speech.

2a. Prepare to listen

It is not necessarily instinctual to take the time to prepare before a situation that requires skilled listening.

1 Banish distractions, get physically set

In our multitasking society, we are used to doing many things at once. When listening is a priority, we need to break that pattern by sitting up straight, looking at the speaker, and clearing away all materials except those needed for note taking.

2 Stop talking

Beyond the obvious, this applies to keeping up a running internal commentary that hampers genuine listening as you focus on composing rebuttals. (See **2b**.) Also, when interviewing someone, don't do most of the talking.

3 Decide on your purpose

There are many possible objectives to listening, including to learn, to understand a new point of view, to evaluate an argument, or to enjoy a narrative. Marshal the resources you need to draw on—your empathy, your curiosity, your critical analysis, your concentration—to meet your goal as a listener.

2b. Be both curious and critical

Effective listeners balance a charitable and open receptiveness against a critical assessment based on their real-life experiences and common sense.

1 Show respect for the speaker

Recognize that speaking in public takes courage and effort. Give the gift of your full attention, and adhere to the courtesies of a public situation.

> **KEY POINT** **Listening to Nonnative English Speakers** We encourage native speakers of American English to make a special commitment to understanding the speech of those for whom English is a second or third language. Learn to listen past any unusual pronunciations or inflections that may be by-products of the speaker's original language. Remember that, to communicate with you, the speaker has learned American English vocabulary, grammar, and syntax, and then has risked speaking publicly in that new language. In return, the only contribution required of you is to accustom your ear to a somewhat different pattern of sounds.

2 Be open to the speaker's point of view

Although people cannot help evaluating everything they hear as they hear it, you can avoid a harshly critical attitude toward the speaker and make a conscious effort to substitute an attitude of curiosity. What, exactly, is this person saying? What led to that position? How did the person come to these conclusions, with what assumptions?

3 Follow the structure of the speech

Try to identify the thesis, main points, supporting materials, and crucial links, whether these are explicitly stated or not. Discerning the structure aids your retention of content and your evaluation of its validity.

4 Assess the speaker's claims

As you listen to any speaker who makes a controversial claim, engage your critical thinking skills to test the validity of the argument.

CHECKLIST

Evaluating Claims Critically

❏ Do the main points taken together justify the thesis? (See **18a**.)

❏ Is each claim stated clearly? (See **21a**.)

❏ Is this claim a proposition of fact, value, or policy? (See **11d**.)

❏ Is the support offered for each claim relevant to the point? (See **16**.)

❏ Does each piece of evidence meet the appropriate tests for examples, testimony, or statistics? (See **16**.)

❏ Are the links between the points logically drawn? (See **24d**.)

❏ What premises are taken for granted without being stated? Are these assumptions valid? (See **21c**.)

❏ Are any fallacies present? (See **21f**.)

❏ Does the speaker misuse emotional appeals or substitute them for intellectual argument? (See **25d**.)

---

5   At the designated time, ask questions

Frame questions that deepen your understanding of what the speaker is trying to get across.

2c. Provide constructive feedback

In one special situation, as a consultant to a speaker, you agree to listen to provide feedback on the decisions the speaker has made and the effectiveness of the presentation. The role of critic/consultant requires a special blend of honesty and tact. The supportive critic bears in mind the fragility of partially formed ideas and the close connection between the person's speaking personality and the person's self-image. The following guidelines are for listeners who have been asked to give feedback.

■ *Start with the positive.* Acknowledge what the speaker has tried to do and how it has succeeded. Try to communicate some sense of priority. There is no profit in refining the phrasing of a sentence if the whole point is going to be cut from the speech. Think first about whether the message makes sense and whether the overall strategy is effective. When those issues are settled, move on to the refinements.

■ *Be specific.* It is more helpful to say, "You were discussing causes of the problem in Point 1 and then again in Point 3" than "This speech was disorganized." The same is true for positive comments.

■ *Give suggestions, not orders.* Your comments should acknowledge the fact that your response is the reaction of just one listener and that others may differ. For example: "I have never cared for a big dramatic introduction, though I know it works for some people. Have you thought about . . . ?"

- *Be realistic about the amount and kind of feedback a speaker can receive.* Always consider the speaker's feelings when deciding what to say and how to phrase it. Be aware of the time constraints a speaker faces. Early in the development of the speech you can make some major suggestions for revision, but if the speech is in final rehearsal, it's too late to suggest going back to the drawing board.

- *Use the 90/10 principle.* This principle, developed by one of the authors in teaching interpersonal communication, states that people's weaknesses are rarely the *opposite* of their strengths. More often, they are the *excesses.* This awareness suggests a way of phrasing feedback: "The first 90 percent of quality A is a positive addition to your speech, but the last 10 percent of quality A begins to work in the opposite way." You are not suggesting that speakers eliminate a characteristic behavior, but that they hold it in check. Actual feedback phrased this way might sound like this: "Your informal conversational style works wonderfully for most of the speech, except that at one or two points it becomes so colloquial and casual that your credibility suffers a bit."

CHECKLIST

Constructive Feedback
- ❏ Start with the positive
- ❏ Be specific
- ❏ Give suggestions, not orders
- ❏ Be realistic
- ❏ Use the 90/10 principle

2d. Listen to optimize learning

Effective listening will enable you to reach a deeper understanding of your topic and to use your time more efficiently when you seek information from other people as you research your speech. (See **15**.)

- *Paraphrase.* Check your understanding of the points being made by paraphrasing and clarifying. This involves restating what you think you heard so the speaker can confirm or correct your interpretations.

- *Ask follow-up questions for clarification.* As the expert answers your open-ended questions, careful listening will enable you to follow up with more-specific questions in response to those answers: "You said a minute ago that the issue of class size may be more important in the long run than teacher development. Why do you say that?"

- *Take notes.* Be sure to take notes as you gather information from another person. Because the object is to optimize learning, it can make sense to employ this tool, which forces you to think about what is being said so that you can write notes that make sense as well.

2e. Avoid common listening pitfalls

1   Daydreaming, doodling, and disengaging

It's easy for your mind to wander, in part because it takes a speaker longer to state an idea than for a listener to think the same thing. Listening experts recommend using that time differential constructively. Fill in your own examples. Think of questions to ask later. Stay mentally active in ways that connect to the speech topic. (See **2a**.)

2   Being distracted by superficial qualities of the speaker

You may notice that a speaker sways back and forth, or has a vocal inflection that makes every statement sound like a question. Or you may notice that the speaker looks wonderful in that shade of blue. In either case, letting yourself be distracted by these traits hinders your listening to the message of the speech.

3   Uncritically accepting a message

Don't automatically assume that if a speaker makes a statement it must be true. If something sounds wrong, it may be because it *is* wrong. Listeners share ethical responsibility for the meanings that come out of speeches. Give ideas the scrutiny that respect for them requires. (See **2b**.)

4   Prematurely or totally rejecting a message

Hear the speaker out. Listen attentively, and you may hear a new argument or find an intriguing point you hadn't considered. (See **2b**.)

5   Planning your response or rebuttal

You can certainly be critical and analytical, but unless you are in a debate that requires on-the-spot refutation, don't divert your attention to the extent of composing your own responses. (See **2a**.)

6   Failing to monitor your nonverbal behaviors

As a matter of courtesy and respect, assume a supportive and responsive listening demeanor. (See **2b.1**.) The International Listening Association website **http://www.listen.org** provides some short articles on the value of listening as well as a compendium of irritating listening habits.

CHAPTER 3

Speaking Ethically

Sometimes, a speaker succeeds in getting a point across or in persuading an audience but does so in a manner that is manipulative, exploitative, dishonest, or otherwise offensive. These cases raise questions about the ethical obligations of all speakers. Ethical questions do not ask, What works? but rather ask, What is right?

Fortunately, effective speaking and ethical speaking usually go together. There are no guarantees, though, that audiences will always respond best to those speakers who take the moral high ground; history is replete with examples of speakers who used all sorts of questionable tactics and were rewarded with great success. Ultimately, the question transcends the simple yes/no choice of, Can I get away with it? and moves to the more complex realm of personal values, where each speaker has to decide what is ethically justifiable, based on beliefs about such fundamental matters as how people should treat one another and what counts as honesty.

In one sense, ethical beliefs are so individual that they seem almost to be a matter of each person's own conscience. Yet our beliefs about right and wrong are highly influenced by other people. The National Communication Association has established a code of ethics to guide communicators that can be reviewed at **http://www.natcom.org/policies/External/Ethical/Comm.htm**. Other, less formal, codes of ethical conduct come to us through family, religion, and culture.

3a. Be aware of ethical implications of your choices

Every human action has an ethical dimension. No decision a speaker makes is morally neutral. We speak because we believe that what we say will make a difference. And it does. The results of a speech can be as serious as persuading others to follow a dangerous course of action or as apparently harmless as wasting their time with an unprepared and unfocused message. Every time you speak, you exercise power and assume responsibility for the consequences of what you do or do not say.

1 Ethical decisions are rarely clear-cut

Often, the answer to questions about what works in public speaking is, It depends. Questions about what is the right or ethical course of action are just as complex. Our ethics grow from our values, and values sometimes conflict. Rarely are there black-and-white choices. The best we can do most of the time is to select the lighter shade of gray. As communicators, we are obligated to think hard about each case and to develop our judgment through experience and reflection.

2 Ethical decisions vary with context

In a speech tournament, a debater might argue for legalized prostitution at 9:00 and argue against it at 10:30. In this context, it is understood that the rules of the game are to defend the assigned side of a topic as vigorously and skillfully as possible. This is considered no more unethical than the case of the football team that defends the north goal in the first and third quarters and just as vigorously defends the south goal in the second and fourth. However, we judge as very unethical a candidate who takes one position when addressing voters in Oregon and the opposite position in Kansas. This is because, as critical listeners in the political arena, we view such public speeches not as part of a game but as sincere statements of the speaker's true beliefs.

What you can pass off as your own words varies as well. Political leaders are assumed to employ speechwriters who draft many of their speeches for them. This is considered ethical because the demands on public servants make it impossible for them to personally prepare each speech they give. However, in an academic speech class, it is well understood that students are expected to create and deliver their own speeches because the learning experience depends on acquiring a variety of skills and being assessed in them. To use your friend as a ghostwriter is clearly plagiarism in this context. (See **3b**.)

> **KEY POINT** **Be True to Yourself and Your Listeners** As a public speaker, you are not simply a transmitter of messages; you also put yourself (your individual self) in contact with an audience. Though you may adapt and adjust and accommodate to meet your goals, you have an ethical obligation to be true to yourself. When you've finished a speech, regardless of how anyone else responds, you should always feel good about what you said and how you said it.
>
> Public speakers have a special kind of power. When audience members entrust you with their time and attention, you take on an obligation to treat them with fairness and concern. You have every right to pursue your own reasons for speaking, but not at the expense of your listeners' welfare.

3b. Respect the integrity of ideas

A commitment to this principle requires that you take a larger view of how each individual speech act either reinforces or abrades the fabric of society. To live and work together, people have to trust that, on the whole, communication proceeds honestly and reliably.

1 Don't plagiarize

Besides yourself and your audience, there are others, not present, to whom you have some ethical obligations. These are the people whose ideas and words you draw into the speech situation. Some individuals who would never dream of stealing another person's property seem to think it is somehow acceptable to steal a scholar's solution to a problem or to borrow a friend's outline for a speech. The ethics of public speaking generally proscribe using another's major ideas or exact words—or even paraphrasing them—without giving credit to the source. Plagiarism is a serious offense in academic institutions and in the world of publishing. Careers have been ruined when public leaders have been exposed as plagiarists.

To avoid even the appearance of unethical appropriation of speech content, form the habit of taking careful notes of the sources of all your ideas, statistics, and evidence. And when you hear a wonderful anecdote, story, or turn of phrase you might like to quote someday, make a note right then so you will remember to give credit to the source. (See **16d, f.**)

There are several resources to guide you in avoiding even the appearance of plagiarism. Refer to **http://northwestern.edu/ uacc/plagiar.html** or **http://washington.edu/courses/tc231/ course_info/plagiarism.htm** or **http://owl.english.purdue. edu/handouts/print/research/r_plagiar.html**.

2   Don't lie

Rarely do we live up to the standard of "the truth, the whole truth, and nothing but the truth" in everyday interactions. The phrase *it depends* always crops up in conversations about what counts as a lie, a white lie, a fib, a prevarication, or tactful phrasing. In public speaking, however, the following categories of behavior cross the line between honest and dishonest speech.

- *Making statements that are counterfactual.* This is pretty obvious. Saying, "I have no financial interest in this fitness center. I just care about your health" when you receive a commission for every new member you enroll is dishonest.

- *Playing word games to create a false impression.* Sometimes, a speaker can use words with precise definition, being technically correct but totally misleading: "In response to allegations of illegal drug use, let me say that I have never broken the laws of this country" [when the drug use was in another country].

- *Leaving out some part of "the whole truth" that, if known, would reverse the impact of the statement.* Saying "We have totally dominated the Smurge Company in our market" is misleading if you neglect to mention that the domination happened in only one quarter out of four.

3   Don't oversimplify

Another dimension of the integrity of ideas has to do with faithfulness to the facts and realities of your subject matter. Although we can hardly say that there is one "real truth" on any complex issue, we can say that some accounts are so shallow or oversimplified as to provide a basically false picture. Before you speak in public, thus contributing to and shaping the public discourse on a topic, you have an ethical obligation to look beneath the surface.

CHECKLIST

Finding a Balance in Ethical Decisions

❏ Balance the value of using language in a lively and forceful manner against the risk of causing pain and offense.

❏ Balance the importance of appealing to your audience at an emotional level against the risk of abusing emotional appeals.

❏ Balance the right to use compelling persuasive appeals against the obligation to avoid simplistic persuasive techniques.

Another form of oversimplification is exemplified by the classic list of propaganda devices identified by a group of journalists some decades ago that sets forth the techniques unethical speakers can use to short-circuit an audience's rational processes.[1]

- *Name-calling.* By attaching a negative label to an idea or a person, a speaker can provoke fear or hatred in an audience. The speaker hopes this tide of emotion will gloss over the lack of substance in his or her position.

- *Glittering generalities.* At the other extreme is the use of words or phrases that represent some abstract virtue like patriotism or motherhood to generate a positive response rather than dealing with the merits of a position.

- *Testimonials.* Another way to generate positive emotions is to link a popular figure with some cause or product. Here, the speaker replaces sound argument with a possibly inappropriate extension of the person's credibility from another area.

- *"Just plain folks."* It is fine to build identification with an audience so that members are receptive to the ideas presented. This process goes too far, though, when the speaker implies, "You should believe me, not because of the inherent validity of what I say, but because I'm just like you."

- *Card stacking.* In this method, a speaker carefully uses only facts or examples that bolster a particular position, and the highly biased selection is passed off as representative.

- *The bandwagon.* This technique is useful to a speaker who wishes to discourage independent thinking. The "everyone is

---

[1]Adapted from Alfred McClung Lee and Elizabeth Briant Lee, *The Art of Propaganda* (New York: Harcourt and Institute for Propaganda Analysis, 1939), 23–24.

doing it" approach appeals to the need for security and plays on fears of being different or left out. A proposition should be sold on its merits, not on its popularity.

This list is far from comprehensive. Effective persuaders also use such techniques as snob appeal (the opposite of "just plain folks") and stand-out-from-the-crowd (the opposite of the bandwagon). Such persuasive appeals are questionable whenever they serve to distract listeners from important issues, cloud important distinctions, introduce irrelevant factors in the decision-making process, or use emotional appeals inappropriately or excessively.

CHAPTER 4
Overcoming Fear of Speaking

Stage fright, communication apprehension, speech anxiety, reticence, shyness—these are among the most researched and analyzed variables in the literature on communication, precisely because the problem of feeling fearful about a public presentation is so widespread. Experts offer some ways of thinking about this problem that can help you become more comfortable and confident when you speak in public. There are techniques you can use to work toward this goal as well.

4a. Put your fear into perspective

Many speakers try to be calm in every speech situation. This is unrealistic.

1 Accept some fear as normal

All speakers feel some fear, and for most of us the feeling can be managed and sometimes even turned to positive effect. The more speeches you give, the more confident you will become. You will recognize that fear is usually worst just prior to the speech and during the introduction. Once your speech is under way and the audience responds to you, negative emotions are often replaced by exhilaration.

2 Analyze your fear as specifically as possible

"I'm scared to death" is a common statement that describes the emotional intensity of stage fright, but in reality, few people expect the experience to be fatal. An amorphous, ill-defined fear cannot be dealt with, though. Dealing logically with this fear requires examining its components so you can isolate a number of specific problems to be solved.

It is helpful to list your fears on paper. Be as specific as possible. If you write statements like "I'm afraid I'll make a fool of myself," ask yourself these follow-up questions: "How will I do that?" ("I'll forget my speech"); and "What will happen next?" ("The audience will think I'm dumb"). Use this format for your list:

I am afraid that [specific event] will occur and then that [specific result] will follow.

When you have generated your list, you can classify the fears you have. For items like "I'm afraid my visual aids won't be clear," the solution is simple. Check out the clarity of your visual aids with a few people, and if there is any problem, redesign them. As **4b** points out, many fears have roots in inadequate preparation. The mere act of writing the fears down makes them manageable and often points immediately to a solution.

Other fears on your list may relate to physical responses: "I'm afraid my hands will shake and my voice will crack." If many of your concerns fall into this category, pay special attention to the suggestions in **4c**.

A number of items on your list may relate to your failure to meet your own high standards. Recognize this concern as a positive motivation to do the best you can. But also realize that the power of suggestion is great and that dwelling on failure can cause it to happen. Use some of the visualization and verbalization techniques recommended in **4d** to create positive self-expectations.

> **KEY POINT**   **Reconceptualizing the Role of the Audience**   If one technique in particular has helped people cope with stage fright, it is seeing their listeners as "recipients" rather than "critics." A speaker must break out of the self-absorption of speech fright: "How do I look? Will they like me? Is my speech good enough?" Remind yourself that you are there not to perform but to share. How will the ideas and information you offer enrich their lives?
>
> Some recent research findings suggest that the best way to reduce communication apprehension is to change how you view the public speaking event. It is not easy, but if you can think of yourself more as "talking with" the listeners and less as "performing for" them, you will feel much more comfortable.

4b.   Prepare and practice thoroughly

Although good speakers can make delivery seem effortless, their skill is based on extensive preparation over a period of time. The confidence they exude is also a result of preparation, not genes or fate or dumb luck.

If you feel uneasy about starting your speech, perhaps your introduction needs more work. If you are fearful of losing the continuity of the speech, you may need to practice it aloud several more times to internalize the flow of ideas. If you find yourself becoming generally anxious, use this as a stimulus to review your preparation. Whatever else you do, remember that time spent fretting about the outcome could better be used taking positive action to ensure a positive outcome.

As you prepare, follow the suggestions on practice sessions in chapter **33**. Avoid making last-minute changes in the speech.

4c. Use techniques of relaxation and tension release

When too much adrenaline makes you jumpy, physical activity usually helps you cope with the physical effects of fear. Avoid heavy exercise, but a brisk walk around the block or a little pacing in the hall—or a few arm swings and neck rolls—can be enough to bring your body back to normal. Once the speech begins, take advantage of the extra energy that the adrenaline provides to make your delivery more vigorous. Appropriate, dynamic gestures will help you discharge the nervous residue.

You can also handle symptoms of nervousness by learning and practicing relaxation techniques. Explore such methods as tightening and then relaxing certain muscle groups, breathing deeply, visualizing serene settings, or imagining sensations such as warmth or heaviness in parts of your body.

Chemical aids to relaxation—alcohol, drugs, tranquilizers—are highly inadvisable.

4d. Use positive self-suggestion

When you experience fear, you are visualizing the most negative outcome for your speech. It is possible, however, to turn these fearful visions around. For example, tennis players, field goal kickers, and concert pianists, among others, have found it helpful to visualize what they are striving for.

1 Visualize success

When you prepare a speech, do not let yourself think about failure. When you detect such thoughts in your mind, replace them with a positive scenario: "I will approach the lectern calmly, smile at the audience, and begin. My voice will sound strong and confident." Do not, however, set unrealistic standards of perfection. Build some contingencies into your fantasy: "If I forget a point, I'll look down at my notecard and concentrate on the main idea I am conveying." Run through these positive visualizations a few times a day before you speak. As you practice, picture the audience responding favorably to the speech. And just before you get up to speak, remind yourself of the general tone and image you wish to project: "When I get up there, I am going to communicate my sincerity and concern in a warm, natural, confident manner."

2   Replace negative internal statements with positive ones

One approach to reducing fears is to use "cognitive restructuring" to probe our mental commentaries, identify the unrealistic or irrational statements that cause fear, and replace them with more positive, logical, and realistic beliefs. We all have constant narrations running through our minds, so familiar that we are barely conscious of them. With some introspection, you can bring them to the mental fore and examine the effect they have on your behavior. It is helpful to remember that these are not statements of fact but statements that you yourself have created and that you can choose to replace if they interfere with your efficient functioning. Once you become fully aware of the commentaries that govern your response to public speaking, you can work on replacing the unproductive beliefs with more positive ones. Table 4-1 gives some examples.

TABLE 4-1   Replacement Statements

False Belief	Positive Replacement
A good speaker never says "uh" or "er."	A few nonfluencies aren't even noticed unless attention is called to them.
I'm going to go blank.	I've practiced several times, and I know the basic structure of this speech.
I can't handle this tension!	Even though I feel uncomfortable, I'm able to cope with tense situations.
No one will be able to understand me because of my accent.	My listeners will want to hear what I have to say, not how I say it.

Your unproductive responses are habitual and will not change easily. At first, you will have to repeat the replacement sentences mechanically, over and over. Because the replacement sentences are so reasonable and logical, a large part of your mind will want to accept them. The reassuring nature of the words often helps you to become physically calmer, and this more comfortable sensation acts to reinforce the new beliefs.

4e.   If necessary, seek further assistance

Some fear of speaking is too deeply rooted to be remedied by the methods suggested here. If your fear of speaking is almost paralyzing, if none of the preceding suggestions work, you may need help in coping with it. Research shows that even severe fear of speaking can usually be reduced to a manageable level when treated by a qualified professional.

2 Tailoring Your Speech to Its Context

CHAPTER 5. **Analyzing Speech Contexts**

Learn all you can about the contexts in which you will speak: general expectations, specific formats, and unspoken norms for speakers and listeners.

CHAPTER 6. **Educational Context**

Understand the essentials of speaking in the educational context.

CHAPTER 7. **Workplace Context**

Understand the essentials of speaking in the workplace context.

CHAPTER 8. **Civic and Political Context**

Understand the essentials of speaking in the civic and political context.

CHAPTER 9. **Social and Ceremonial Context**

Understand the essentials of speaking in the social and ceremonial context.

CHAPTER 5

Analyzing Speech Contexts

The skills and recommendations discussed throughout this handbook are necessarily general. They become useful to you when you are able to tailor them to the demands and expectations of a particular context. A person with excellent generic speaking skills may still be at a loss if a situation requires knowledge of a particular format. For example, it does a concerned citizen no good to prepare a compelling persuasive argument if the person cannot penetrate the rules of parliamentary procedure to gain recognition to speak. Ultimately, what is important to a speaker is not what is said but what meaning is created through the saying. Any given message or *text* takes on meaning from the circumstances that surround it—from the *context*. (See **1c**.) Both speakers and listeners rely on the context to make sense of messages. So knowing the rules and customs of a given speaking occasion will reduce the uncertainty you feel and thus minimize your fear.

5a. Take time to think about the basics

You will save time and work more efficiently if, before you even begin to plan a speech, you think carefully about the overall context of the speech. You can do this by starting with some fundamental questions: Who, where, what, when, why, and how?

■ *Whom will you be speaking to? And **where** will you be speaking?* It's virtually impossible to begin to design a speech without having some picture of the situation that you will be entering. The people gathered in a particular place, or linked electronically, constitute the audience that will help define the meaning of your speech. As soon as you identify them, you can use chapter **12** to guide your more detailed audience analysis.

■ *What will you speak about?* Topic selection is rarely completely under your control or completely out of your control. In every case an early determination must be made to map out the general content area you will be working with. Then, and only then, can you begin to gather materials and organize, develop, and craft them into an effective speech.

■ *When will you be speaking?* Both the calendar and the clock have much to do with your overall approach to the speech. Be realistic about how soon you need to have the speech ready and how long you will be talking. This information is necessary to manage your preparation time (chapter **10**) and to practice your speech (chapter **33**).

■ *Why are you giving the speech?* You always have some *reason* for speaking. Maybe you were invited to speak at some event, assigned to speak in a class, or have sought an opportunity to address a particular audience. Additionally, you have some *purpose* for speaking. In this handbook we classify general speaking purposes as to persuade, to inform, and to evoke, but we hasten to add that most situations involve a blend of these goals. Chapter **11** goes into more depth about how to identify these purposes and how to refine them into specific objectives and thesis statements.

■ *How will you be presenting the speech?* From the outset, make the decision as to whether your speech will be extemporaneous (carefully planned and outlined but not planned word for word), delivered from a written manuscript, memorized, or impromptu (off the cuff). The decision will influence how you prepare, following the guidelines for each mode of delivery as presented in chapter **28**.

5b. Identify relevant speaking formats

Just as there are genres of literature—fiction, nonfiction, poetry—each with multiple subgenres such as the thriller, romance, and space opera, there are familiar categories of speaking. When one conducts a training workshop, delivers a sermon, or participates in a debate, there are some well-known, albeit general, expectations about the shape that speech will take. In other cases, there are more specific formats speakers typically follow. Examples of some workplace, civic, and ceremonial formats are found in chapters **7**, **8**, and **9**. On our website you will find other examples of some detailed speech formats used in classroom speaking assignments in various disciplines and in particular professional settings. Whenever such standard formats exist, it is your responsibility to learn about them and to adhere to them.

If you are not given a particular format to follow, your first research task should be to seek out models and exemplars to study. How do social workers present case reports at staff meetings? What is included in a progress report on an engineering project? What kind of speeches been presented as keynote addresses to this particular organization? There may be a set of written guidelines to follow. If not, ask for manuscripts, outlines, and videos of previous presentations. Interview members of the organization about what is expected. Whenever possible, sit in as an observer on presentations of the type you will be making. Make note of the steps that are followed, the kinds of arguments and evidence that are used, the style and tone that are common; from these observations generate a template for your presentation.

5c. Analyze each specific context

Besides finding out the essential information about a speech situation and researching existing formats, speakers benefit by thinking about the many factors that define every context for speaking. These dimensions might be arrayed along several continua. Locate where your speaking situation falls within each category.

← **Public sphere** ————————————— **Private sphere** →

A context is established in part by the venue or domain in which speaking occurs. One set of expectations accompanies a meeting in a legislative hall, a large city square, or a cathedral. Even if the same topics are being talked about, quite different expectations will come into play if the speech takes place in a private office or a living room.

← **Formal demeanor** ————————————— **Informal demeanor** →

Some contexts are highly formal and require dressy attire, use of titles and respectful forms of address, dignified word choice, and a setting that is orderly and perhaps ceremonial. The informality of other contexts is signaled by casual dress, use of first names, colloquial speech forms, and everyday physical arrangements.

← **Monologic** ————————————— **Dialogic** →

Contexts are also defined by the role of the participants. In monologic situations, it is assumed that a featured primary speaker will dominate the event, taking primary responsibility for what is talked about. In dialogic situations, other participants can direct both the topic and the form of the interaction. As with all the other continua, there are many contexts that fall between the extremes or that blend the norms. At a public lecture, for example, the expectation is that the main speaker will be listened to without interruption or heckling until the question-and-answer period begins. Then the norms of dialogic speech take precedence and it is considered inappropriate for the speaker to give another speech.

← **Highly prescribed rules of speaking** ————————————— **More open rules of speaking** →

All public speaking is rule-bound to some extent, but there is tremendous variation in how explicit or specific those rules are. Some contexts have very rigid rules about who may speak, for how long, and on what topic. In a formal parliamentary meeting, a speaker must receive recognition and then link the discourse to a particular motion before the house. In a legal proceeding, advocates can ask questions only in certain ways and at certain times, and they can present arguments only during opening and closing statements. Contrast this to a meeting of a small task force, in which participants might seize the floor at any time and change subjects at will. The rules in the latter case either are implicit—group members may subtly sanction those who talk too much or too long—or evolve on the spot—as when someone suggests that each person take a few minutes to state a position on the topic.

←————————————————————————————————→
Power resides with speaker   **Power resides with listeners**

Power differences between speakers and listeners inevitably influence context. Sometimes, the power resides with the listeners: Bosses control paychecks, teachers assign grades, judges make rulings, and homeowners' association boards approve projects. Whether motivated by common sense, self-preservation, or genuine respect, speakers usually show a degree of restraint in addressing those in higher-power positions. At other times, power resides with the speaker. Here, the expectations differ: The speaker doesn't deny the power but often chooses to downplay it to avoid being intimidating or threatening to listeners.

←————————————————————————————————→
Existing community   **One-time assembly**

The context of a speech differs based on the relationship among the participants. When an already established group comes together, speeches typically include in-group jokes, use of abbreviations and shorthand expressions, and references to shared history. There is no need to spend time building a sense of community as there would be in a situation in which individuals have gathered for the first time, primarily because they are interested in a common topic or in the speaker.

←————————————————————————————————→
Immediate audience   **Extended audience**

Most often, a speech is intended for those who are present. But there are occasions when everyone understands that the real context of the speech involves a much wider audience that will read it or hear it broadcast.

These dimensions illustrate the uniqueness and complexity of speech contexts. A speaker could be right on target in analyzing most of the relevant factors in a situation but, by misreading just one of these—say, the expected level of formality—could jeopardize effectiveness. Do not be afraid to ask questions about any new situation that you enter. If you are in charge of an event, be sure that invitations and announcements communicate shared expectations.

An additional and important determinant in each speaking context is culture. Mastering the marketing presentation in a U.S. business context will not prepare you to give a similar presentation in Japan. Knowing about different cultural norms and expectations also helps listeners to be respectful of international guests.

The chapters that follow in part 2 offer some preliminary suggestions for four kinds of contexts: the educational, the business and professional, the civic and political, and the social and ceremonial. We offer these suggestions with caution, because even these generalizations need to be adapted and combined for each specific event. For example, a training workshop within a company would combine the expectations of workplace communication and the education setting. Or, an inaugural address would draw in elements of both political and ceremonial speaking.

CHAPTER 6
Educational Context

Though it is common to contrast academic life with the "real world," the classroom speaking context is a real one in all important respects. Classroom presentations involve real people who are involved in the mutual creation of meaning with significant consequences. Speakers are challenged to analyze the expectations and requirements of each educational context. To adapt the recommendations from other sections of this book, begin by determining why an oral assignment is being used in a particular classroom.

6a. Oral assignments to develop speaking skill

Academic speech classes, presentation skills training programs, speech contests, and Toastmasters' groups represent the few types of contexts in which the presentation of a public speech is treated as a primary activity rather than as a means to some other end. In these situations, the assignment is typically designed around the skills students need to practice. You may be required to give a speech to inform or to persuade, to include a variety of types of supporting material, or to use different kinds of reasoning. Admittedly, such speech experiences are artificial in some ways, such as asking you to cover a great deal within a restricted time limit, requiring detailed outlines with speech components labeled, or asking audiences to shift their attention from topic to topic. To succeed in these contexts, it's important to learn exactly what each assignment entails and to touch every base. But there is no need to chafe against the constraints of classroom speaking. You are still speaking to real people. Try to select topics that excite you and engage your listeners. Take advantage of this special opportunity to receive detailed feedback on both the overall impact of your message and the technical aspects of your presentation.

6b. Oral assignments to provide practice in specific professional contexts

Most introductory speech classes are set up to teach the most generalizable skills of analysis, research, organization, and delivery that will apply across contexts. But in advanced academic classes and in organizational training programs, you will have opportunities to learn how those generic speaking skills are modified in various contexts. In presenting a literary critique, a social science research report, an engineering design review, a health care plan for a patient, a training program for employees, you must master a new set of conventions. Oral assignments are designed to simulate situations you will face in career settings. Audience members may be asked to role play colleagues, customers, or clients. Outside experts are sometimes invited to presentations to give you feedback. It is particularly important in these projects to get detailed information about the purpose of your presentation and the expectations of your listeners.

Though we always encourage you to "be yourself," assignments of this sort invite you to project yourself into a new persona to some extent. If you aspire to be a chemist or a journalist or a physical therapist, the classroom setting provides a safe environment to explore how you will communicate in those roles. Step up to class assignments and try on the conventions, speaking style, and even the clothing that will be expected in the new contexts you will face later.

6c. Oral assignments to facilitate learning subject matter

In contrast to situations where learners speak for the purpose of improving speech skills, the most common use of oral assignments in educational contexts is as a means to a broader end. Educators in almost every field have found that oral reports, debates, and group presentations are powerful ways to explore and master subject matter. When student presenters know they have to talk about ideas in public, they are forced to engage material deeply to synthesize points and make them clear to others. Members of classroom audiences often find that peer presentations help reinforce course content, possibly because their classmates explain things in more accessible ways than professors sometimes do. And instructors find oral presentations to be one important way to assess student learning, sometimes superior to papers or exams in showing how fully students understand course material and how creatively they can apply it. For these assignments, success depends on taking the extra time, after studying the topic and doing research, to follow the principles of effective speaking. For example, don't assume that the oral presentation consists of just reading an academic paper. Clarify the expectations and time limits and then plan and rehearse a lively, well-organized presentation that engages the audience and boosts your credibility.

CHAPTER 7

Workplace Context

Generally, presentations in business and professional settings are, well, businesslike. That is, in the formats that have been created and the norms that have evolved, the emphasis is on efficiency and clarity. Speech in workplace settings is expected to be streamlined and unadorned. A routine report to a work group typically does not begin with an attention getter, but rather features a detailed logical orientation step to locate the topic within the organization's multiple tasks. Visual aids (including handouts) are considered central to professional presentations, in part so that technical details can be available for examination and reference without the speaker having to spend a great deal of time going over them orally. Within organizations, because goals are assumed to be shared, listeners may ask each other tough questions and play devil's advocate.

In a team environment, internal communication is a way to test ideas so that they can be improved before costly mistakes are made. Of course, organizational communication must include a healthy dose of team building, and sales and marketing presentations to persons outside the organization will involve a very different set of expectations.

Typical presentations in a business and professional context include the employment interview, the sales interview, the marketing presentation, the technical presentation, annual or periodic business reports, and the project status report. We discuss two of these.

7a. Follow common guidelines for job interviews

Traditionally, the job interview consists of an applicant and a personnel director, with a desk as a prop. However, more interviews are now being done in a group, with a number of people from different departments and levels talking with the applicant. Other events that resemble interviews are the performance review and the sales presentation to a committee. In any of these situations, you may not be successful if you come prepared only to answer questions. When you speak to a group, even a small one, you should apply several public speaking concepts, of which the following are the most important.

1 Analyze your audience

Learn all you can about the people who will be interviewing you. (If the organization has a website, mine it for information as your first step.) If possible, get a list with their names, so you can learn to pronounce them, and their positions, so you can think about the various perspectives and interests they represent. When you are introduced, you can quickly associate faces with the names and roles you have studied. Throughout the interview, you can adapt your answers to their perspectives: "That brings up the whole question of the cost effectiveness of surveys. I'm sure you confront that issue all the time, Mr. Keenan, being director of marketing research."

2 Prepare an opening statement

The first question likely will be, "Well, tell us a little bit about your background—how you got to where you are now, and how you describe your orientation to our field." Seize this opportunity to set the tone. Make a brief statement that serves the purposes of a speech introduction: gets their attention, creates rapport, and establishes a framework for the main content to follow. Do not assume that on the day of the interview your résumé or sales brochure is fresh in the interviewers' minds. Besides reiterating what you sent earlier, you can also update it if further developments would be of interest to the group.

You can use your opening statement to develop a general philosophy or position. You may highlight aspects of your experience to show trends or directions that led you to the present interview. Whether you are selling yourself, a service, a product, or an idea, use this opportunity to establish credibility.

It seldom hurts to compliment their organization. Be as specific as possible to show your knowledge of it and its workings.

3 Answer questions directly and concisely

Before any interview, review the guidelines for answering questions in chapter **37**. Try to tie questions together in a group interview: "This question spotlights another side of the training issue Ms. Herman raised a few minutes ago." You can demonstrate your powers of synthesis by relating certain common threads to your opening position.

4 Prepare problem–solution–result (PSR) statements

A PSR is a brief, memorable personal success story. In it, you succinctly state a *problem,* describe your *solution* to that problem, and then list the components of the beneficial *result* of your solution— and all in 90 seconds or less. Describing the problem should take about 50 percent of your time. You set the stage, laying out what was at stake, what the consequences would have been if the problem had not been solved, and what constraints you may have operated under. The solution should take no more than 25 percent—what actions you took and what skills and abilities of yours were brought into play. Summarize the key steps, and avoid the temptation to go into the kind of detail that comprehensively demonstrates your understanding of your field (save this for follow-up questions). The result should be brief as well, showing quantifiable results if possible, but it should be a concise and powerful description of the immediate and long-term benefit of your actions, along with any awards or recognition that came with them.

Here is a sample:

Problem

When I was the publications manager for a small software company, there was one time when my leadership, management, and organizational skills were really put to the test. We had a telecommunications management package under development and in trial at a large potential customer. At a status meeting it was let drop that Sales had promised a complete documentation set for a week from Friday, eight days away, instead of the eight weeks agreed upon in the original development plan. Well, this was a problem, certainly, because the documentation consisted of 10 manuals, many of which were not started yet. But if we failed to produce the manuals, no matter how ridiculous the deadline, the image of the company would suffer, as would the chances for landing the customer.

Solution

I immediately pulled my staff off all other projects and divided the workload according to their various talents. I made the rounds of the other departments in the company, negotiating new delivery dates for their existing projects while gaining assurance of easy access to subject matter experts for my staff. As the days passed, I adjusted workloads to respond to evolving needs, did subprojects where necessary, and continued to work on interdepartmental cooperation.

Result

On the appointed Friday, three sets of a 10-manual, 800-page documentation suite went into the arms of DHL for delivery. As a result, my team was stronger, with the confidence that comes from meeting an impossible goal; the other departments knew they could count on us in a pinch; the potential customer was very pleased with the documentation and became a customer-in-fact not long after—which landed the company a $12 million receivable.

By preparing a collection of PSRs, you can ensure that in an interview you are primed to respond positively to a variety of questions concerning your skills and achievements. Ninety seconds is not much time at all, but for PSRs, brevity is important. By keeping them brief, you make them more memorable, and you also allow your interviewer to set the level of detail on any particular subject. If the interviewers want to know more, they can ask more questions, and, of course, you will have prepared more PSRs to cover the more in-depth questions. In the preceding example, an interviewer could ask to find out more about how the speaker negotiated the new internal delivery dates or what the most difficult project assignment was.

PSRs are not only for job interviews. They are also very handy in performance reviews and salary adjustment meetings, in which having such a store of examples demonstrating the benefits that accrue to the organization because of your presence can only work to your own benefit.

Prepare the PSR when events are still fresh in your mind. Don't wait until the annual performance review, or until you start job-hunting, or until you've finished school.

Although by no means exhaustive, Table 7-1 lists a representative set of topics for PSRs.

TABLE 7-1   Subjects for Problem–Solution–Result Statements

Specific personal attribute	Decisiveness Creativity Spoken/written communication Fast learning curve Adaptability	Versatility Leadership Confidence Analytical problem solving Organization
Specific work skill	Report writing Supervision Manual dexterity Crisis management Negotiating experience	Accounts receivable Medical knowledge Government relations Facility with computers Budget preparation
Accomplishment	Designed and implemented X Lowered costs Staffed X Set record for X Recruited and trained X	Improved productivity Organized and directed Enhanced customer relations Met goals and objectives Devised new strategies

5   Maintain effective delivery skills

You are "on stage" the entire time, even though you are seated and in an informal setting. Look at chapters **34** and **35** for a review of delivery skills.

When you answer a question from one group member, be sure to include the entire group in your eye contact.

7b. Team presentations

Often, teams form within an organization to present information on products, processes, or decisions to internal and external audiences. Usually, the information to be presented is complex enough to require an interdepartmental approach. This means that, in addition to good speaking skills, success depends upon planning, coordination, and teamwork.

1   As a group, establish an overall preparation plan

In the workplace, everyone is already overtasked, so it is crucial at the beginning of a project to make the investment in a plan that ensures people's time is used efficiently. This responsibility falls to the project manager, who should initiate the first planning session well before the date of the presentation.

> **CHECKLIST**
>
> ### Key Tasks for Group Planning
> 1. Clarify the purpose, including identifying who the stakeholders are, what their expectations are, and what constitutes success. (See **11c** and **22a**.)
> 2. Agree on the core message, the equivalent of the thesis statement, which will serve as a touchstone against which all content will be evaluated. (See **11d**.)
> 3. Divide the labor among team members.
> 4. Establish the timeline, making sure to cover intermediate milestones and practice sessions.

2   Create a content outline that includes speakers' responsibilities

If you have understood the benefits of the various steps in organizing an individual presentation (see **10, 17, 18, 19**), you will see why we recommend that a team presentation be thought of as one "macrospeech" rather than as a series of individual presentations given at the same time and place. We have all heard group presentations in which the speakers contradicted each other, overlapped in content, left out some key points altogether, jumped ahead and stole the thunder of upcoming presenters, and even squabbled publicly about the order and coverage of points. To provide coherent content and project a professional image, it is crucial that each team member have a picture of the whole presentation and how each piece relates to that whole.

Before an outline can be decided upon, the group will have engaged in initial brainstorming and preliminary decision making. When the topic is narrowed and focused, someone needs to create a detailed outline of the speech, complete with an introduction and a conclusion, transitions, time limits for each segment, and a list of visual support and equipment needed.

In this process of decision making and outline crafting, the group should come to agreement on several issues.

How will the presentation be introduced? This may be done by the team leader, though it might be added to the responsibility of the first speaker. In any case, it should cover the basics of an introduction, making the audience want to listen, telling them what will be covered, and introducing the team members. (See **31**.)

What are the main points of the presentation? Thinking about it this way reinforces the need for each segment to serve a clear purpose in developing the core idea. If the group merely decides that Andrea will talk about her part of the project, and then Clint will talk about his, and so on, there is no guarantee that the components will be relevant and will fit together. As with a speech, it is prudent to have only a few key ideas and, generally, a few speakers. However, in an extended presentation, each group leader can present the main idea, and additional speakers can present segments that function as subpoints under that topic. However simple or complex the organization, there needs to be prior agreement on the goal of each part of the presentation and on the time allotted for it.

How will transitions be handled? Listeners need to be reminded of the overall road map for the presentation. The transition from segment to segment can be handled by a group leader who acts as an emcee of sorts, or each speaker can be charged with building a bridge to the next. In either case, it is important to review the principles of transitions (see **31**) and to go beyond "Here's Johnny" to offer a statement like "Once the basic design is completed, it needs to be tested. Here is where John Carlton and his able group come in. John is now going to tell you about the steps they go through to make sure our clever designs actually work."

How will the presentation be concluded? Again, the functions of reviewing and integrating the material presented can be done by a group leader or by the final presenter. The important point is that there be a planned wrap-up that ties things together and ends on a positive note. (See **31**.)

How will questions be handled? The plan either needs to build in a question-and-answer period after each segment of a longer or more technical presentation or to allow for questions at the end. Decide who will field questions and direct them to the appropriate person. Sometimes, individuals are present who do not actually participate in the main presentation but are available as resources during the question-and-answer period. (See **37**.)

3   Agree on unifying elements

Think of projecting the impression of unity, mutual respect, and teamwork as one of the goals of each presentation. Having a clearly organized presentation is the most important way to make this point; however, there are a few additional steps a team can take to show they are "on the same page."

- *Make the segments parallel.* This may involve common phrasing of the main idea of each piece: "With our technological Innovations, we will own this marketspace next year. . . . With our dedicated and knowledgeable sales force, we will own this marketspace next year. . . . With our uncompromising support, we will own this marketspace next year." Or, in some cases, it may be appropriate to use the same suborganization in each part of the presentation. In a cross-departmental status report, each department might follow this pattern: (1) review the goal, (2) report on progress to date, (3) report on problems encountered, (4) identify solutions, and (5) provide a current timetable.

- *Use common themes and phrases.* Develop a glossary of technical terms, abbreviations, and acronyms, and get agreement within the group to adhere to the "approved list," so that listeners aren't confused by multiple words meaning the same thing. Once the substance of the presentation is in place, look for ways to emphasize certain points that capture the unique approach of your organization or the special features you are offering. Just as the main ideas can have common phrasing, other integral concepts and themes can be consciously constructed in parallel language woven throughout the presentation.

- *Find opportunities for cross references.* Speak of your copresenters with respect and admiration. Use terms like *colleague.* Briefly forecast or refer back to their points, and direct questions to them acknowledging their expertise.

- *Present a consistent visual message.* Slides, presentation software, and diagrams should have a common look-and-feel. Agree on a template at the beginning of a process, and have a designated specialist to polish and unify the material coming in from disparate sources.

4   Practice the presentation

Busy professionals who know their topic well and talk about it often are reluctant to have formal practice sessions. Practice is important for an individual talk, but it is *essential* for pulling together a team of speakers.

- *Schedule at least one early run-through even if some pieces are still under construction.* The goal is to get a sense of how the presentation fits together and to find opportunities to improve it.
- *Schedule at least one final run-through.* This will serve to polish the transitions and to familiarize the speakers with the equipment and visual aids used.
- *Arrange for feedback on the presentations during the practice stage.* Participants may comment on one another's content and clarity. It is also common for managers or other organizational members to sit in on practice sessions to make suggestions. For very important presentations, simulations may be staged with persons role-playing potential audience members, and communication consultants may be brought in to videotape the rehearsal and even coach individuals on presentation skills.
- *Pay attention to the timing of the overall presentation, whatever the level of rehearsal.* It is not inappropriate to have someone give time signals during the actual presentation to keep the team on track.

5   Debrief after each practice or presentation

Shortly after a presentation, whether it was successful or disappointing, the team should meet to talk candidly about what worked and what can be improved in the future.

CHAPTER 8
Civic and Political Context

When you speak as a member of a community or a political unit, you may be entering a context in which there are conflicts of interest. For a diverse group to come to consensus, communicators have to work to build bonds. These contexts are often characterized by explicit affirmations of respect and common ground. Notice, for example, how representatives from opposing political parties continually say things like "My highly distinguished colleague from South Carolina . . ." and "The esteemed senator and I have cosponsored legislation in the past, and it is with regret that I must reluctantly disagree with her remarks." In a democratic society, we allow for the testing of ideas through vigorous debate and argumentation. We maintain social order by setting fairly strict rules constraining the form of speech. The ideal is that personal attacks are taboo, as are arguments from pure self-interest. We do not argue for restricted parking in the neighborhood around a university campus by saying, "I am inconvenienced, and my property value may be jeopardized." Instead, we state that the community needs to maintain its special character and to continue to attract residents who will be good neighbors to the university.

Passion and eloquence are not out of place in this context. Sound argument and evidence are frequently combined with appeals to common values.

Typical speaking situations in this context include public debates, community forums, legal arguments, panel discussions, political conventions, appearances before community agencies, rallies, and talk shows.

8a. Tailor your individual presentation to a group format

Group formats include, among others, the symposium, panel, forum, and debate.

1   Confirm the format and clarify expectations

There are many versions of group presentations, and too often, their standard labels are used interchangeably and inconsistently. You may be invited to be part of a "panel" and prepare accordingly, only to discover that the organizer has actually set up a debate. Here are the definitions most commonly used by speech communication texts:

Symposium: A series of short speeches, usually informative, on various aspects of the same general topic. Audience questions often follow.

Panel: A group of experts publicly discussing a topic among themselves. Individually prepared speeches, if any, are limited to very brief opening statements.

Forum: Essentially a question-and-answer format. One or more experts may be questioned by a panel of other experts, journalists, and/or the audience.

Debate: A structured argument in which participants speak for or against a preannounced proposition. The proposition is worded so that one side has the burden of proof, and that same side has the benefit of speaking first and last. Speakers assume an advocacy role and attempt to persuade the audience, not each other.

Do not assume that the person arranging the program uses the terms this way. Find out as much as possible about the program.

2 Prepare as carefully for a group presentation as for a speech

Do not be lulled into thinking a group presentation is merely a conversation. Even if you already know your topic very well, brush up on your research, plan a general outline, and bring along notes with key facts and statistics. Prepare visual aids if appropriate. Plan an introduction and a conclusion for your formal part of the session.

Be prepared to adapt, however, in your best extemporaneous style. Because you are in a group, do not give your talk in isolation; make frequent references to the other panelists: "Ms. Larsen has pointed out some of the reasons mental health care is so expensive." Also, unless the panelists coordinate beforehand, overlap is inevitable on related topics. When you hear your favorite example or best statistic being presented, quickly reorganize and substitute the backup material you wisely brought along. Review the principles in chapter **37** for use in the question-and-answer exchange.

3 Be aware of your nonverbal communication

When you speak in a group, you should still follow the guidelines for effective delivery. The fact that you might be seated does not allow you to be offhand or overly casual. On the contrary, you may need to project a little more energy to compensate for the lack of visibility and movement.

What far too many speakers seem to overlook is that they are "on stage" during the whole presentation. While other speakers are talking, look attentive and be courteous. Nod and respond facially in ways sufficiently subtle that you do not upstage the speaker. Above all, do not distract the audience by whispering, fidgeting, or grimacing in disbelief. Do not hurt your own credibility by looking bored or by frantically going over your notes.

The previous suggestions, combined with general speaking skills, should get you through most group situations. The public debate presents some additional challenges.

8b. Follow common guidelines for a public debate

Formal academic debating and competitive tournament debating require skills beyond the scope of this handbook. Any good public speaker, though, can handle informal debates—such as are held during election campaigns or at public meetings or club functions—by remembering and applying the following prescriptions.

1   Consider the opposing point of view

Research both sides of the topic to see what evidence you will encounter. Look at the strongest points of your opponent's case and the weakest points of your own. This helps you anticipate the arguments and prepare for them.

2   Organize your ideas, arguments, and evidence

First, develop your own best case for your position, which will be your opening statement or constructive speech. Next, plan attacks on or challenges to the opposing position, which you will use to respond to or refute their case. Finally, compile defense material, which you will probably need to answer challenges to your position.

3   Prepare your opening speech carefully

Pay particular attention to organizational clarity and to sound support of assertions. Follow the general suggestions for speaking to an unfavorable audience. (See **23b.3**.)

4   Address major issues during the refutation phase

When you refute a point, explain the argumentative impact and show what damage you have done to the underlying logical structure of your opponent's argument. If you weaken an opponent's case, drive home the point by issuing a specific challenge for the opponent to repair the damage.

5   Save time for a summary of the argument

Debates can be confusing, with points flying back and forth. So, even if you have to skip some additional specifics, use the final few minutes to focus the controversy, interpreting how it has emerged during the discussion. End with a persuasive closing statement and a clincher that capitalizes on your strongest point.

6   Maintain a calm and professional demeanor

As with sports, poker games, or any other competitive activity, emotions can sometimes get out of hand. Do not lose perspective—getting the last word on every single point is less important than maintaining your long-term credibility. Even if another debater distorts or misleads, you should remain courteous and unflappable. Your tone may be vigorous, but it should never be hostile. Address your arguments to the audience, and refer to the other speaker by name, and not as "my opponent." Treat the person's arguments respectfully, and grant good points that are made. Always assume the honesty and good intentions of the other speaker. Never say, "That's a lie"; rather, say, "I think those figures are inaccurate. Here's what I found." Keep in mind the wisdom of the maxim, "you can disagree without being disagreeable."

CHAPTER 9
Social and Ceremonial Context

Arguably, the most ancient forms of speech are those that people developed simply to affirm their connectedness. We make small talk to share our everyday experiences, and we draw together to share joy, grief, outrage, and reverence. The expectation in social and ceremonial contexts is that the participants are united. This is not a time to mention difference or to actively build consensus. Just assume consensus and celebrate it.

Some speeches, classified in this book as evocative, are designed more to fill a ritualistic function than to transmit information or change behavior. These follow standard forms, and, as with all rituals, the familiarity of the form is one source of the emotional satisfaction participants derive. Happy moments like winning an Olympic medal and sad ones like mourning a death take on added meaning when accompanied by traditional, familiar ceremony. Certain words, gestures, and acts are expected—the Olympic athlete would undoubtedly be disappointed if the medal award ceremony and playing of the national anthem were replaced by a gift certificate presented at a pizza house get-together. As you might imagine from the preceding, you are by necessity forced to tread near that line separating tradition and triteness when you give a ceremonial speech.

Cover the expected bases no matter how predictable they are. Do not be *too* creative, but at the same time, strive to find ways to make these ceremonial moments special and fresh. Above all, this means avoiding overused phrases and constructions. Unless you prepare carefully, you will hear yourself ad-libbing clichés you would never use otherwise:

On this auspicious occasion . . .

This small token of our esteem . . .

With no further ado . . .

Information exchange is of secondary importance in these speeches; style becomes crucial. Because the two or three ideas you transmit will be fairly basic, you should expend your energy crafting ways to express them, polishing your language and timing. This is made easier by the fact that ceremonial speeches are usually short. Frequently, a memorized or partially memorized mode of delivery is best. (See **28d**.) Your language should be more elevated than in everyday speech, but not so formal as to seem stiff or unnatural.

9a. Identify the needs of the people involved

In preparing all ceremonial speeches, consider two questions.

What are the needs of the person to whom or about whom I speak?

Suppose that as company president you give a safety award each year, and so for you it is old hat. However, it is a special moment for the recipient. What can you say that he or she will remember with pride? Address the *uniqueness* of that person. Although the form of the speech may be stylized, the content should be personalized.

What are the needs of the people for whom I speak?

In most ceremonial or ritualistic addresses, you can think of yourself as speaking on behalf of some group or community and not just for yourself. People have come together to share emotions as well as—or instead of—information. Yet these emotions may be unfocused. When you deliver a thoughtful and moving speech, you symbolize the feelings of audience members and are thus bonding them. You also help them gain perspective and find deeper meanings in their experiences. Early in the preparation for this sort of speech, envision yourself as a vehicle for group expression. Typical speaking situations in this context include presenting an award, proposing a toast, and nominating a candidate.

9b. Follow common guidelines for various contexts

When presenting an award or honor

1. Unless a surprise is part of the tradition, announce the person's name early in the speech.
2. Explain how the person was selected for the honor, and by whom.
3. Besides listing achievements or qualities, use a brief anecdote or description to capture some unique qualities of the person.
4. If a tangible object—plaque, certificate, key to the city—is presented, explain what it symbolizes.

When delivering a eulogy or memorial address

1. Do not accept this assignment unless you feel able to keep your composure.
2. Acknowledge shared feelings of sadness, loss, and anger, but do not dwell on them.
3. Highlight and celebrate the value of the one being eulogized. Some people present may have known the person only professionally or only socially, or only long ago or only recently. Touch on several aspects of the person's life. Do not be reluctant to share light, and even humorous, moments.

4. Use phrases that bond the group together: "All of us who cared for Eleanor . . ." or "I see many people here who . . ." or "We all know how persistent she could be when she believed in an idea."

5. Try to place the loss in some larger, more optimistic perspective. Themes of the continuity of life, appreciation of each moment, and growth through pain are timeless and universal. These philosophical concepts are still a source of comfort.

6. Do not play on the grief of a captive audience to promote a specific religious belief or social or political cause.

When giving a toast

1. If the toast is a formal part of the event, make arrangements ahead of time so that everyone will have a beverage in hand at the proper point. Be sure that nonalcoholic beverages are available so that everyone can participate.

2. Refine your basic idea into a short message of goodwill, and memorize it.

3. Choose the words carefully. Humor, wordplay, rhymes, metaphors, and proverbs all find their way into toasts. If no witty inspiration comes to you and if the toasts in books all seem corny and contrived, then there is absolutely nothing wrong with taking a sincere thought and stating it gracefully.

4. If the toast is more than a few sentences—really, a short speech—do not make listeners hoist their glasses the full time. Start out as a speech. Then at the end say something like, "Let's raise our glasses to our new laboratory director. Sheila, we wish you luck, and success, and may all your troubles be microscopic!"

When accepting an award or a tribute

1. Unless asked in advance to prepare a major acceptance speech, limit your remarks to a few sentences.

2. Accept the honor with pride. Do not let humility and embarrassment make you seem to reject the gesture.

3. Share the honor with those who deserve it. But do not get into an endless thank-you litany of the sort that always makes the Academy Awards presentation run overtime.

4. Give a gift back to the audience. Can you offer them a genuine tribute, an insight, or even a funny story related to your relationship with them?

5. End with a future-oriented statement about what the honor means to you.

PART **3** # Planning Your Speech

CHAPTER 10. **Managing Your Preparation Time**

Have a schedule to structure the preparation of your speech.

CHAPTER 11. **Topic Selection and Analysis**

Select an interesting and manageable topic and determine what response you hope to evoke with the topic.

CHAPTER 12. **Analyzing Your Audience**

Base your speech preparation on thorough audience analysis.

CHAPTER 10

Managing Your Preparation Time

One way to avoid false starts and wasted effort when preparing a speech is to give yourself the time to organize your preparation from the outset. An effective plan balances the needs of creativity against the constraints of a deadline.

10a. Allow time for the four phases of creativity

It has been proposed that there are four phases to the creative process: preparation, incubation, illumination, and refinement.[1]

- The *preparation* phase, for speakers, includes gathering the materials, analyzing the topic and audience, and making the first attempts at putting the parts together.

- *Incubation* is a phase marked by frustration, and even despair, when the problems seem insoluble and the speech is set aside. During this phase, your unconscious mind and your peripheral awareness work on the problems.

- *Illumination* occurs when, suddenly, the pieces fit together, or there is a dawning awareness that grows in intensity. Illumination may occur while you are working on the project, but it is just as likely to occur when you are driving down the freeway, taking a shower, or even sleeping. Exhilaration and relief accompany this phase. You work eagerly and fluidly, accomplishing more in a few hours than you have in several days.

- *Refinement* comes next. After the creative burst, there follows a comparatively long period of checking details, fine tuning, and polishing. Like the preparation phase, this phase is largely cognitive and requires concentration and discipline.

This delineation of the four-phase creative process is provided to stress the importance of allocating time for *each* phase. Many creative products have never been shared with the world because the creator gave up during the refinement phase. Other fine ideas have failed to be appreciated because the speaker presented them directly after the illumination phase, without spending the needed time on refinement. The rest of this chapter supplies guidance for optimizing your planning so that none of the creative phases is slighted.

---

[1]Based on Catherine Patrick, *What Is Creative Thinking?* (New York: Philosophical Library, 1955), 1–48.

10b. Make a realistic timetable

At one university, a group of public speaking instructors infor-
mally survey their students at the end of each term, asking what
advice they would pass on to the next group of students. Consistently and overwhelmingly, the surveyed students' response is,
"Start early." They all regret underestimating the time necessary to
prepare a speech that reflected what they knew they could do. To
know what is "early" enough for you, you need to invest the effort
to create a realistic timetable.

When professionals plan major projects—whether it is organizing a sales convention, designing a recycling campaign, or tooling
up to manufacture a new product—they use a number of structured time management techniques. Without getting into the intricacies of PERT systems or Gantt charts, there are a few valuable
principles that you can adapt.

1   List the tasks and estimate the time needed

Be sure that you include intellectual tasks such as analyzing your
topic, and not just physical tasks like going to the library or making
visual aids. For each task, jot down the most optimistic and least
optimistic estimate of the time needed. When setting a timetable
for preparing your speech, always provide extra time to allow for
emergencies. Speech research and rehearsal can go on when you
have a headache or when you are in an emotional funk, but the
creative aspects of speech organization require physical and psychological alertness.

Invest time at the beginning to gather the information you
need on schedules and availability of resources so that your time
estimates for each task are accurate.

2   Determine the order in which tasks must be completed

This is what professional project managers call *determining the critical path*. It is not enough to schedule three hours for speech practice and call that "planning." Those three hours must occur after
the speech outline is completed. The outline cannot be completed
until you have articulated your speech purpose and goals, and so
on. When you lay out the entire project in this linear fashion and
add up the time estimates for each task, you will see if it is possible
to reach your goals. Often, you will realize that, in order to succeed, certain preliminary steps must be taken *now*.

To take this further, suppose your speech is due in three weeks,
and the critical path adds up to five weeks. If your plans are unrealistic, it is better to discover this now than two days before the
speech, giving you time to scale down your plans.

Ultimately, what's most important is that you decide at the outset on a schedule you can meet. Otherwise, you will end up skip-
ping the final and crucial steps of practice and refinement altogether.

3   Set intermediate deadlines for major stages

In Figure 10-1, speech planning and practice is divided into four stages: initial decisions and analysis, research, development of speech materials, and practice. For each stage, the central tasks are contained in a box with a solid border. The related but less time-bound tasks are surrounded by a broken border. Generally, time flows downward and to the right in this chart. The figure also shows the transitions between stages where deadlines fall naturally. That is, the central tasks of one stage cannot really be started until the central tasks of the previous stage are completed. At some point, you must make preliminary decisions regarding a narrowed and focused topic, purpose, and thesis, and then get into your serious

Initial decisions and analysis	Research	Development of speech materials	Practice
Select topic Narrow topic Clarify purpose Frame thesis statement Analyze topic Analyze audience	*Preliminary research* Do background reading Locate resources		Ongoing talk
	Main research effort Investigate articles, books, and websites Conduct interviews	Jot down possible points Develop rough working outline	
	Continuing research Check details Locate a few specific facts/statistics Watch daily paper/newscasts for latest applications	Develop full-sentence outline of points to be covered Add supporting materials and attention factors to outline Prepare introduction, conclusion, and transitions	
		Prepare presentation aids and handouts Prepare speech notes Make minor revisions to content and style	Developmental practice sessions Feedback practice sessions Refinement practice sessions

FIGURE 10-1   Speech Planning and Practice

research. And, at some point, you must stop gathering material and put the speech together. If you do not have a speech outline soon enough, you cannot begin the first stage of practice. There is no point in scheduling your feedback practice sessions so late that you cannot take advantage of the feedback.

Sometimes, however, you must briefly retrace your steps. For instance, important new evidence may present itself, or a feedback session may show that more visual aids are needed. Such movement should be minimal, and under almost no circumstances should you be returning to tasks "way back." We feel very strongly that you should not be making any substantive changes to the speech at the last minute. During the final practice sessions, you should have complete mastery of the organization and basic content so your consciousness can center on refinement of phrasing, delivery, and timing, and on attainment of the desired audience response.

10c. Make your speech preparation an oral and collaborative process

Because a speech is delivered orally, it should be composed orally. And because the meaning of a speech is dependent on the interaction between speaker and listeners, it should be created collaboratively. Keep the "speech as conversation" theme foremost even during those parts of preparation that require you to draw on your skills as a writer or performer.

Although you cannot practice "the speech" until your basic outline exists, one form of oral preparation begins with your first idea. This is the ongoing talk suggested by the large, dotted section in the Practice column of Figure 10-1. Talk to yourself about your topic. Talk to other people. Try out your ideas and words; see if they make sense. You are not, however, practicing your speech in front of other people. Work your ideas into conversations over lunch and chats with colleagues and friends. You do not need a reaction to every idea from each individual you talk to. After talking to a number of people, you will find that you have begun to word the speech.

If you are fortunate, you may be able to add continuity to this oral and collaborative process by structuring it to embrace a more formal method for obtaining feedback and support. (See **33**.)

CHAPTER 11

Topic Selection and Analysis

Do not settle on the first topic that occurs to you. Consider a number of different topics and examine their various facets. When you have chosen a promising one, narrow it down and crystallize your reasons for speaking about that subject.

11a. Select a speech topic

As a speaker, you have varying degrees of freedom in topic choice, according to the situation. At one pole is the office manager who is told to give an oral report on the effectiveness of the current secretarial assignment system. At the other is the student who is told, "Friday morning you will speak third and persuade us to do something, anything." Most speaking situations fall between these extremes. You may be asked to welcome delegates to a conference or to speak to the Rotary Club about the economy. In these cases, you still have to select a theme for your talk. Even when the general topic is set, you need to home in on an approach that will fit you, the audience, and the situation.

1 Draw from your own experience, expertise, and interests

You bring a body of knowledge to the speech situation. Perhaps this is why you have been asked to speak about your experiences in the stock market. Or your background may be the springboard for discovering a topic or a slant on a topic that can be developed into a compelling and substantial speech. You should ask yourself a number of questions to help you do this.

In answering the questions that follow, do not stop to evaluate every answer as you write it down. You want to generate a list of possible topics by brainstorming. Respond to these questions in as many different ways as you can think of, even if some seem silly. Later, you will select your best topic in terms of audience and occasion.

- *What unusual experiences have you had?* Consider places you have traveled, jobs you have held, and events in which you have participated. Do not overlook aspects of your experience that you take for granted but that might be interesting to others.

- *What special knowledge or expertise do you have?* Each of us has developed mastery in certain areas. This may be in relation to how you make your living, or to people you meet in that context. Your course of study in school has increased your knowledge in areas that perhaps are obscure to your potential audience. Think, too, about the talents, hobbies, and skills you have developed.

- *What strong opinions and beliefs do you hold?* What topics stir your passions? These issues, which probably touch on your core values (see **25**), frequently make good speech topics. Besides those issues that can provoke you into heated debate, there are others that fascinate you intellectually. Explaining the basis of a pet theory or favorite area of inquiry can make an excellent speech.

- *What would you like to know more about?* Use the occasion of giving a speech as an opportunity to research some topic that has piqued your curiosity.

2 Select a topic appropriate to the audience and occasion

By brainstorming answers to the questions in **11a.1**, you have created a possible subject list of great variety. To choose the one topic on which you will speak, you next need to think about who the audience members are and why they have gathered together and what they expect. This step can help you rule out a number of topics. The occasion for a speech is closely related to its context (see **part 2**).

When you have removed the inappropriate subjects from your list, you then need to find the *most* appropriate of the remainder. Empathy is your best tool. Imagine sitting on those hard chairs in the boardroom or classroom. What would you sit still to hear?

3 Select a topic that is both timely and timeless

You may still have more than one possible topic on your list even after going through the processes in **11a.1** and **11a.2**. Other things being equal, the best topics are those that are both timely and timeless. Certain issues have always been and always will be part of human discourse. The rights of the individual versus the rights of the group and the need for security versus the need for adventure were being discussed 1,000 years ago, 100 years ago, and this past year; they will continue to be discussed by our descendants. When you tie a contemporary event to one of these enduring human dialogues, you link the timely and the timeless.

Neither one of these conditions by itself is an indication that the topic will be a good one. Consider the criterion of timeliness. If an event has been front-page news for two weeks, a speech on that topic may be timely. But unless you can tell your audience what it all means in more universal terms, you probably will give them little that they do not already know. You have wasted their time. The reverse is true as well: Your audience can miss or fail to be interested in the profundity of your topic if you do not tie it into the fabric of their current existence. A profound, timeless topic should have a timely application. A timely speech should point out the timeless implication of the subject.

Table 11-1 shows how topics that are too narrowly contemporary or too broadly universal may be altered to meet these criteria.

TABLE 11-1   Timely and Timeless Topics

Timely (but Potentially Trivial)	Timeless (but Potentially Diffuse)	Timely and Timeless
There was a major confrontation last week when the Ku Klux Klan held a rally downtown.	Freedom of assembly must be protected for everyone.	Last week's confrontation over the Ku Klux Klan rally raised important questions about what restrictions, if any, should be placed on freedom of assembly.
I took a trip to Quebec.	Travel helps people understand diversity of human cultures.	My trip to Quebec helped me to understand my own culture by contrasting it to another.
Our company has adopted a new profit-sharing plan.	The best management philosophy is one that treats the employees like partners.	Our new profit-sharing plan will benefit the employees directly and reflect an enlightened philosophy of management.

Notice the different kinds of speeches to which the timely/timeless standard can apply.

11b. Narrow your topic

An important principle is that the selection of a topic is not complete until that topic has been narrowed to accommodate the constraints of time. The main advantage of limiting a topic is to ensure depth of analysis. To avoid superficiality, you have to keep one eye on the clock while preparing your speech. To delve into a topic, you have to limit yourself to the number of points that can be adequately developed in the time available. You can expedite your research and preparation by narrowing your topic from the beginning. Thus, instead of looking up all the books and articles about higher education, you can focus on those related to the financing of community colleges, or to pass/fail grading, or to coed dormitories, as the narrowed topic warrants.

1   Determine the number of ideas time allows

The average speaker utters 100 to 150 words per minute. If you speak very rapidly or very slowly, you may fall outside this range. Chances are, though, that your rate of speaking is somewhere near 125 words per minute. Conveniently, a typical journalistic paragraph of simple sentences runs about 125 words. Thus, on average, a speaker delivers roughly one short paragraph per minute. If your material is highly technical or interspersed with statistics, dialogue, and dramatic pauses, or if you speak slowly, you had better allot two minutes per paragraph. This system, though basic, allows you to do some realistic narrowing of your topic.

For instance, if you plan on speaking informatively for 8 to 10 minutes on the U.S. criminal justice system, you need to set aside at least 1 to 2 minutes for the introduction and 1 minute for the conclusion. This leaves 6 to 7 minutes for the body of your speech.

The same principle can be applied to longer speeches, business presentations, and lectures. A 20-minute speech can be thought of as 20 short, simple paragraphs or 10 longer, more developed paragraphs.

2 Select a few main ideas to cover

Knowing that a speech should be limited to two or three main points does not tell you *which* two or three to select. Consider the following questions, which can help you narrow your topic effectively.

Which aspects of your topic are best covered in the public, oral mode? A speech should not be used to transmit routine information, to discuss specialized problems of a small portion of the audience, or, of course, to indulge the speaker's ego.

Which aspects of your topic are best suited to this audience and occasion? Select those points that relate most directly to the needs, attitudes, knowledge, and expectations of your listeners. (See **12**.)

Which aspects of your topic can you present most effectively? Select those points on which you have the most knowledge, in which you have the most interest, and that best fit your speaking personality.

11c. Clarify the purpose of your speech

Each speech has a general purpose, a specific purpose, and a set of desired outcomes. Like a speech's occasion, these aspects of a speech are also closely related to its context (see **part 2**).

1 Identify the general purpose

What is your intention? Are you trying to change people's minds? To teach them something? To move them?

The general purpose of a speech can be classified in one of three ways:

Inform: A speech designed to explain, instruct, define, clarify, demonstrate, or teach

Persuade: A speech designed to influence, convince, motivate, sell, preach, or stimulate action

Evoke: A speech designed to entertain, inspire, celebrate, commemorate, or bond, or to help listeners relive

You will quickly discover that no speech has only one purpose. Most have a combination, but with one purpose usually dominant. For instance, a classroom lecture is used primarily to teach, but at the same time it can be used to shape attitudes. The purpose of a campaign speech is to drum up support for the candidate, but the speech can also entertain. An excellent sermon might do all three: inform, persuade, and evoke. Even though most speeches have multiple purposes, they are sometimes grouped as types of speeches that correspond to the purposes. Within these general categories of informative, persuasive and evocative speeches, of course, there are many more specialized formats and genres. Strategic guidelines for informative speaking (**22**) and persuasive speaking (**23**) give insight into how these purposes are realized in common types of speeches, and all of Part 2 addresses adapting speeches for different contexts.

2 Determine the specific purpose

Knowing which of the three purposes—to inform, persuade, or evoke—is predominant in your speech will help you in the next step: deciding what you really want to accomplish with your topic. In phrasing this purpose, isolate your central reason for speaking. Do not go any further until you can complete this sentence:

If there is one goal I want to achieve in this speech, it is to . . .

At this point, your topic should have a clear focus:

Not: My specific purpose is to inform the audience about politics.

But: My specific purpose is to inform the audience about the role of the two-party system in American politics.

Not: My specific purpose is to persuade the audience against drunken driving.

But: My specific purpose is to persuade the audience of the need for stiffer penalties for those convicted of drunken driving.

3 Specify your desired outcomes

Once your goal is phrased in the terms of what *you* want to do, turn it around and phrase it in terms of what you want your *audience* to do:

If there is one action I want my listeners to take after my speech, it is to . . .

In other words, if your speech is a success, what will your audience do? This is called the *primary audience outcome.*

Not: My desired outcome is to sell this product.

But: My desired outcome is to have you buy this product.

Not: My desired outcome is to explain photosynthesis.

But: My desired outcome is to have you understand the workings of photosynthesis.

Notice the significance of the verbs in each case. The emphasis is on the behavior you want the audience to adopt.

Next break the primary audience outcome into a series of *contributing audience outcomes.* In phrasing these components, continue to use verbs that describe overt actions rather than general states of mind.

"I want my audience to *appreciate* art" is fine for a primary audience outcome, but you must go further and ask yourself how you will know if you have succeeded. What, exactly, are people doing when they are appreciating art? If you think about the specific behaviors or operations that contribute to appreciating art, you will come up with a list like this:

- *Go* to galleries
- *Read* books on art
- *Create* pieces of art themselves

Observe how speech purposes and outcomes can be crystallized for a persuasive speech:

General purpose: To persuade.

Specific purpose: To convince the audience that changes in individual behaviors are needed to protect our environment.

Primary audience outcome: I want my audience to commit themselves actively to environmental concerns.

Contributing audience outcomes: I want my audience to

- use public transportation when possible
- minimize the use of nonbiodegradable materials
- recycle paper, glass, aluminum, and steel
- make their dwellings energy efficient
- support environmentally oriented political candidates and contribute money and time to environmental causes

11d. Develop a clear thesis statement

Every topic analysis needs a thesis statement that gives you something concrete against which to test ideas.

1   Formulate a single declarative sentence

In contrast to your "purpose" and "outcomes," your thesis sentence states your topic as a proposition to be proved or a theme to be developed. This sentence, sometimes referred to as the *central idea*, gives your speech a focus. It helps you make the transition from thinking about where you want to end up (your goal) to how to get there.

A thesis statement should not merely announce your topic. It should capsulize what you plan to say about the topic. The rationale for insisting on the complete sentence is the clarity of thought that comes when you must delineate both what you are talking about (the subject of the sentence) and what you are saying about it (the predicate of the sentence). A thesis statement whose single declarative sentence is "Today I will talk about roses" makes *you* the subject and makes the fact that you *are talking* the predicate—hardly the essence of your speech content.

However, "Roses are beautiful" makes the topic (roses) serve as subject and the point being made about it (they are beautiful) the predicate. See **11d.3** for further discussion of the role of propositional phrasing in testing the relevance and completeness of ideas.

Be sure that the thesis statement includes enough information to differentiate your approach from other possibilities.

Informative Speech

> *Not:*   My speech is on gangs.
>
> *Or even:* Young people find gangs attractive.
>
> *But:*   There are a number of sociological and developmental reasons for gangs being attractive to youths.

Persuasive Speech

> *Not:*   Something must be done about tuberculosis.
>
> *Or even:* Drug-resistant TB is on the increase and should be combated.
>
> *But:*   The threat of a resurgence of TB requires a major governmental program of education, research, and treatment.

2   Break your thesis statement into a list of questions

As a speaker, you need to break up a topic to find all the subtopics within it. By committing yourself to developing a thesis, you take on an obligation to discover and answer a set of questions. These questions are the ones your listeners will be asking themselves before they accept your thesis. Thus they are the ones you should identify before proceeding with your research.

Do not be restricted by the wording of your thesis. In analyzing the grammatical structure of a sentence, you probably learned to fill in the understood subjects and predicates. "Pick up that book

55

and then let go" has to be seen as "(You) pick up that book and then (you) let go (of it)."

Consider this thesis for a persuasive speech:

> Like other industrialized nations, the United States has a caste-like social system based on race, sex, and age.

Embedded in this thesis are six questions your audience will be asking as they listen:

- Does the United States have a castelike system?
- Is the stratification based on race?
- Is the stratification based on sex?
- Is the stratification based on age?
- Is the United States an industrialized nation?
- Are these characteristics shared by other industrialized nations?

For a speech about comic books, you might develop the following thesis sentence:

> With their scope, history, and influence, comic books are an interesting component of American popular culture.

For this informative speech, four questions present themselves:

- What is the scope of comic book themes?
- What is the history of the comic book?
- What influence have comic books had?
- Are comic books an interesting component of American popular culture?

The answers to these questions will not necessarily be the main points of your speech, and you might not develop your ideas in this order. However, the analysis serves to direct your research and prevents you from any glaring oversights.

3   Identify the kind of proposition you are advancing

In a persuasive speech, the thesis of a speech and the claim of an argument are described as propositions—the speaker *proposes* something to the audience. There are three kinds of propositions: the proposition of *fact*, the proposition of *value*, and the proposition of *policy*. When you are developing a persuasive speech, discovering which kind of proposition lies at the heart of your speech is essential to identifying your obligations and planning your persuasive strategy. See **23**.

Proposition of fact   It may seem that if something is a fact there is no need to use persuasion to establish it, but there are issues in the factual domain that cannot be verified directly. For instance, there either is or is not life on other planets. The question is one of fact, but because we lack the means to find out, we must argue from the data we have, drawing the most logical inferences therefrom. Here are some other examples:

> More than two cups of coffee a day increases the chance of cancer of the pancreas.

> Converting to solar energy can save the average homeowner money.

Proposition of value Persuasive speakers are often attempting to prove evaluative positions. Their goal is to judge the worth of something, to establish that it is good or bad, wise or foolish, just or unjust, ethical or unethical, beautiful or ugly, competent or incompetent. For example:

> It is wrong to try to avoid jury duty.

> Charlie Parker was the greatest sax player ever.

Proposition of policy Most common and most complex among persuasive theses is the proposition of policy, which advocates a specific course of action. Here are some propositions of policy:

> The federal government should legalize marijuana for private use.

> You should send your children to private schools.

K E Y P O I N T   **Kinds of Propositions**

Propositions of fact: IS/IS NOT
Propositions of value: GOOD/BAD
Propositions of policy: SHOULD/SHOULD NOT

11e. If necessary, select a speech title

Although every speech needs a thesis and a purpose, not every speech needs a title. A title is necessary when there is to be advance publicity, when there is a printed program, and, usually, when the speaker is going to be formally introduced. Unless there is a definite deadline to announce your title, you can defer selecting one until after the speech is composed. An effective title should pique interest in your subject and make the audience eager to listen. Sometimes, a metaphor, quotation, or allusion that is central to the speech can be part of the title.

A title can take any grammatical form. It can be a declarative sentence, question, phrase, or fragment:

> "Freedom of Speech Is in Jeopardy"

> "Is Free Speech Really Free?"

> "Threats to Free Speech"

> "Free Speech: An Endangered Species"

> **KEY POINT** **Thesis Statement versus Speech Title** Do not confuse the thesis statement with the speech title. The thesis statement is a declarative sentence essential for organizing and composing the speech. The title is not.

CHAPTER 12

Analyzing Your Audience

The ultimate outcome of any speech situation is a product of what the speaker actually says and how the listeners process and interpret what is said. Audience analysis therefore is much more than a step in planning a speech. It involves the constant awareness of those who are the "coauthors" of your speech—your listeners.

You speak to a particular group of people because you want a certain response from them. If you do not know the composition of that group, you cannot make intelligent decisions about what to include, what to emphasize, and how best to arrange and present your ideas. Research your audience thoroughly. Their age, sex, attitudes, and expectations are all relevant to your planning. Within a given audience, the degree of homogeneity or heterogeneity can differ for each of the characteristics discussed in this chapter.

We approach each of these characteristics as a discrete factor and describe the techniques to be used with various kinds of homogeneous audiences. *You* have to "mix and match" these techniques as you uncover the actual composition of your potential audience.

12a. Seek information through numerous channels

When you ask an audience to listen to your ideas, you are asking them to come partway into your experience. It is your obligation, in turn, to go partway into theirs.

The following are valuable sources of information about your audience. But it's important not to limit yourself to any one of them:

- *Use direct observation.* If you have enough lead time, try to observe the audience, perhaps at a business meeting or while they listen to another speaker.

- *Do systematic data collection.* One excellent way to become informed about your audience is to ask them about themselves. Do not discount even a simple form of data gathering, such as distributing a three- or four-item questionnaire at a meeting before the one at which you will speak.

- *Conduct selected interviews/focus groups.* When you cannot get information on the whole audience, arrange to talk to some members of the group. In these individual or group sessions, try to find out not just what people think but also how they think. Ask open-ended questions and encourage respondents to expand on their answers by framing follow-up questions in a nonargumentative tone. Ask them for examples and anecdotes.

- *Talk with the contact person.* The person who asked you to speak has certain expectations about the interaction between you and the audience. Ask this contact person as many specific questions as occur to you to elaborate on his or her perceptions of the audience.

- *Use intelligent inference and empathy.* When you do not have any specific information about an audience, draw on your general knowledge of human behavior and groups. Let empathy round out the image. Get outside yourself and adopt your listeners' frames of reference.

12b. Analyze audience demographics

Obtaining each audience's vital statistics enables you to make certain general predictions about their responses. However, there is no such thing as an average audience. A speaker would be more than a little surprised to stand before a group of listeners whose composition followed exactly the distribution of the most recent census with regard to age, sex, race, socioeconomic status, and religion.

CHECKLIST

Pertinent Demographic Questions

❏ What is the average age of the audience members?

❏ What is the age range?

❏ What is the sexual breakdown of the audience?

❏ What racial and ethnic groups are represented, in about what proportions?

❏ What is the socioeconomic composition of the group?

❏ What occupations are represented?

❏ What religious groups are represented?

❏ What is the political orientation of the group?

❏ How homogeneous (similar) or heterogeneous (diverse) are the audience members for each of the preceding characteristics?

Obviously, all demographic characteristics are not equally important for any given speech. Knowledge of the religious configuration of your audience will be important in preparing a speech on abortion, as will knowledge of the age distribution for a speech on Social Security reform.

But religion and age might have no bearing whatsoever on another topic. Despite differences in relative importance to a particular topic, each demographic characteristic should be noted, if only to give you a general picture. It is disconcerting to face a roomful of ethnically diverse teenagers if you had expected middle-aged professionals of northern European descent.

KEY POINT   Limitations of Demographic Generalizations

Very few generalizations can be made on the basis of demographic factors. The studies from which data are drawn are often flawed. Also, social change occurs so rapidly that by the time this research is reported the situation has changed. And by the time the findings have reached the average layperson through synthesis or summaries, even more time has elapsed. Social science research, even when carefully controlled and well designed, provides *probability statements* about how one group *on average* differs from another group *on average*. For example, with respect to almost any trait you might select, the differences among individual women and among individual men are far greater than the differences between the average man and the average woman. You can say that many people in an audience *are likely to* respond in a certain way; you cannot say that any individual in that audience definitely *will* respond in a given way.

Notwithstanding the limitations of demographic analysis, you will benefit from identifying various audience characteristics that may affect audience response—including the following.

1   Age/generation

Maxims like "You're as young as you feel" and "Age is a state of mind" tell us to be careful when we make assumptions based on chronological age. Most of us have been exposed to octogenarians who routinely question authority and are open to new experiences, and to 18-year-olds who have already ossified their thought patterns. Despite these exceptions, some generalizations can be justified. Current theory holds that psychological development does not stop at the threshold of adulthood but continues through life in fairly predictable stages. Works by Erikson and Sheehy offer insight into the most common crises and value realignments of people in their twenties, thirties, forties, and so on.[1] (For our purposes,

---

[1] See, for example, Erik Erikson, *Identity and the Life Cycle* (New York: Norton, 1980), and Gail Sheehy, *Passages: Predictable Crises of Adult Life* (New York: Dutton, 1976).

younger refers generally to people going through adolescence, formal education, or the early phases of establishing career directions and of confirming life goals; *older* covers most everyone else.)

- *Younger people tend to be idealistic.* They respond positively to arguments based on change and innovation. They are impatient about social change and want to see results in the near future.

- *Younger people are strongly affected by the values of their peers.*

- *Younger people like a speech to be organized in a fluid, narrative fashion.* They prefer a rapid, exciting tempo and a delivery employing several media or channels of communication.

- *Older people are more conservative.* They are responsive to appeals to traditional values. They tend to have a stake in the status quo and to be reluctant to risk major changes. They are more patient in waiting for results.

- *Older people prefer a linear, highly structured speech organization, with clear previews, transitions, and summaries.* They are most comfortable with a slow, deliberate delivery.

KEY POINT **Generational Identity** In addition to thinking about the life stage of your audience, you can infer from the members' ages certain specific experiences they have had, based on their generational identity. For instance, it's not merely that your audience members in the first year of the twenty-first century are 60 years old that is important. Unlike other 60-year-olds of the past and future, they were children during the post–World War II era of prosperity, students during the idealistic 1960s, disillusioned young adults during the Watergate era, and so on. This is a different audience from one of 60-year-olds in the mid-1980s, who were adolescents during the Great Depression and who came of age during World War II. Think about what current events have inspired and traumatized the particular audience you are addressing. What movies, TV shows, songs, and sports figures were central to their lives? What generational stereotypes might they have become weary of?

2 Sex/gender

Sex is the demographic category that relates to biological maleness or femaleness. *Gender* refers to the socialized roles we have learned as appropriate for our sex. There may be a very few experiences that are directly linked to sex; a speech on breast-feeding or circumcision might take the actual male–female composition of an audience into account. Far more commonly, however, gender issues enter into audience analysis. The issue is not how many males and females are present, but how audience members of either sex think about masculinity and femininity. These gender expectations are highly culture bound and change rapidly in contemporary life.

Traditionally, women were socialized to be nurturant, sensitive, compassionate, and emotional. So, in the past, appeals to home, family, and the safety of loved ones usually were effective with women. Traditionally, men were socialized to be dominant, aggressive, ambitious, and unemotional (except when it came to sports). So, a speech to a predominantly male group used appeals to power, success, competitive values, and logic.

In recent decades, many more women and men have become more aware of how sex role socialization has limited their avenues of expression and growth. They are experimenting with new roles and divisions of labor in both public and private life. And men and women undergoing this process bridle when presented with stereotypical assumptions about social roles and power relationships.

3   Race/ethnicity

As with women and men, the differences between ethnic groups are not innate. The differences that do exist result from variations in socialization and experience. In the United States, we daily encounter newcomers who migrated here voluntarily to be with their families or to enhance their opportunities, or who came involuntarily as refugees. Conversations with such diverse members of our communities encourage those of us who have been in the United States longer to remember why our ancestors came: some seeking opportunity, some escaping economic hardship or political and religious oppression, some involuntarily as slaves.

This expanding ethnic and cultural diversity can be seen as either a problem or an interesting opportunity. In the past, when there were three or four predominant ethnic groups in an area, it might have been a reasonable goal to become somewhat expert on the cultural values and symbols of those groups. Today, when dozens of cultures are part of a single community or organization, this approach to audience analysis becomes overwhelming. To further complicate the challenge, it is not just that audiences are multicultural groups but also that they are composed of individuals who are themselves multicultural persons. It is increasingly rare to find someone whose heritage is monocultural in any real sense.

Because people's experiences, not their traits, shape them as listeners, there are no prescriptions for how to relate to predominantly white, African American, Native American, Latino/Latina, Hispanic, or Asian American audiences. Instead, you need to familiarize yourself as much as possible with the experiences of each group. The common experience of nonwhite racial groups and most other ethnic minorities in the United States has included discrimination and oppression. Members of these groups, like women, are justifiably sensitive to any communication that reduces their status or reflects old stereotypes. Forms of address, both collective and individual, are very important. Never refer to people by first names, diminutives, or nicknames unless invited to do so. And never address white males by titles such as "mister," "doctor," or "colonel" while addressing anyone else more casually. Find out what group designations your audience prefers, and respect their wishes.

Beyond showing sensitivity to the relationships between members of dominant and nondominant cultural groups, a speaker can also demonstrate an appreciation of cultural diversity. People of any ethnic group can tend to look at things from the standpoint of the group's own history and culture. Taking the time to investigate other cultural views can open up a number of refreshingly different avenues to good communication. Making the effort to pronounce unfamiliar names and phrases correctly, and avoiding the most stereotypical cultural generalizations, shows your goodwill and openness.

KEY POINT   **Multiple Identities of Audiences**   Because speakers are not transmitting information, but rather are jointly constructing meanings with listeners, no part of audience analysis is as important as learning *how a particular group of people makes meaning.* The demographic data you collect can be useful, but only if treated within the context of this complex process. We know that age, race, and sex all contribute to a person's interpretation of the world. But so, too, do religion, social class, educational level, economic status, sexual orientation, health, physical ability, and many other factors. As the incredible diversity and constantly changing profile of U.S. society have made clear, no formula can tell a speaker how each of these variables relates to a particular topic, let alone how they all interact. In a sense, as a speaker, you have been freed from the unrealistic goal of making predictions based on static traits of your listeners. Instead, your task is to thoughtfully consider how they engage in a constant process of constructing, and reconstructing, the world. In this sort of audience analysis, you are trying to glimpse what some describe as *core values* (or *worldviews, personal construct systems, frames of reference, informal theories,* or *master narratives*). (See **25c**.) What do your listeners draw on to organize their experience and make sense of it?

12c. Determine the audience's attitudes toward your topic

You could spread every possible reaction a person might have to the thesis of your speech across a continuum that ranges from extreme disagreement to extreme agreement. Much social science research is based on asking people to clarify their attitudes on scales like this one:

Strongly disagree	Moderately disagree	Slightly disagree	Neither agree nor disagree	Slightly agree	Moderately agree	Strongly agree

If your goal is to bring about some specific act, your listeners' responses will range across these categories:

←————————————————————————————————————→
Opposed to action   **Uninclined to act**   **Ready to act**   **Taking action**

If the majority of your audience falls to the left on either continuum, that audience should be considered *unfavorable,* and if it falls to the right, it is *favorable.* If in the middle, it is *neutral.*

Most speakers agree that knowing the audience's predisposition toward the topic is the single most important bit of information in planning their speech strategy. If your speech deals with a controversial topic, it is crucial that you interview people who differ from you in terms of attitude and experience. Listen carefully and respectfully to their accounts of the world. At the information-gathering stage, your goal is not to plan a strategy for changing them, but rather to try to see how their views and yours might be connected. This means letting go of your predispositions and judgments about people who disagree with you. Once you determine whether your audience is favorable, neutral, or unfavorable, you can follow the specific suggestions offered in chapter **23**. Although attitudes toward your topic are most obviously relevant to persuasive speaking, they can influence the speech to inform or evoke as well.

12d. Gather details about the specific speech situation

Anticipate your audience's expectations. We have stressed the importance of knowing your purpose in speaking, but what is your audience's purpose in listening? Why are they sitting there giving you their valuable time? Perhaps they are required to as part of a class or job assignment. Maybe they are present voluntarily but for a reason unrelated to you or your topic. Or perhaps, if you are fortunate, they are there because of an interest in what you have to say. In any audience, you will find combinations of these and other motivations. Knowing the predominant audience expectation is vital to the preparation of your speech. An excellent speech can fail miserably if the audience expected a different sort of talk altogether.

This is not to say that you must be bound by the audience's expectations. You can lead them to a new mind-set, but to do that, you need to discover what they know and expect.

CHECKLIST

Audience Expectations

❏ *What do they know about your topic?* Make no blanket assumptions about sophistication of your audience; rather, use the techniques of audience analysis to find it. People listen best and learn best when exposed to information that is just beyond their current level of comprehension.

❏ *What do they think about you?* Learn what your audience has heard, read, or assumed about you. You want to build on their positive expectations and overcome their negative ones. Knowing what your credibility is prior to the speech helps you decide how much you need to bolster it during the speech. (See **26a**.)

❏ *What is the history of your audience as a group?* Audiences come in many different forms, with varied levels of group cohesion. Most audiences have some common history, which may range from a long association in a business or club to a few weeks together in a classroom. Learn all you can about this collective history.

❏ *What is the program surrounding your speech?* To understand an audience's expectations of you, it is essential to learn your speech's place in the context of their immediate situation. Familiarize yourself with the agenda and where you fit into it.

Finding and Using Resources

CHAPTER 13. **Having a Research Strategy**

Use a research strategy that enables you to gather information effectively.

CHAPTER 14. **Finding Print, Internet, and Other Electronic Resources**

Execute your research strategy by gathering materials from the library and from electronic sources.

CHAPTER 15. **Interviewing People About Your Topic**

Execute your research strategy by seeking information directly from other people.

CHAPTER 16. **Identifying and Recording Evidence**

Extract examples, statistics, and testimony from your research for use in your speech.

CHAPTER 13

Having a Research Strategy

Plan a research strategy that optimizes your effort for the time allotted. This requires you to reflect before dashing off for research. How much time? What themes require investigation? What are your objectives? Other questions center on where you will get your information. What can best be found in the library? Which research can be done electronically? Whom can you approach to discuss your topic?

13a. Fit your research to the time allotted

Chapter **10** advises having a realistic timetable for preparation. With one day's notice, you cannot make an exhaustive study of the literature, but you can draw from general references like encyclopedias, whether at the library, on CD-ROM, or online. With more time, a broader effort is possible.

13b. Progress from the general to the specific

Start with an investigation of the "big picture." You do not want to commit yourself prematurely to only one avenue of research; you may miss signs of other paths important to your topic. As you move further into your research, you can get more specific when you have enough general understanding to be able to follow those trails effectively.

There are two basic sources to tap for research: other people and recorded information. It is usually best to start with the recorded information, saving the use of human resources for later when you know how best to take advantage of their expertise. Here, too, is where the general references become your initial and primary resource.

One of the most useful talents in the early stages of research is the ability to skim. Because you will not have time to read everything, try to get a feel for the most important approaches and theories: look at the table of contents, skim the first and last chapters of the book, or read the first and last paragraphs of the chapter or article. Jot down the names of the key people who are frequently cited, as well as recurring concepts and studies.

You need to develop a similar technique as you search online. Especially on the web, it is easy to be seduced by a long set of links that are fun and interesting but that have absolutely nothing to do with what you are researching. One way to sidestep this problem is to start with subject directories rather than search engines. See **14b**. But if you are using search engines, you should be able to develop, after a time, a sense for the ranking algorithm used by each engine and be able to skip some highly ranked hits that really don't match your criteria.

As you begin, look for summary or state-of-the-art articles and books and sites that synthesize current thinking on your subject. Pieces that trace the history of your topic are also useful. Often, these sources are readily identifiable by their titles:

> "The Lasting Changes Brought by Women Workers" [*Business Week*]
>
> *Women in the American Economy* [Juanita M. Kreps, Prentice-Hall]
>
> "Women and the Workforce" [Alice Kessler, *The Reader's Companion to American History,* via web search]

13c. Develop a terminology lexicon

As you start exploring your topic, make a list of key terms that come up. You will notice that certain phrases are widely used in the discourse. Familiarity with the language of your topic is essential as you continue your research because you need to identify key words as you search through the literature. This is particularly useful in searches for electronic information—one way to reduce an Internet search engine's "hits" from 98,000 to a more manageable number is to use precise language.

13d. Use questions to direct your research

When you've made one pass through for background research, but before you launch your main research effort, go back and analyze your topic. Consider whether you want to narrow your topic, adjust your speech objectives, or fine-tune the wording of your thesis statement. Carefully follow the suggestions in **11d.2** to list what your audience will want to know. These questions become the basis of your research objectives.

Suppose that your thesis is this:

> Since the beginning of the Industrial Revolution, women in the United States have been exploited as a cheap and expendable source of labor.

Your audience will want to hear the answers to questions like these:

> Are women a cheap source of labor?
>
> Are women an expendable source of labor?
>
> Can the labor practices appropriately be labeled as exploitation?
>
> Has the treatment of women been rather consistent since the Industrial Revolution?

Clearly, then, your list of research objectives will include goals like these:

> Find out how women's salaries compare with those of men who do the same job.

Find specific examples of women having been treated as an expendable source of labor.

Find an expert definition of *exploitation.*

Find out how women's work changed at the time of the Industrial Revolution.

And so on. Armed with this list of research objectives, you are ready to make the best use of your research time and to ask for the help you need.

CHAPTER 14

Finding Print, Internet, and Other Electronic Resources

The vast amount of information available, literally at your fingertips, can seem overwhelming. Stay focused on your research objectives (see **13**) as you explore various electronic and print resources.

14a. Use the library

It is not by chance that we start our discussion of where to go for research with the library. Even with the advent of the Internet, it is still the place to find the widest variety of research tools (including access to the Internet) and the place to find professional researchers primed to give you direction and help.

KEY POINT **Talk to a Librarian** Librarians are service-oriented information specialists, there to help you find the materials you need. Do not hesitate to ask them questions. They welcome the challenge of trying to understand your requirements and direct you to the answers you seek.

14b. Locate printed books and articles on your topic

In addition to the librarian, important library resources include the book catalogue, periodical indexes and databases, and special dictionaries and encyclopedias.

The book catalogue In most libraries, the book catalogue is a computer database. These database systems let you search for entries in a number of ways. For instance, you may choose to search by some combination of subject, author, and title. Or you can focus on topics as they are grouped in the Dewey decimal system or the Library of Congress classifications. Or you can search by keywords or *descriptors*—words or short phrases that the database uses to identify entries on related topics. Or, in some cases, you may make a *free text search,* in which the computer does not limit itself to defined descriptors, but rather looks for words and combinations of words that you have chosen within the titles and content summaries of the books in the database. The lexicon you developed in **13c** will be extremely helpful in both keyword and free text searches. Special collections may have separate catalogues; check with the librarian to see which catalogues you have access to.

Periodical indexes and databases   You can locate magazine, journal, and newspaper articles on your topic using the periodical indexes and databases available at the library. Some of these are general in their coverage; others can be quite specific to a field or area of interest. Once again, do not hesitate to approach the librarian to ask for guidance in finding these sources. There also are indexes for many major newspapers.

Special dictionaries, encyclopedias, and similar resources   Special dictionaries and encyclopedias are useful tools, especially for clarifying terms and concepts as they are used in fields in which you may have little knowledge. The library may have other sources of information available, including filmstrips, microforms, records, compact discs, cassettes, films, and videotapes.

14c. Use electronic information retrieval

To retrieve information electronically, you can use: an institutional search service that provides access to databases at remote sites; a computer terminal at the library that provides access to databases on-site or to the Internet; a personal computer to connect to an online service; a computer to access a general Internet search tool. These choices run from the highly structured (the institutional search service) to the highly unstructured (the Internet).

LEXIS-NEXIS, DIALOG, BRS (Bibliographic Retrieval Service), and Wilson OmniFile are services that provide information retrieval. A service can have hundreds of databases to choose from, each of which can cover hundreds of thousands of articles and papers. You can gain access to one of these systems via a public library, or a college or university library. Many companies have access to at least one of the major systems.

InfoTrac College Edition is an electronic virtual library that is available 24 hours a day via an Internet connection. It consists of

Typing the keywords "comparable worth" and "equal pay" with the Boolean "OR" results in ...

356 hits and shows the list of results.

From the list you may select the articles that best fit your research needs.

FIGURE 14-1   A Search Using InfoTrac College Edition

full-length articles collected from hundreds of scholarly and popular periodicals, a range that embraces diverse publications. Figure 14-1 shows a search conducted on InfoTrac College Edition.

Online services accessible by personal computer offer information in a variety of areas, from an online edition of an encyclopedia or news magazine, to stock market performance, to government statistics, to news on sports and entertainment.

Seeking out information may be more esoteric on the Internet, where you can use such things as Gopher servers and the World Wide Web to track down what you are looking for. There are a number of ways you gain access to the Internet and, once there, a number of ways you can move around in it. In fact, its combination of flexibility and arcane global structure can make it a daunting prospect for casual users. Tools for finding information include newsreaders to gain access to Usenet newsgroups or e-mail discussion groups, search engines and metasearch engines to perform keyword searches on the web (e.g., Google, Northern Light), subject directories consisting of links organized by subject (e.g., INFOMINE, the Librarian's Index to the Internet), and directed query engines that gain access to the databases of the "deep web" not available through standard search engines (e.g., Complete Planet, invisibleweb.com).

1   Search effectively and efficiently

Approach the available search engines and directories with a search technique that maximizes focus and minimizes ambiguity. Use Boolean operators ("this AND that," "this OR that," "this NOT that"), if the search engine allows, to keep from being overwhelmed by tens of thousands of "hits." Many engines permit users to specify that one word in the search should be near another and use other tools (such as wildcards and required terms) to be as precise as possible at the beginning.

An excellent place to find information on the various search engines and strategies for using them is the Librarians' Index to the Internet (**www.lii.org**). See especially its "Searching the Internet" directory. Also extremely valuable is the UC Berkeley Library's "Finding Information on the Internet: A Tutorial" (**http://www.lib.berkeley.edu/TeachingLib/Guides/Internet/FindInfo.html**).

For the most efficient use of any of these electronic resources, you must create a concise research strategy by narrowing your topic after considering different avenues of approach. (See **13**.) Then you can decide what are the most likely categories, keywords, and search texts to identify information related to your topic. Coming prepared to do a search will help you avoid going down blind alleys and investigating topics before discovering their lack of relevance.

Table 14-1 lists some useful reference sites that could be the starting point for your Internet researching. This is just a drop in the bucket, though, and you will find many other sites through links on the sites listed, and also through links on the *The Speaker's Compact Handbook* website.

TABLE 14-1 **Some Useful Reference Sites**

General Reference	Science
Internet Public Library—annotated subject directory http://www.ipl.org	Eric Weisstein's World of Science—resource for math, chemistry, physics, astronomy http://scienceworld.wolfram.com
Librarian's Index to the Internet—annotated subject directory http://www.lii.org	**Government (U.S.) and Law**
LibrarySpot—virtual library resource center http://www.libraryspot.com	FirstGov—U.S. government official web portal http://www.firstgov.gov
Martindale's the Reference Desk—subject directory http://www.martindalecenter.com	GPO Access—access to U.S. government printing office databases http://www.gpoaccess.gov/databases.html
RefDesk—index to reference sites http://www.refdesk.com	Library of Congress—the National Digital Library (NDL) http://www.loc.gov
Information Please—online encyclopedia, dictionary, atlas http://www.infoplease.com	U.S. National Archives and Records Administration—archives and records http://www.archives.gov
Virtual Library—noncommercial network of indexes http://vlib.org	FedStats—links to statistics collected by the U.S. government http://www.fedstats.gov
Bartleby—index to reference and literature sites http://www.bartleby.com	World Legal Information Institute—access to law databases worldwide http://www.worldlii.org
Literature	**Urban Legends and Misinformation**
Project Gutenberg—access to free electronic books in the public domain http://Gutenberg.net	The AFU & Urban Legends Archive http://www.urbanlegends.com
Perseus Digital Library—Greek and Latin classics, along with early modern English http://www.perseus.tufts.edu	Urban Legends Reference Pages ("Snopes") http://www.snopes.com

2   Carefully evaluate Internet sources

Scrutinize web-based materials with special caution. Although *any* information you gather in the course of research should be subjected to tests of credibility and reliability as described in **16c** and in chapter **26**, the wide-open nature of the World Wide Web invites a particularly critical eye. In contrast to the various review processes applied to getting ideas into print or onto film, all it takes to mount a website is the software and a server.

CHECKLIST

Evaluating a Website

Ask yourself these questions as you look at a website:

❑ *Who is it?* Is it a personal page? If so, what credentials does the person present, and how compelling are they? If it is an organization's page, does it provide enough background information (e.g., "About us" page) for you to make a judgment about its credibility?

❑ *What's its slant?* Why was this site created? Was it to provide information, advocate a position, or just rant? If it's providing information, how is that information influenced by the underlying assumptions embraced by the site creator?

❑ *Is it up to date?* Does the site have regular maintenance that keeps it on top of developments?

❑ *What company does it keep?* That is, who does it link to, and who links to it? How would you assess the credibility and competence of those linked sites?

For more on evaluating websites, see the UC Berkeley tutorial and the Librarian's Index to the Internet previously cited.

CHAPTER 15

Interviewing People About Your Topic

You are surrounded by potential sources of information in the form of other people—either as individuals or as members of informal or formal information networks. These sources can complement and supplement your library and electronic research.

15a. Locate human resources

Look for human resources at home, at school and work, and in the community.

1 Acquaintances, family, and coworkers

As you start developing ideas on your topic, begin to talk about them with the people you come in contact with every day. On many topics, what these people can offer you is not so much expertise as a lay perspective that you will not find in any book.

2 Experts

In every community there are people with specialized expertise in your topic, and who can often direct you to obscure sources.

- *Educators.* Dissemination of information is an educator's business. Call the appropriate department or school. They will direct you to someone knowledgeable.

- *Public officials and agencies.* People elected to public office consider it one of their duties to make information available to their constituents. If you do not know where to start, call the main switchboard of the local or regional government and outline the direction of your research.

- *Independent agencies and special interest groups.* Groups such as the American Cancer Society or the National Hot Rod Association can be excellent sources of information. When possible, interview experts with differing orientations toward your subject, especially if the subject is controversial. A useful resource for making contact with such groups is the *Encyclopedia of Associations*, available at the library or through DIALOG.

- *Potpourri.* Athletes, businesspeople, police officers, doctors, accountants can all be experts. If you do not know a person in the particular field, see if you have a one-step link to one through a colleague or friend. You can also tap into an enormous pool of talent in the electronic community accessible by computer. The newsgroups and conferences available online can introduce you to knowledgeable human resources at a national, and even global, level. Thousands of forums exist, covering just about every area of interest you could think of, and probably many that you would never think of. In these groups and on message boards, people carry on extended dialogue on many issues. Join in by asking your own questions. Before asking a specific question, check to see if it is one that has come up many times before. Questions of this sort, along with their answers, are usually posted in a Frequently Asked Questions (FAQ) file. If there is such a posting in your area of interest, read it first—you may find many answers immediately, and you may also find answers to questions that you had not yet thought to ask. Links to Usenet FAQs of all kinds can be found at the Internet FAQ Archives: **http://www.faqs. org/faqs/**.

15b. Conduct interviews

As with all aspects of public speaking, in interviewing, preparation is just as important as the process itself.

1   Preparing for the interview

Ask yourself in what ways your interviewee can best contribute to your research. Devise a list of questions that are specific enough that you will not be wasting this person's time by asking for information you could have found in the encyclopedia. Prepare open-ended, but focused, questions. For instance:

> *Not:* How many women are there in the workforce in this county? [You could have looked up the figure before.]

> *Not:* What are the problems working women encounter? [This is too vague.]

> *But:* I've read that in this county the average woman's salary is 32 percent less than the average man's. To what do you attribute this?

2   During the interview

First establish rapport and set a context. Explain who you are, why you need the information, and how far you have gotten. Also, confirm your understanding of the time available. If you wish to tape the interview, ask permission at this point, but be ready with a notepad in case you do not get it. Either way, take notes.

When you begin to ask questions, be sure to let the expert do most of the talking. (See the suggestions on listening in **2d**.) Use questions to summarize and direct the interview: "So far you've talked about four problems working women face—unequal pay, lack of training, sexual harassment, and inadequate child care. Are there others?"

Allow for a closing phase for the interview. Respect the interviewee's time limit, and if you are approaching it, stop—even if you have gone through only half of your questions. Summarize your perspective of the interview. Often, it is productive to ask if the person would like to make a wrap-up statement.

> **KEY POINT**   **After the Interview** Just as it's essential to be well prepared going into an interview, it's equally important that you do the necessary follow-up after an interview. The focus of this follow-up is two-fold: ensuring that your notes or recording, or both, will be as useful as possible, and thanking your interviewee. As soon as possible after the interview, read through your notes, making sure they are legible and make sense. You can also use this review to jot down any additional details that may come to mind. If you recorded

the interview, label it clearly. Whether or not you need to contact your interviewee to have information clarified or a quote verified, follow up an interview with a written thank-you note. An e-mail message is fastest and easiest, but a handwritten card or note might be appreciated more.

CHAPTER 16

Identifying and Recording Evidence

Carefully review the print and electronic texts you have gathered and the interview notes you have taken. Glean from these the materials that will make up the real building blocks of your speech, ones that are crucial to its success. Select the support for your ideas first on the basis of relevance, then on soundness, and then on interest value. Form the habit of using a variety of the following methods to develop your speech.

16a. Make frequent use of examples

Beyond the universal appeal of a good story, examples provide audience members with a chance to check their perceptions of a speaker's message. As a speaker, you need to make decisions about whether to use real examples or hypothetical ones and about how brief or how extended these examples should be.

1   Use factual examples

A fact is an assertion that is universally accepted. Sometimes, it is directly verifiable, as in "Sandra Day O'Connor is a justice of the Supreme Court." Even if you were not at the swearing-in, there is enough corroborative evidence from many sources to satisfy you that this is a factual statement. "The earth is 93 million miles from the sun" is another assertion accepted as a fact although it is not directly verifiable through any of the five senses. But we do accept it, because we have constructed theoretical frameworks based on consistent results of observation and can make predictions of near-absolute certainty.

When you use examples to prove a point, though, specific logical tests must be met.

> CHECKLIST

Tests of Factual Examples

❏ *Are sufficient examples given?* The more examples you give, the less likely your listeners are to dismiss the phenomenon as the product of chance.

❏ *Are the examples representative?* To be credible, examples should represent a cross section of cases.

❏ *Are negative instances accounted for?* When you reason by example, you must look into and account for dramatic negative examples. Your obligation, if you wish to carry your point, is to show how these examples are atypical and this should not detract from your conclusion.

2   Use hypothetical examples

Sometimes, when no factual example quite suits your purpose, or when you are speculating about the future, you might give a brief or extended hypothetical example. Here is an illustration of an *extended hypothetical* example:

> How should you develop an investment portfolio? Well, let's imagine that you have a monthly household income of $4,000 and that your expenses run to about $2,800. Let me show you how to calculate what portion of the remainder should go into fairly liquid, low-risk areas like the money markets or short-term T-bills and what portion can go into higher-risk areas like commodities.

Hypothetical examples do not have to be extended ones. Here is a speech segment that uses three *brief hypothetical* examples in quick succession:

> What would happen if this tax law were to pass? Well, Miguel over there couldn't deduct his business lunches. Audrey wouldn't be able to depreciate her buildings. You, Tom, with kids about to start college . . .

Be aware that the examples you pick reflect a set of assumptions about the world. Be sensitive to racist or sexist implications of your illustrations.

> K E Y P O I N T   **The Appropriate Amount of Detail**   When you use examples, you must decide how long or short to make each one. The factual and hypothetical examples in a speech can be kept brief when you can safely assume that the audience is already familiar with them. If a succession of quick references will not illuminate a point for your listeners, however, you need to develop the example into an illustration.

Ideally, a speech blends several short examples with a few extended ones. Properly selected, these show the audience both the breadth of your subject and some in-depth aspects of it.

16b. Use statistical evidence

When examples are systematically collected and classified, they are reported as statistics. An excellent source of governmental statistical information, classified by topic, state, and agency, can be found at **www.fedstats.gov.**

1 Check the accuracy of statistical evidence

For any statistics you cite, investigate the methods and motivations of those who collected them.

CHECKLIST

Tests of Statistical Evidence

❑ *Who collected the data?* Investigate the qualifications and competence of the researchers. Was the work done by a professional pollster or the host of a call-in radio show?

❑ *Why were the data collected?* The motivation behind collecting certain information can make the data suspect. Most people have more confidence in inquiries rooted in a desire to advance knowledge rather than to sell a product or promote a cause.

❑ *When were the data collected?* Be sure your evidence is up to date. Attitudes change as swiftly as prices, and some data are obsolete by the time they are published.

❑ *How were the data collected?* Find out as much as you can about the design of the research and the details of its execution. Track it back to the original study. Check how the cases were chosen. Evaluate the method of data collection—observation, experiment, or survey conducted by phone, mail, or personal interview.

---

2 Avoid misleading statistics

We know that language is ambiguous, but we tend to believe that numbers make straightforward statements; there is no mystery in $2 + 2 = 4$. However, numbers *can* be just as ambiguous, with statistical pitfalls to trap the unwary.

The fallacy of the average Although the average can be a useful tool for analysis, it sometimes gives a picture absurdly at odds with reality. An example of how this can mislead is the Smurge Company report that shows an average of 6 computer scanners per department when, in fact, the marketing department has 40 scanners, and most other departments have 1 or none. As this demonstrates, calculating the arithmetic *mean* is not appropriate when one or two extreme cases skew the distribution. The *median* (the number or score that falls at the midpoint of the range of numbers or scores) or the *mode* (the most frequently occurring score or number) can be more meaningful averages to use in this example, although they, too, can be abused. See Figure 16-1 for a graphic representation of the scanner distribution in the Smurge Company. In this case, although the *mean* is 6, the *median* is 2 (scores of 0 and 1 below it, scores of 3 and 40 above it), and the *mode* is 1 (the largest number of departments—three—have this score).

The fallacy of the unknown base A speaker using percentages and proportions can sometimes give the mistaken impression that a large population has been sampled. In fact, data are sometimes reported in this manner to give credence to unscientific or skimpy evidence: "Two out of three mechanics recommend this synthetic oil." Most listeners would see this as shorthand for "We polled 300 mechanics around the country, and 200 of them recommended this synthetic oil." How valid would this recommendation seem if it came to light that in reality only *three* were polled?

The fallacy of the atypical or arbitrary time frame Recently, an executive of a computer circuit board company told us that sales in February were double those of the previous month. These data could be misleading unless you know that January is always the worst month in the yearly cycle of the computer industry.

3 Make your numbers clear and meaningful

The stereotypical dry, plodding speech is one that is overloaded with statistics. After a short while, the audience becomes overloaded too, and listeners start to build a mental dike against the numbers flowing over them. When you do use statistics, round

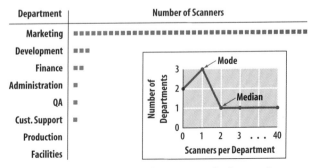

FIGURE 16-1 Distribution of Scanners at the Smurge Company

them off. Say "about fifteen hundred" instead of "one thousand four hundred eighty-nine point six." Use visual representations such as charts and graphs. See **27a**. Use comparisons to make the numbers more understandable:

> For the amount of money they propose to spend on this weapons system, we could provide educational grants in aid to all the needy students in the 11 western states, or triple the government funding for cancer research, or upgrade the highway system in this state and its three neighbors.

16c. Draw on testimony from authorities

Often, we call on statements from other people to get our point across. For instance, even if you have never been arrested or never been a public safety officer, you can give a credible speech on the penal system by making judicious use of testimony from experts or eyewitnesses.

1 Evaluate the credibility of the authorities you cite

It is easy to find citations that say almost anything; it is much more difficult to select those that provide legitimate support for your points. This requires scrutinizing the people you quote for support.

CHECKLIST

Tests of Testimony

❑ *Does the authority have access to the necessary information?* A person does not have to be famous to be an authority. When you use an authority, be sure that the person had firsthand experience, direct observation, or personal access to relevant facts and files.

❑ *Is the authority qualified to interpret data?* When a person starts making interpretations, forming opinions and conclusions, and proposing recommendations, the standards of credibility become stricter. People earn the right to be considered experts either by holding specific credentials or by establishing a record of success and experience.

❑ *Is the person acknowledged as an expert on this subject?* Just because a person is an expert in one field, it doesn't follow that she is an expert in other fields.

❑ *Is the authority figure free of bias and self-interest?* We give more credence to the opinion of an authority who appears to have no personal stake—ideological or financial—in an issue. If you can find testimony from a person speaking *against* his or her interests, then it certainly will be an effective addition to your presentation.

2 Do not distort quotations

Shortening quotations to highlight the basic thrust of the message is perfectly acceptable. What is unacceptable is editing a person's statements to such a degree that they appear to support positions other than or even opposite those espoused in the actual quotations. There is the old joke about the movie critic who wrote that "the wretchedness of the acting in this film is nothing short of amazing!" only to find later that an advertisement for the movie quoted him as saying "this film . . . is amazing!"

Do not edit a quotation so radically that it loses all substance. Virtually content-free quotations are sometimes deliberately used to confuse listeners or to overwhelm them with an apparent preponderance of evidence.

> **KEY POINT** **Finding Quotations** In addition to specific testimony, it is often effective to use the timeless words of famous individuals who have said something about your topic. There are several resources to help you locate brief generic quotations on your topic: **www.quoteland.com**, **www.quotationspage.com**, and **www.Bartleby.com** provide lists of famous quotations indexed by topic.

16d. Maintain a complete record of your sources

Form the habit of identifying the source for every piece of information you use and of recording complete bibliographic information for each source. With electronic catalogues your task often will be easier—you may be able to print out the bibliographic information for each of your potential sources or perhaps download it onto a portable storage medium. When you print pages from the Internet, make sure your print command will include the headers and footers from your browser, which contain the page title and the page's uniform resource locator (URL). In other situations, you will need to record it yourself. Writing down volume numbers of journals, or the cities of publication of books, or the telephone numbers of interviewees—details that you will never mention in your speech—may seem unnecessary, but routinely recording all such information will help you retrieve sources if you need to check them again.

> **KEY POINT** **Citing Sources for a List of References** We recommend that you master one of the standard formats for citing references so that if you need to append a reference list to an outline or decide to produce a handout for your audience, the sources of your research will be appropriately laid out. Three of the most popular formats are found in *The Chicago Manual of Style (CMS),* 15th edition (2003), usually referred to simply as Chicago style; the *MLA Handbook for Writers of Research Papers,* 6th edition (2003), abbreviated and referred to as MLA style; and the *Publication Manual of the American*

Psychological Association, 5th edition (2001), or APA style. MLA and APA styles are the ones most likely to be used in the context of a speech class. More information about these two styles and their organizations is available online at **www.mla.org** and **www.apa.org.** Individual variations notwithstanding, all three styles require an alphabetical listing of research sources that includes author, title, date, and publication details. In addition to the conventions for citing books, articles, chapters, and abstracts, there are correct ways to cite nearly every known type of source, including interviews, personal correspondence, photographs, TV shows, websites, and e-mail. Appendix B shows the APA and MLA styles for 13 types of reference citation. Keep in mind that this list is just a sampling of the types of publications and communications that can end up in a reference list.

16e. Capture information and ideas in discrete units

In the process of doing your research, you want to gather and record your information and ideas in a way that makes it as easy as possible to find things later on and to work with them creatively. The ability to photocopy whole chapters of books or to download pages and pages of text from the web does not make it any easier to review the information you have. Smaller, more manageable units will promote creative flexibility as you arrange and rearrange, structure and restructure your thoughts and data.

We talk about "notecards" in this section, but the important thing is not the media or the cardstock but the activity—and if you use an outlining tool or idea development software on a computer, these suggestions are as pertinent.

1   Notecards from print and electronic sources

As you read the book or article, jot down each discrete idea or bit of information on a separate card, being sure you add the identifying code and page number. Use only one side of each card. There are three kinds of data you might record: direct quotations or citations, paraphrased ideas, and references for later use. Do not neglect to do this for materials obtained online. Even if you have a printout, it is valuable to go through the process of paraphrasing or quoting so that you isolate and internalize the key points that drew you to the source in the first place.

If you copy entire articles or chapters, be sure to make a bibliography card for each. Many people find it helpful to photocopy the title page and copyright page of the book or periodical.

2   Notecards from interviews and surveys

The suggestions in **16e.1** relate to printed information but are easily adapted to information acquired through interviews and surveys. Make a bibliography card for each interview, citing the person interviewed, his or her qualifications, the date of the interview, and the person's telephone number or address. As you listen to the tape or review your notes, transcribe the information on cards.

3 Grouping your cards

When you have gathered many notecards, you may want to stack them under cover cards with titles such as "History," "Causes," and "Solutions." Or you may decide to put these keywords in the upper-right corner.

16f. Citing sources in the speech itself

In **32a** we talk about weaving supporting materials smoothly into the speech while citing the source. The form this citation takes is, like many choices in speaking, dependent on the context. In some cases there is a rigid and stylized form, in others there is a lot more flexibility available to the speaker. The college debate or speech contest may have a strict form, developed by tradition. Otherwise, you can choose the "density" level of your citation—how much information you need to include about the source as you speak—according to how much you think your audience has to hear to accept the source as legitimate (although they don't have to agree with it).

One context is your listeners' attitude toward you and your topic: in **23b** we go into adjustments you may have to make depending on whether your audience is *favorable, neutral,* or *unfavorable.* As you might imagine, the more unfavorably your listeners regard your position, the more useful it may be to include denser citations as you introduce your supporting material (and to have a complete reference list printed up and ready to hand out). Another determinant in the density of your citations is your judgment on projecting credibility. See **26c.** You may find that in some cases citing your sources more fully would be to your advantage, especially if a goal is to impress upon your listeners your competence and trustworthiness.

Here are three examples along the continuum of citation density. The first introduces the information with no citation at all. The second presents the name of the source, which indicates that you are not picking numbers out of the air. The third example is fairly dense, giving your listeners enough information that they can jot down and use to check your source if they so wish.

No citation Only 17 percent of all bicycle accidents are car–bike collisions, and in only 10 percent of those collisions was the car overtaking the bike from the rear.

Light citation According to transportation engineer John Forester, only 17 percent of all bicycle accidents are car–bike collisions, and in only 10 percent of those collisions was the car overtaking the bike from the rear.

Dense citation In his 1993 book, *Effective Cycling,* published by MIT Press, transportation engineer John Forester notes that only 17 percent of all bicycle accidents are car–bike collisions, and in only 10 percent of those collisions was the car overtaking the bike from the rear.

> **KEY POINT** **Make Dense Citations Conversational** In the interest of weaving your supporting materials *smoothly* into your speech, we urge that if you must be dense in your citing, you make it as conversational as possible. Avoid the "big parenthetical speed bump" that interrupts the flow of a sentence, as in "Transportation engineer John Forester notes (*Effective Cycling*, MIT Press, 1993) that only. . . ." It may take a few more words to come up with a smooth version, but the result will be more natural to the ears.

PART **5** # Organizing Your Ideas and Information

CHAPTER 17. **Exploring Your Ideas and Potential Points**

Look for logical groupings of ideas that could be developed as points of your speech.

CHAPTER 18. **Choosing Points That Work**

When you choose your main points, determine which ones work best to convey your ideas.

CHAPTER 19. **Arranging Points**

When you arrange your points, consider the traditional patterns of speech organization, and select or create the one that is best suited to your topic and purpose.

CHAPTER 20. **Outlining**

Use a formal outline as an organizational tool.

CHAPTER 21. **Building Sound Arguments**

Use sound reasoning to develop your speech.

CHAPTER 17

Exploring Your Ideas and Potential Points

You may have lots of good ideas, but you need a procedure to assess which are important and where you want to go with them—a process that cannot be given short shrift. This entails four stages:

1. Generating many ideas

2. Grouping them into clusters

3. Labeling each cluster

4. Reworking, adjusting, and culling the ideas until you have two to five major groupings that cover the most important ideas and that can be developed in your allotted time

17a. Assemble all the possible ideas and information

When you begin to prepare a speech, do not limit yourself. Jot down every item you might possibly cover in your speech, whether drawn from your research or from ideas that have been percolating. Follow the techniques of brainstorming; go for quantity rather than quality at this point. Do not judge or dismiss any idea, but instead write them all down in no particular order and don't worry about duplication. You cannot start the process of organizing until you have some raw material to organize.

17b. Use a variety of tools to identify potential points

Look back over the brainstorming list you made and consider how you might cluster the entries. There is no one correct way to group these ideas. Almost certainly, some ideas will be omitted altogether, and others will have to be forced a bit to fit into any category. Sometimes, one or more of the ideas from your brainstorming list will serve as a category around which to group lesser points. Other times, you will group several minor ideas first and then devise a superordinate heading.

1 Create a working outline

Perhaps the most traditional technique of speech organization is to arrange ideas in the hierarchical, indented outline format. At this stage of development, however, you do not want to be constrained by the requirements of the formal full-sentence outline. (See **20a** and **20b**.) The full-sentence outline has a very important role in ensuring that you properly elaborate your points and subpoints, but a less rigid form, the *topic outline*, is more useful at this point.

Because you are likely to experiment with several alternative groupings of ideas, don't spend time on phrasing or format. Just try to fit ideas under one another, nesting them in various ways until you discover the pattern that seems to make the most sense.

If this is a comfortable method for you, you will have a head start on developing the full-sentence outline, but there are other, more spatially oriented ways to marshal your thoughts, which we describe next.

2   Use concept mapping

Concept mapping is a visual method of showing how your ideas relate to each other. In its most basic form, you quickly draw a simple diagram made of labeled circles and squares, connecting them with lines.

Starting with your central idea—your topic—you write it in a box or circle in the center of a sheet of paper. Thinking about the points from your brainstorming list, you jot some major ones around the topic, leaving enough room to add more subpoints. Your ideas will start to cluster around certain points; as you write each new one down, draw a line to connect it to its related point. This doesn't have to be done hierarchically, however. Subpoints might come to you before a broader point does. You can redraw as new relationships become clear.

There are a variety of styles for doing this, under the names of *clustering, mindmapping, branching,* and *ballooning.* Figure 17-1 shows a simple concept map, one that could have been part of the organizational process that led to the comic book outline in **Appendix A.**

3   Manipulate movable components

This manipulation can be similar to concept mapping in that you organize things spatially, or it can be similar to outlining in that you put things together in linear form. It depends on the components you use. For example, you can jot your ideas on Post-it notes and stick them to a wall or desktop. You can cluster them according to themes, moving items from group to group until you are happy with the total grouping.

Another possibility is to start with your research notecards and supplement them with cards on which you've written your own thoughts. In **16e,** we suggest grouping the research notecards under subject cover cards. You can write ideas, transitions, and syntheses on additional cards and plug them in where you think they fit. As with the Post-it notes, you can easily change the organization to experiment with a variety of approaches to your subject.

These two paper-based approaches can also be duplicated on a computer, using the simple outlining facility of word processing software or specialized idea development software.

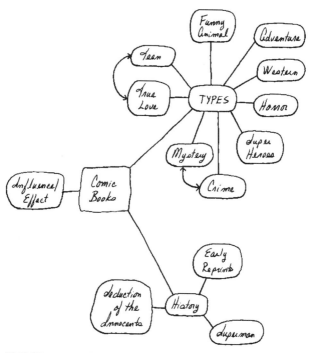

FIGURE 17-1 **Simple Concept Map**

As a result of this process, you will have a set of potential points for your speech. The next step is to choose the points that are most suitable for your purpose and that work best together.

CHAPTER 18
Choosing Points That Work

Experience has shown that following a few basic principles while selecting main points and subpoints from your pool of potential speech points will enhance your ability to craft a speech that is well structured, coherent, and effective.

18a. Choose main points that correspond to your thesis

To decide which main points to include in your speech, first look at your thesis statement. Follow the steps discussed in **11d.2** to identify the essential questions you must answer. For persuasive speeches that develop propositions of fact, value, or policy, consult **11d.3** for information on how to identify the essential questions with more precision. Once you know what a complete development of your topic requires, use the thesis statement as a standard against which to test your main points. Ask yourself:

- Is there any part of my thesis that is not developed in the speech?

- Is there any main idea of the speech that is not reflected in the thesis?

18b. Select main points that are mutually exclusive

Main points are those few ideas that are central and indispensable to the development of the thesis. They should be mutually exclusive for maximum clarity. That is, each category should exclude the ideas that are covered by any other category: "A place for everything and everything in its place." The challenge for the speaker lies in finding a scheme in which each idea fits in just *one* place.

Sometimes, when you are grouping ideas under potential main points, you will find that many fit into two or more categories. When this overlap occurs, you know that you have not yet found an effective system for classifying your ideas. Settling on a single organizational pattern is essential. If you do not know where an idea fits, your audience certainly will not.

For example, let's examine a speech on the topic of great films. Our speaker has come up with an outline that looks at great dramas with the first point, great comedies with the second, and great black-and-white films with the third. A little reflection shows that the topic was not completely thought through before the speaker began to lay out the structure of the speech. Apparently, the speaker was unable to decide whether the discussion of film should be framed along lines defined by dramatic category or by color or the lack of it. Whether a movie was shot on color or black-and-white stock does not have any intrinsic relationship to the subject (being more a matter of the history of the technology). Thus, having the three main points deal with drama, comedy, and black and white presents a problem: These three main points are not distinct categories.

Ideally, with a system of mutually exclusive main points, you will know how to classify any film and list it under one point only. If we put the sample organization to the test, however, we encounter uncertainty. *Raging Bull*, for instance, is a drama, but it could be listed under black and white, or drama. If we take a film like *Bringing Up Baby*, a black-and-white comedy from 1938, the uncertainty continues. There is no basis to exclude it from either the comedy or the black and white categories. So, although each main point taken alone seems a plausible way to classify some movies, the three main points taken together do not constitute a sensible way to look at the topic.

What *would* be a sensible way to organize it? One possibility is to divide the topic into main points along a single dimension: color, or lack of it. These main points could each be broken down into two categories, drama and comedy, that are then repeated for each main point. This same topic could be divided many other ways. For instance, the main points might also form along chronology (1920s, 1930s, etc.) with each decade having subpoints that break the films out by comedy and drama. Still other classification systems might include categories for language, director, and genre.

What is most important is that you choose *one* classification scheme for your main points that gives you a rule by which to include each item under one and only one main point.

18c. Have between two and five main points

As a speaker, you should be able to cluster your ideas around a few main themes. Otherwise, if every thought is treated as a main point, you will have no opportunity to *develop* any of them. With many random subpoints, you never extract meaning from an unorganized barrage of information. And if you have only one main point, you basically have a topic and no organization to speak of.

Understand, too, that your audience will not be able to remember more than a few main points.

18d. Express points to reflect relationships

Ideas of equal importance or of parallel logical function are called coordinate points. Points of lesser significance that support, explain, or contribute steps of logical development to other ideas are called subordinate points.

The relative importance of main and other points must be very clear in your own mind. Every point in the speech is subordinate, coordinate, or superordinate to every other.

CHECKLIST

Relationships Among Points

❑ Subordinate points (and subpoints) should fit inside, or support, a larger idea.

❑ Coordinate points (and subpoints) should be of equal importance.

❑ Each subpoint should directly relate to the point it supports.

CHAPTER 19

Arranging Points

Once the main ideas of a speech are selected, you need to arrange them in the order that will maximize effectiveness. In some cases, the decision is virtually made for you: many ceremonial or special occasion speeches are so stylized that they follow a formula. (See **9**.) For the usual informative or persuasive speech, though, there is no given pattern. You, as a speaker, must select the best arrangement of ideas.

19a. Arrange your main points

Patterns arise either inherently from the subject matter or from the requirements of the thesis statement. There are several traditional patterns of speech arrangement: chronological, spatial, cause–effect, problem–solution, and topical.

1   Using the chronological pattern

Probably the most ancient form of extended discourse is the narrative unfolding of a story. A time-ordered format that sequences information still undergirds many contemporary speeches. *Historical* development is the most common chronological pattern. If you were giving a speech on the course of European music from 1600 to 1900, you might arrange it this way:

> I. The Baroque period (1600–1750)
> II. The Classical period (1720–1810)
> III. The Romantic period (1800–1900)

Also look at the outline on women workers in **20b**.

A second way to look at a subject chronologically is to analyze a process *step-by-step*. A speech on keeping fit through aerobic exercise could generate this outline:

> I. Determine the resting and working heart rate for your age.
> II. Begin each session with stretching exercises and low-level cardiovascular warm-up.
> III. Through vigorous exercise maintain your working heart rate for 30 to 40 minutes.
> IV. Allow at least 10 minutes for cool-down and stretching exercises.

Another chronological pattern might divide a topic into *past–present–future*.

2   Using the spatial pattern

The spatial pattern is often based on geography, or location. For example, the outline for a speech on crime might look like this:

I. Crime on the Eastern Seaboard
II. Crime in the Midwest
III. Crime on the Pacific Coast

Other geographical arrangements might divide this topic into crime in Europe [Asia, Latin America] or crime in Manhattan [Brooklyn, the Bronx]. Geography need not refer just to areas on a map but can show up as other ways of dividing the world spatially, such as rural, suburban, urban crime.

The spatial pattern might also be applied to much smaller areas, such as the floor plan of a house. The following example of a spatial pattern for main points describes a very small area indeed—an aircraft instrument panel:

I. Instruments needed to maintain controlled flight are on the left side of the panel.
  A. Compass
  B. Altimeter
  C. Artificial horizon
  D. Turn and bank indicator
  E. Air speed indicator
II. Instruments providing information on the operating condition of the aircraft are on the right side.
  A. Tachometer
  B. Manifold pressure gauge
  C. Oil temperature gauge
  D. Oil pressure gauge
  E. Fuel gauge

3 Using the cause–effect pattern

This pattern is used to move from a discussion of the origins of a condition to the ways it manifests itself, and to show that events that occur in sequence are, in fact, causally related. A cause–effect structure is well suited to a speech in which the goal is to achieve either understanding or agreement rather than overt action, as here:

I. There has been a sharp increase in housing costs over the past generation.
  [as a result]
II. It is extremely difficult for a one-income family to purchase a house.

Occasionally, the pattern may be reversed to an effect–cause sequence:

I. It is extremely difficult for a one-income family to purchase a house.
  [this is because]
II. There has been a sharp increase in housing costs over the past generation.

Of course, when using the cause–effect pattern, you must be sure that the causal relationship you propose is a valid one. (See **21d**.)

4   Using the problem–solution pattern

This pattern is used to examine the symptoms of a problem and then propose a remedy. It is often seen in persuasive speeches that advocate a new policy or a specific course of action, as in the following:

> I. The current system of financing health care in the United States is inadequate.
> [to remedy this]
> II. A system of national health insurance would provide medical care to all citizens.

5   Using the topical pattern

This is the most frequently used speech pattern, where it is employed to divide a speech into elements that have no pattern exclusive of their relationship to the topic itself. It is also the most difficult pattern; many subjects do not lend themselves readily to any of the arrangements discussed so far. In these cases, you need to generate an original system for structuring the speech.

Often, the best structure for a speech involves listing the components of a whole or listing reasons that add up to the thesis. The following is an example of a topical pattern that lists reasons for a conclusion:

> Thesis statement: Capital punishment should be abolished.

> I. Capital punishment does not deter crime.
> II. Capital punishment is ultimately more costly than life imprisonment.
> III. The risk of executing an innocent person is morally unacceptable.

19b. Group subpoints according to a pattern

After your main ideas are set, look at the subpoints under each. These, too, need to be arranged in some effective order—topical, chronological, whatever. You do not have to repeat the pattern used for the main points; you can choose the format that makes the most sense for each set of subpoints. Notice the different arrangements in the detailed outline in **Appendix A**.

CHAPTER 20

Outlining

The speech outline is an indispensable tool of speech organization. A clear outline helps you keep track of the points you want to cover, and laying your ideas out on paper forces you to select points that support your thesis and fit together well. As the planning and practice chart in chapter **10** illustrates, you must develop a logical outline of your points and supporting materials before you can finalize the oral version of your speech. Because full-sentence outlines are so much like actual writing, they must not be used too early in the process (thus producing writer's block) or too late (thus resulting in a speech delivered in a written rather than an oral style). Oral composition and oral practice should surround this one excursion into writing.

KEY POINT **The Handbook Concept of Outlining** Although some outline formats include the introduction and conclusion as main points of the speech, we do not. Rather, the outline as used here is a detailed, logical plan of the *basic* ideas in the body of the speech. Do not confuse the formal speech outline with informal research notes (see **16d**), preliminary organizational tools (see **17b**), or speaking notes (see **33b**). Also, this outline is not an essay; don't let your outline transform itself into a manuscript speech. (See **28c**.)

20a. Use the conventional outline format

By following certain rules of outlining, you will be able to visualize the relationships among the ideas of your speech.

1   Follow a consistent set of symbols

It is conventional to use roman numerals to label the main ideas of the speech and to alternate between letters and numbers for each successive level of subordination, in this manner:

I. Main point
   A. First level of subordination
      1. Second level of subordination
         a. Third level of subordination
            (1) Fourth level of subordination
               (a) Fifth level of subordination

Do not skip levels. If your speech has only main points and one level of subpoints, use I, II, III and A, B, C. If your outline includes a second level of subordination, use 1, 2, 3.

2   Show logical relationships through indentation

Each subordinate idea should be indented several spaces to align with the first word—not the labeling numeral or letter—of the point it supports. This makes the relationship among ideas visually obvious. Note how your eye is directed down the levels of subordination. Your outline should not look like a piece of prose. Your outline exists only to illuminate and clarify the structure of your ideas.

3 Develop each level of subordination with two or more parts

English teachers are fond of saying, "Never have a 1 without a 2 or an A without a B." Generally, this is good advice. The concept of dividing an idea into parts—subordination—becomes nonsensical if a major point is "divided" into only one subpoint. Categories are useful because they encompass several related things. Suppose you outline a main point of your speech as follows:

> I. Redwood City is the best California city in which to live.
>   A. It has the best climate.
> II. ....

If this is your only example, you are guilty of hasty generalization. To avoid this fallacy, outline your speech following the rule of having *at least* two supporting points at each level of subordination. The rule "No 1 without a 2 and no A without a B" is a good one to ensure depth of analysis.

20b. Use a full-sentence outline

The full-sentence outline is a tool to ensure coherent development of your speech. Your thesis statement (see **11d**), the main points, and at least the first level of subpoints should be stated as declarative sentences. The declarative sentence is, in effect, a proposition. As such, it can be proved or disproved, accepted or rejected.

Look at the following sentence:

> I. Secondhand smoke harms nonsmokers.

If this sentence were presented to you on a true/false test, you could, with adequate knowledge, answer one way or the other. But what would you do if you encountered these items on a true/false test?

> I. Nonsmokers' rights

or:

> I. What is the effect of secondhand smoke on nonsmokers?

Obviously, an answer of true or false to either of these examples is impossible. Far too many speeches are constructed around just such vague phrases, questions, and uncompleted ideas. Listeners can identify the speaker's general topic but cannot always recognize the specific points the speaker is trying to make. Consider these examples:

Wrong: I. What are the causes of crime?

Right: I. Crime is caused by a combination of sociological and psychological factors.

Wrong: I. The history of the feminist movement in the United States

Right: I. U.S. feminism can be divided into four historical periods.

Besides rendering the speech more coherent for your audience, the use of declarative sentences in your outline makes you more conscious of the exact points you want to make and forces you to frame them explicitly. Once the thesis and main points are stated in propositional form, they will provide a basis against which you can test all other speech content.

The following outlines deal with a topic, the history of working women in the United States, that could fill many volumes. Here is how a *full-sentence outline* covers the topic. Observe how the thesis statement and full-sentence main and secondary points provide a basis for the speaker to decide what to include.

Full-Sentence Outline

Thesis Statement: *Since the beginning of the Industrial Revolution, women in the United States have been exploited as a cheap and expendable source of labor.*

   I. In preindustrial colonial settings, the boundaries between men's and women's spheres were indistinct.
      A. Colonial women ran self-sufficient factories in their homes.
         1. Women produced candles, the major source of artificial light.
         2. Clothing and bedding were made by women.
         3. The making of soap was a major contribution by women.
      B. The rigors of frontier life decreed a more equal division of labor between women and men than was found on the rapidly industrializing eastern seaboard.
         1. Men and women shared long hours of joint farmwork.
         2. Women were often left alone for long periods to run the farm.
   II. Between the Revolution and the Civil War, increased industrialization led to increased exploitation of women workers.
      A. Factories undercut home production.
      B. When the western migration caused shortages of male workers, women became a cheap source of labor for the factories.
         1. The percentage of women in the workforce increased.
         2. In 1829, women earned one quarter of what men did.

   C. Working women's efforts to improve their lot were not successful.
     1. The first women's strike was in 1824, but poor organization made it and others ineffective.
     2. Associations of working women failed because of the women's isolation and inexperience.

III. In spite of increasing unionization between the Civil War and World War II, women's position in the workforce remained inferior.
   A. Women were an unwelcome minority in trade organizations.
     1. Male union leaders did not believe in equal pay for equal work.
     2. According to men, women were barred from union offices because "no conveniences were available."
   B. Attempts by women before 1900 to organize among themselves met with failure.
     1. Women's unions were not taken seriously.
     2. Female workers were usually too impoverished to strike successfully.
   C. Important gains by working women in the first decades of the 20th century yielded little net improvement.
     1. Women's situation had improved in some areas.
       a. Unionization of the garment industry was successful.
       b. New job classifications were opened to women during World War I.
     2. Female workers still had neither security nor equality.
       a. Men got their jobs back after the war.
       b. Women received one half of comparable men's pay.

IV. During World War II and after, women were used as a dispensable and secondary source of labor.
   A. Traditional views of femininity were conveniently set aside according to economic needs.
     1. Three million women were recruited to replace our fighting men.
     2. "Rosie the Riveter" became a mythic ideal.
   B. After the war, labor, government, and industry cooperated to push women out of their new jobs.
     1. Although most women wanted to keep working, by 1946 four million were gone from the workforce.
     2. When plants began to rehire men, women's seniority was often ignored.
     3. With the unions' tacit approval, many jobs held by women during the war were reclassified as men's jobs.

    4. Many of the laid-off women were denied unemployment insurance.

    5. Articles and pamphlets exhorted women to return to their "primary role."

       a. Women were needed to provide a haven for returning men.

       b. Women were needed to nurture the nuclear family.

For contrast, here is how a *topic outline* on the same subject might have covered the first main point.

Topic Outline

Topic: *The history of working women in the United States*

  I. Preindustrial

    A. Colonial women

      1. Soap

      2. Clothing

    B. Frontier women

      1. Indian attacks

      2. Farmwork

At first glance, the topic outline seems to be a coherent, tidy arrangement of points. But can you form a sharp image of what the speaker is saying about working women in the United States? For example, the first main point of the speech is "Preindustrial." Yet "preindustrial" is so broad that it could include the first humans to appear in America, thousands of years ago. In fact, this point will probably deal with the work that women did between the first European colonization and the advent of the Industrial Revolution, but it ought to be phrased to leave no doubt.

This is only half the job, though. No matter how refined, a *subject* still needs a *predicate*. Although a speaker can delimit a subject with precision by using sufficient modifiers and qualifiers, it still may not be clear what she or he means to say *about* that subject. Even if the speaker refines point I of the topic outline to describe a specific group of women in a specific era (e.g., "Colonial life for women, 1620–1783"), it is still not clear what idea is being developed: That there were many working women? That their lives were hard? That they participated in all spheres of work? As these questions are raised and answered, the speaker transforms a loose phrase into a full sentence. If it turns into something like main point I in the full-sentence outline, the speaker will probably decide that stories about Indian attacks, however interesting, do not belong in this speech.

Full-sentence outlines are not extra work but rather are a needed tool to demonstrate logical relationships in the speech. Once you think these issues through, you can proceed to a more spontaneous and fluid oral form of expression, confident that the underlying structure of your speech is sound.

20c. Phrase main points to forecast subpoints

It is not enough to have an outline with full sentences as main points. The sentences must logically encompass the main ideas of the speech. Suppose a speech outline has the following main point:

I. Many people are unaware of the origins of the paper they use every day.

If this is *really* the main idea being developed in this section of the speech, the subpoints should look something like this:

A. Ursula is utterly unaware of the origin of paper.
B. Clint is clueless about where paper comes from.
C. Ned never thought about paper for a minute.
D. and so on . . .

Obviously, the speaker does not intend to spend this whole portion of the speech exposing the ignorance of the general public. More likely, the person will talk about where paper comes from. And the main point should reflect this. The phrase "many people are unaware" does not have to be jettisoned altogether, but it can become merely a transitional lead-in, not an essential component of what is to follow.

Each main point should be cast as a *subthesis sentence* that answers two simple questions about the section of the speech being covered by the point: What's it about? and What about it?

Wrong:

Subthesis sentence:	I first would like to take a few minutes to discuss the origin of paper.
What's it about?	A speaker talking for a few minutes.
What about it?	The topic being talked about is the origin of paper.

Wrong:

Subthesis sentence:	Another interesting point is the origin of paper.
What's it about?	The origin of paper.
What about it?	It is interesting.

Right:

Subthesis sentence:	The origins of paper can be traced to the use of papyrus in ancient Egypt.
What's it about?	The origin of paper.
What about it?	It can be traced to papyrus in ancient Egypt.

Do not include in the outline transitional phrases that might be part of your oral presentation. They make for pseudosentences. Also, do not include your supporting evidence in the phrasing of a main point; keep statistics, testimony, and examples at the subordinate levels. Your main points should express the more general ideas of the speech; these are supported by evidence or data.

KEY POINT **Phrasing for Impact** Once you have framed your main ideas so that they are logically and grammatically complete, take time to recast your points in language that highlights them for your audience when you speak. In this final phase of refining the outline, you move from one aspect of composition—organizing points logically—to another—sometimes called "writing for the ear."

Listeners are not as quick to see the relationships between points when the perspective and the focus keep changing. Whenever possible, strive for grammatical consistency of structure, person, number, and voice. Ideas that are phrased in concise, colorful, parallel language are more likely to be remembered by both speaker and listeners. (See also **29**.)

CHAPTER 21

Building Sound Arguments

Reasoning is the process by which we come to understand something previously unknown, through analyzing and integrating those things we already know. Any remotely intelligent group of listeners will not be moved by hearing *what* you think; they want to know *why* you think it. Consequently, the reasoning that should be the foundation of every speech can also be seen as "the giving of *good* reasons."

To develop a logical line of thought and test its validity, you need to understand a little more about how reasoning functions to link key points of a speech together. You also need to become familiar with standard patterns of reasoning and with a few of the common fallacies. Only then can you decide how best to use reasoning in putting your speech together.

21a. Identify where reasoning is needed to provide an essential link

In all persuasive speeches and some sections of evocative and informative speeches a challenging task confronts the speaker: You must develop lines of argument through reasoning to explain why you reached your conclusion. This *conclusion* can also be called a *claim*. Claims are any statements that you need to substantiate because they are not taken for granted by your listeners. Your thesis sentence is a claim, your main points are claims that support that claim, and even some of your subordinate points have to be reasoned through before they become acceptable.

1 Evidence can lead to more than one claim

Suppose you have a conclusion or claim that you want your listeners to accept, and you have some evidence or data that you believe support that claim. Clearly, everyone who confronts the same facts and figures does not automatically come to the same conclusion that you do. What links the data to the claim, or *warrants* its acceptance, is the process of reasoning. For example, suppose two different people are confronted with the fact that more people go to the doctor in countries with national health care programs than in countries with privately funded health care. Person A concludes that this is an argument in support of adopting national health care in the United States. Person B concludes that it is an argument against national health care.

As Figure 21-1 shows, there is no connection between evidence and claim except through the reasoning link that you provide.

2 People look for links that fit familiar patterns

In the health care example, Person A is drawing on a pattern observed in the past—namely, that people who cannot afford a service they need will seek out that service when it becomes affordable. This is perfectly reasonable and logical; we all can think of plenty of commonsense examples.

Person B is also being logical and reasonable in linking the evidence of increased medical visits to the claim that national health care would be undesirable. This person is drawing on another observed pattern of human behavior—that people who see a re-

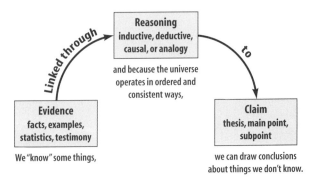

FIGURE 21-1 Reasoning Links Evidence and Claim

source as free and unlimited may use it inappropriately and wastefully. There is also plenty of support for this view.

The issue here is not what the facts *are*, but what the facts *mean*. For our purposes, the significance of these opposing views is to show that there are many sensible ways to interpret the same piece of evidence. A speaker who uses evidence to support a claim cannot simply present the evidence and hope it speaks for itself. The speaker must explain the relevance of the evidence and justify the link to a particular claim.

21b. Inductive reasoning

You use an inductive pattern of reasoning when your argument consists of combining a series of observations that lead to a probable conclusion. Dozens of times a day, we draw inferences that go beyond what we observe directly. We could not function unless we trusted regularities in events, unless we believed that much of what has happened before will happen again: We step in front of oncoming traffic because we believe from previous experience that the cars will obey the traffic signals. Figure 21-2 depicts the process of inductive reasoning.

1   Base your inferences on sufficient and representative cases

Inductive reasoning consists of collecting enough instances to establish a pattern. Remember the logical tests in **16a.1**. A typical line of inductive thought can be portrayed as follows:

Orchid 1 has no fragrance.

Orchid 2 has no fragrance.

....

Orchid *n* has no fragrance.

Therefore, it is probable that all orchids have no fragrance.

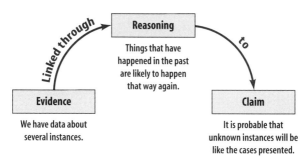

FIGURE 21-2   Inductive Reasoning Draws Inferences from Observations

The extent to which you can generalize from such observations is linked to the extent of your sampling. If you smelled only a few orchids or only the orchids in one corner of one hothouse, you would be less able to make a general conclusion than if you had smelled orchids in different hothouses throughout the country.

Be cautious in drawing inferences from limited data. How many cases did you examine? Were they selected fairly? Are the contrary instances accounted for? (See **16b** and **21f**.)

2   Recognize the degree of probability of your claim

The conclusions drawn from induction are always *probable* rather than *absolute*. An inductive conclusion can fall anywhere along this continuum:

The degree of certainty depends on the methods used in making our observations and on the number of observations made.

How strong must this probability be before you can consider the conclusion of an inductive argument to be valid? A 51 percent probability? or 75 percent? or 99 percent? It depends. There is no mathematical or logical answer to the question.

Would you leap off a 20-foot wall for $1,000? Many would say yes. It is *possible* that you could be killed, but it is probable that you would escape with no worse than a sprained ankle or broken leg. Would you jump from the roof of a three-story building for $1,000? Most people would say no. It is *possible* that you would be unharmed, but not very probable. In both cases, you set the acceptable level of probability by weighing potential risks against potential gains. In inductive reasoning, the acceptability of a probable conclusion always depends on cost–benefit analysis.

21c. Deductive reasoning

You use a deductive pattern of reasoning when your argument demonstrates how the relationships among established premises lead to a necessary conclusion. Unlike induction, in which the emphasis is on collecting observable data, *deduction* consists of manipulating verbal statements, or premises, according to formal rules. Deduction, then, does not involve bringing new data into play. Rather it is rearranging things you already know to discover something meaningful about how they fit together, as in scientific breakthroughs, gossip, and the English murder mystery. In our everyday lives, we have that "Aha!" experience when we suddenly discover the pattern underlying separate facts and realize their implication. Figure 21-3 depicts the process of deductive reasoning.

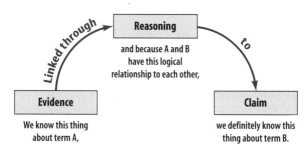

FIGURE 21-3 Deductive Reasoning Finds the Patterns in What You Already Know

Because the correctness of deduction lies in whether it adheres to certain rules, experts in deductive reasoning learn complex symbolic formulas by which they test arguments. For the purpose of this book, we need only touch on the basic concept of deduction: If we know certain things about how two terms (concepts, events, characteristics) are related, we can discover other relationships that are logically entailed or implicated:

Term A is related in a known way to Term B.

We know certain things about B.

Therefore, we can draw certain conclusions about Term A.

To use deductive reasoning in a speech, you need to transpose this into a series of steps:

Step 1: Establish that a relationship exists between two terms (the *major premise*).

Step 2: Establish the actual condition/status of one of the terms (the *minor premise*).

Step 3: Show how a conclusion about the other term necessarily follows.

1 Begin with an absolute statement

Step 1 in deduction—establishing the major premise—takes many forms. It always involves an absolute relationship between two terms. Here are examples of four common relationships.

- One term may be an intrinsic characteristic of the other: All ducks have webbed feet.

- One term may be a category that includes the other: The Food Stamp program is part of the social welfare system.

- One term may be inevitably linked to the other: If corporate taxes are cut, then investment will increase.

- The two terms may be the opposite of or exclude each other: Either that fabric is natural or it is synthetic.

2 Derive a necessary conclusion

When you have established one of these basic major premises, you have set up a formula that will serve as the linking device at the top of your arc of reasoning. When you move to Step 2, you establish something about one of the two terms—in what logicians call the *minor premise*.

A piece of evidence like "Daffy is a duck" might mean many things, or nothing, in some lines of argument. But in the context of the first major premise illustrated earlier, it is the minor premise, and the resulting, relevant implication is that Daffy has webbed feet.

Feed in the data you have, follow the rules of deductive logic, and certain conclusions are inevitably entailed:

> This blouse is made of a synthetic fiber, *so it is not made of a natural fiber.*
>
> Corporate taxes were not cut, *so investment must not have increased.*

The beauty of deduction lies in its certainty. If your listeners accept the premises, they *must* accept the conclusion. The problem with deduction is that, for its conclusion to be absolute, its premises must be absolute. The requirement of having an all-or-nothing beginning premise is so restrictive that true, formal deductive reasoning is rather rare.

21d. Causal reasoning

You use causal reasoning to demonstrate that one event results from another. It is the backbone of all speeches that deal with policy and problem solving. In most cases, if a person says, "I don't favor your policy (or program, or solution)," what that person is really saying is, "I disagree with you that X causes Y." This means that you must carefully scrutinize the relationship between two events to satisfy yourself that it is causal. Figure 21-4 depicts the causal reasoning process.

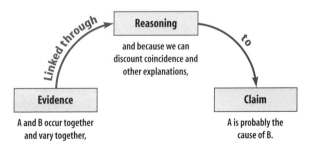

FIGURE 21-4   Causal Reasoning Links Cause and Effect

1 Test the validity of your causal relationships

A causal relationship is stronger than mere correlation or coexistence or coincidence. Two events may occur together or in sequence without one causing the other. For instance, morning sickness and weight gain often occur together, but neither causes the other; they are the result of a third condition, pregnancy. To be sure that the relationship is a causal one, apply these tests.

Do the alleged cause and alleged effect occur together? To prove that a causal relationship exists, at least two formal comparisons must be made, as with a control group and an experimental group. Otherwise, mere coincidence or correlation cannot be ruled out. It is not enough to show that the alleged cause is present with the alleged effect; you must also show that, in the absence of the alleged cause, the alleged effect does not appear:

> If a rash appears every time you eat tomatoes, and never appears when you haven't eaten tomatoes, this is strong evidence that tomatoes cause the rash.

> To prove a causal relationship, you must show both concurrent presence and concurrent absence.

Do the alleged cause and the alleged effect vary together? Another test of causation is to determine whether the magnitude of change in the cause matches that in the effect:

> If one bite of tomato gives you a small rash, and consuming many tomatoes gives you a big rash, this is one more bit of evidence to suggest that tomatoes cause your rash.

2 Do not oversimplify causal relationships

In the worlds of physics and chemistry, there are some clear, straightforward causal relationships:

> Adding silver nitrate solution ($AgNO_3$) to sodium chloride ($NaCl$) will cause silver chloride ($AgCl$) to precipitate.

This type of relationship between cause (*C*) and effect (*E*) could be represented as

$$C \rightarrow E$$

However, in the areas of politics, psychology, medicine, economics, and the like, more complex patterns usually exist.

Some effects have multiple causes

If smoking were the single cause of lung cancer, then every smoker would have lung cancer, and every victim of lung cancer would be a smoker. Obviously, this is not the case. Yet research does show smoking to be one causal factor contributing to lung cancer.

Some causes are also effects, and some effects are also causes in a long causal chain When we designate a cause of a certain event, we can look at the immediate cause or a more distant factor. A doctor might say that the cause of a particular death was a cerebral hemorrhage. What, though, was the cause of the hemorrhage? Perhaps a fractured skull, which was caused by going through a windshield, which was caused by the impact of a car with a tree, which was caused by excessive drinking, which was caused by worry over being unemployed, and so on:

$$C \rightarrow (E/C) \rightarrow (E/C) \rightarrow (E/C) \rightarrow E$$

It is sometimes important to point out the cyclical nature of certain causal chains. For example, ignorance about a particular group may lead to prejudice, which in turn results in lack of contact with that group, which perpetuates ignorance. This sort of analysis is far more interesting than positing a single cause of racial disharmony.

Some effects result from a one-time cause, and some from ongoing causes Effects that are labeled undesirable can be dealt with in two ways, either by treating the effect directly, or by blocking the cause that produces the effect. To decide which strategy makes the most sense in a given context, you need to determine whether the cause is one-time or ongoing, as in a neighborhood with bare dirt for landscaping, shattered windows, broken furniture in the yards, and residents in need of medical care—if you find that a tornado whipped through the area, you may push for emergency relief, but if you learn that the area is chronically depressed you may choose to advocate structural economic reform. A mistake in evaluation, whereby the effect of an ongoing cause is treated as if it resulted from a one-time cause, will lead to the eventual reappearance of that effect.

21e. Reasoning by analogy

You use reasoning by analogy to draw conclusions about unknown events, based on what you know about similar events. Figure 21-5 depicts the process of reasoning by analogy.

Reasoning by analogy is a natural and powerful way to make links. People intuitively look to similar examples when they want to understand something. Suppose the president's foreign policy advisors are trying to decide whether to intervene in a foreign country's internal struggles, or a judge is pondering whether to

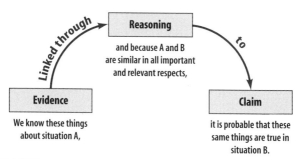

FIGURE 21-5   Analogy Compares Two Things in the Same Category

admit expert testimony on battered wife syndrome, or you are wondering whether to take the freeway or back streets to work. In all these cases, from the most cosmic policy issues to the most mundane everyday decisions, people ask themselves, "What is this like that I already know about?"

Although reasoning by analogy is so innate—or *because* it is—you need to choose your analogies carefully.

Be sure that when you reason by analogy the two cases are similar in all relevant and important respects. No cases are identical, and simply pointing out differences does not automatically discredit an analogy. If they differ in relevant and important ways, the differences are probably significant enough to reject the comparison.

> **KEY POINT**   **Use the Correct Type of Analogy** Do not confuse a literal analogy, which is a form of reasoning, with a figurative analogy, which is used only in a descriptive function. Reasoning by analogy *requires* a comparison of two members of the *same* category. Figurative analogy compares the members of different categories:
>
> > Convincing my boss, Fred, to adopt a new procedure takes as much persistence, luck, and timing as starting my 1972 Fiat on a January morning.
> >
> > Going to war in Vietnam was like tap-dancing on quicksand.
>
> These analogies may have stylistic impact, but they cannot support a conclusion because they compare a human relationship with a human–machine relationship, and a war with an athletic impossibility.

21f.   Avoid common reasoning fallacies

Some people commit reasoning fallacies knowingly, with dishonest intent. Others commit them due to a lack of practice or skill in doing their own thinking. The good public speaker wants to avoid the appearance of either. Once you have built your speech around sound, logical arguments, go through it to detect any constructions that even hint of sloppy thinking. One glaring fallacy in your speech will make all your other conclusions suspect. It is not necessary to learn all the fallacies—over one hundred have been categorized—but you should be familiar with the most common of them.

1 Attacking the person (ad hominem)

This fallacy substitutes character assassination for solid refutation or persuasion:

> Anyone who advocates abortion on demand is a murderer anyway. It certainly wouldn't surprise me to find them taking kickbacks from the clinics that would receive government funds.

2 The slippery slope

This common fallacy consists of making the false assumption that taking the first step in any direction will inevitably lead to going dangerously far in that direction. The image is of someone sliding down a slope without being able to stop.

> If we let the government ban the sale and possession of assault rifles, banning all firearms is next.

> If we let the government abandon support of the arts, artistic freedom will die.

3 The semantic fallacy

The rich, connotative nature of words, which so enhances communication, can also abet fuzzy thinking. When midstream shifts of definition are obvious, they can be funny, as in "blackberries are red when they're green."

More subtle and dangerous shifts in definition can occur in various critical parts of an argument:

> The free enterprise system, which we all cherish, could not exist without competition. This bill to protect small businesses threatens our whole economic structure. There can be no true competition when one group is given special protection.

In the underlying value premise, the word *competition* is used in the general sense of a market mechanism. In claiming that the bill endangers competition, the speaker uses the term in a much narrower sense, as in "a specific contest between individuals." The semantic fallacy is especially difficult to identify and frustrating to respond to because the syllogistic form of the argument appears to be valid. The problem of identification arises from the slight slippage of definition as a term is used with different meanings in different premises.

4   False dichotomy

It is fallacious to base reasoning on an *either/or* statement when the two alternatives are not really mutually exclusive or when other alternatives exist. Many speeches set up artificial choices:

> Either we stand up to naked aggression, or we lose the confidence of our allies.

This basic premise so oversimplifies a complex issue that no conclusions can be drawn from it. Do not set up a deductive argument with a false dichotomy as its major premise.

5   Hasty generalization

This fallacy entails making a premature inductive "leap." (See **21b**.) It is glorified in the pomp surrounding Groundhog Day, when data from an isolated event are blindly accepted as gospel in relation to a much wider range of events.

This statement makes a faulty leap:

> The savings and loan scandal proved that every elected official has a price.

Time may not allow you, as a speaker, to include all the data that led you to some conclusion. It is especially important, then, to have the unused data at your fingertips so that you can respond to any accusations of hasty generalization that may arise.

6   Confusing sequence with cause

The Latin label for this fallacy (post hoc, ergo propter hoc) translates as "after the event, therefore because of the event." It is natural to try to understand the world around us by looking for cause–effect patterns wherever possible. So strong is this motivation that we are frequently guilty of imitating Chanticleer the rooster, who firmly believed that it was his predawn crowing that caused the sun to rise each day.

To avoid this fallacy, never assume causation based on time sequence alone. Test every causal hypothesis against the criteria in **21d**.

PART 6 Getting Your Ideas Across

CHAPTER 22. **Developing Informative Strategies**

For informative speaking, plan a strategy that will aid your audience's comprehension.

CHAPTER 23. **Developing Persuasive Strategies**

Plan a strategy that takes into account the attitudes of the audience and arranges points for maximum persuasive impact.

CHAPTER 24. **Presenting Your Reasoning**

Lay out the basic arguments you have developed in a way that makes the reasoning clear and effective for your audience.

CHAPTER 25. **Using Motivational Appeals**

Motivate your listeners toward your speech purpose through appeals to their emotions, needs, and values.

CHAPTER 26. **Establishing Credibility**

Establish your credibility by projecting the qualities of competence, concern, trustworthiness, and dynamism.

CHAPTER 27. **Designing Presentation Aids**

Design effective presentation aids to support your message.

CHAPTER 22

Developing Informative Strategies

A large part of speaking is merely explanation—stating an idea and then restating it in a way that develops or expands upon the basic notion. Unfortunately, some explanations do more to confuse than to clarify. Usually, this occurs when the speaker has lost sight of which of the many details of a complex process or idea are the essential ones. It is a real challenge to select the most significant details and present them in the clearest order. How can you most economically create the mental picture that will aid your listeners' understanding?

22a. Help your listeners grasp your information

Base your speech structure and content on an understanding of how people acquire, process, and retain information.

1 Avoid information overload

When you speak on a topic that you know a great deal about, there is a tendency to want to bring your audience up to your level immediately. When you give out too much information in too short a time, the result is information overload. The informative speaker has to manage a large mass of information and deliver it at the right pace and in the right-sized chunks so it can be useful and meaningful for listeners. Bear in mind the information-processing principle known as *seven, plus or minus two*. Research suggests that this is how many points the average person can comprehend at one time, so select just a handful of points to develop.

2 Give listeners an organizing framework

Have you ever tried to put together a jigsaw puzzle without looking at the picture on the box? What you have is a jumble of unrelated pieces. Once you see the big picture, you have some idea of how things are supposed to fit together. Do not plunge directly into the specifics of the topic before giving your audience some sense of the whole.

3 Move from the simple to the complex

Even at the risk of temporary oversimplification, it is advisable first to lay out the most basic concepts and later to introduce qualifiers, exceptions, and interesting tangents. Think of each listener as the newcomer to town who first wants to learn the basic route from home to work, and only after mastering that wants to learn about shortcuts and scenic detours.

4   Move from the familiar to the unfamiliar

Any group can learn about any subject if you start where members are and move along at the proper rate. Teachers will attest that learning proceeds best when they are able to adjust the focus of their instruction to a point just beyond the current knowledge level of the group If the instruction duplicates what the group already knows, the material will not be challenging. If the focus is two or three levels beyond them, group members will get discouraged.

22b. Adhere to common principles of clear explanation

If you employ the following, you substantially ease your listeners' path to comprehension.

1   Use organizers

Provide your listeners with cues as to how they should structure the information.

Signposts One organizer is the signpost. Signposts, like their physical counterparts, point the way you are going and can serve as a reminder of where you've been:

> First, I'll show you how to make a simple white sauce, and then move on to three more elaborate sauces that start with the basic recipe.

> So, from this short description of one novel and three of her poems, you can see once again the two themes that permeate Sylvia Plath's work.

Enumeration Numbering is an obvious organizational cue:

> The many steps in building an apartment complex can be grouped into these three phases:

> One: Finding attractive sites with the proper zoning.

> Two: Negotiating for the purchase of a piece of property.

> Three: Contracting with architects and builders.

Acronyms An acronym is a word that is formed from the first letters of a series of words and that can be pronounced like a word. For instance, radar is an acronym formed from RAdio Detecting And Ranging. Other examples are SETI, for Search for Extra Terrestrial Intelligence, and GIGO, for Garbage In, Garbage Out.

Slogans, catchwords, and memorable phrases Like acronyms, these types of cues give your listeners a framework for remembering your points:

So, look at those files in your drawer that you haven't used in a year, and assess their real value. Keep in mind Peg Bracken's advice about leftover food: "When in doubt, throw it out."

Try to do something decisive with each piece of mail as you open it. Apply the "Four D's": Drop the item, Delay the item, Delegate the item, or Do the item.

2   Use emphasis cues

Underline and highlight key points with phrases like "this is very important," "if you don't remember anything else . . . ," and "here's what it all comes down to. . . ."

You can also emphasize points by vocal or physical cues. When you want an idea to stand out, speak more loudly, or occasionally more softly. Pause before and after the big idea. Step forward. Let your facial expression forecast the seriousness of a point.

3   Use examples liberally

When an audience is feeling confused, nothing reassures them like the appearance of a concrete example. You might begin with a simple, even whimsical, example:

> A "win–win" negotiation has occurred when both parties achieve their important goals without perceiving that they have had to make a major sacrifice. Phil and Dave are room-mates, and they both think the other needs to do more around the apartment. After talking about it, they agree that Dave will do all the cooking and Phil will do all the cleaning. Each thinks he got off easy.

Next, you could move to a more complex and realistic example:

> Or suppose that you have a used car for sale and your neighbor wants to buy it but does not have all the cash now. You offer to carry an interest free note due in six months if your neighbor will take care of your pets and plants for three weeks while you are on vacation.

Finally, you might give an example that is sophisticated, subtle, and complex enough for your audience to apply it to situations they may actually encounter:

> Now, let's see how these principles apply to a typical real estate negotiation. On this chart you will see the seller's and buyer's prioritized needs and bargaining chips are listed . . .

4   Use analogies

Continually compare the known to the unknown. For instance, you might use this simple analogy to explain a complex process.

A nuclear power plant is like a steam locomotive. The fireman shovels coal into the furnace, where the heat it gives off turns the water in the boiler into steam. The steam travels through pipes to pistons, where the energy is converted and carried by driving rods to the wheels, pulling long trains of cars down the rails. Substitute a nuclear pile for the coal, a turbine for the pistons, and an electrical generator for the drive wheels, and you have a nuclear power plant.

To reinforce points and reach more listeners, draw analogies from many areas: sports, movies, nature, history, other cultures, and so on.

5   Use multiple channels and modes

Your message will be clearer if you send it through several channels. As you describe a process with words, also use your hands, a visual aid, a chart, or a recording. Appeal to as many senses as possible to reinforce the message. A good rule to follow is this: If a point is very important or very difficult, always use at least one other channel besides the spoken word to get it across.

6   Use repetition and redundancy

People learn and remember what they hear repeatedly. If a principle is important, say it over again, in the same words or different words. Repeat it. Paraphrase it. Reinforce it. Refer back to it. Then mention it again.

CHAPTER 23
Developing Persuasive Strategies

When you try to change others' attitudes or behavior, you need to base your persuasive effort on some guiding principles. This requires an understanding of how and why people change their minds.

23a. Clarify the goals of your persuasion

A strong grasp of purpose is especially important in persuasive speaking. When you try to change people, and not simply educate or inspire them, you are more likely to encounter resistance. It helps to know exactly what your goals are—and what they are not. (See **11c**.) You want to aim for a realistic target.

Some authorities distinguish between persuasive speeches that seek to change actual behavior and those that merely try to influence beliefs and attitudes. Although an attitude is a predisposition to respond in a particular way, holding a certain attitude does not guarantee certain behaviors associated with the attitude. People may say they believe in recycling but never drum up the energy to separate their trash. Generally, if you want action, you should set your goals in terms of behavior and tell the audience what to *do* (or *not do*), not what to *think*.

23b. Adjust your content in light of audience attitude

You should pay attention to your audience's attitude both toward your topic and toward you. Section **12d** asks you to analyze your listeners' possible reactions to your thesis. Based on surveys, observations, or inference, you can make some determination of their predisposition toward your topic. The following continuum classifies audiences according to that predisposition:

Types of Audiences

Unfavorable			Neutral	Favorable		
Strongly disagree	Moderately disagree	Slightly disagree	Neither agree nor disagree	Slightly agree	Moderately agree	Strongly agree

Here are some suggestions on how to deal with such favorable, neutral, or unfavorable audiences.

1   Favorable audience

A speaker facing a favorable audience is relieved of a number of burdens. In this situation, as a speaker, you rarely need to establish credibility. Your listeners, perceiving your position as identical to theirs, approve of you and your good taste already. Furthermore, a favorable audience will not raise internal counterarguments for you to deflect or defuse.

Being relieved of a few burdens, however, does not release you from all responsibility as an effective champion of your position. A poorly prepared speech can actually erode audience support. But if you accept the challenge of speaking to a favorable audience, you can solidify or strengthen their attitudes, or you can cause them to move from theoretical agreement to positive action.

Make use of emotional appeals to intensify support   There is a difference between intellectually agreeing with a position and making a commitment to it. Even once committed, the difference between commitment and action is usually a function of emotional arousal. Out of the vast number of positions you might agree with, there is a much shorter list of issues that you really

117

care about. These issues appeal to your most basic needs, touch on your core values, or have a personal effect on your life.

To get your speech topic on your listeners' short list, make extensive use of appeals to basic values such as patriotism, humanitarianism, and progress; appeals to basic needs such as survival, security, and status; and appeals to basic emotions such as fear, pity, and love.

When listeners agree with you but are not taking action, they probably do not feel personally involved with the subject. A major task in speaking to a favorable audience is the creation of that personal involvement in two ways. First, be very specific about how their lives are affected, and then show them that their actions can make a difference:

> Your 10-dollar check can feed a Sudanese refugee family for a week.

> If you can take that extra second to switch off the lights as you leave the room, you can save yourself 50 dollars a year.

Get your audience to make a public commitment Invite your listeners to offer suggestions, sign a petition, raise their hands to volunteer, lend their names to a letterhead, or talk to others. People who have made a public commitment—oral, or written, or physical—are less likely to change their minds.

Provide several specific alternatives for action Make it easy for listeners to take action by offering several specific choices. For example, with people who have shown up at a rally for a candidate, do not say, "Stop by campaign headquarters sometime." Instead, say, "I'd like everyone here either to walk a precinct or to spend an evening making phone calls. Sign-up sheets are being passed around now." With a favorable audience, do not settle for urging members to do "something." Tell them what you want them to do, and make the execution easy and attractive: If you want them to write letters, give them addresses; if you want them to reduce their sodium intake, give them low-sodium recipes.

Prepare your audience to carry your message to others You can tap the potential of audience members as persuaders in their own right. Each of them may later discuss your topic with coworkers, neighbors, or friends who are neutral or hostile toward it. Give the less facile listeners ammunition for these interactions, and make that material as memorable and quotable as possible. Provide your audience with ready answers to refute standard counterarguments. (See **23c.3**.) Here's an example:

> You may meet people who tell you that the administration's economic policy is designed to help the average worker. Just

ask those people why the greatest tax relief goes to the rich. Have them explain to you why a person who earns $300,000 a year will have a 50 percent reduction in taxes, but a person making $18,000 a year will see a reduction of only 6 percent. They may say, "Ah, but we are creating new jobs." Ask them this . . .

This also serves to inoculate your listeners against the persuasiveness of those counterarguments.

2   Neutral audience

An audience can be neutral toward your position for one of three reasons: They are *uninterested,* they are *uninformed,* or they are genuinely *undecided.*

Stress attention factors with an uninterested neutral audience With this sort of audience, draw on all the attention techniques described in chapter **30** with special emphasis on concrete illustrations of the impact of your subject on their lives. Be sure the facts and statistics you use are relevant to your listeners' experience. Sprinkle your speech with humor and human interest. Make a special effort to have a lively and animated delivery and style to stimulate them.

With an uninformed neutral audience, stress clarification Before you can expect people to agree with you, they must have some comprehension of the issue. The main concern is clarity: Use explanation, definitions, examples, and restatement. (See **16a**.) Visual aids can be helpful. Keep your language simple and your organization straightforward.

A direct persuasive appeal should be saved until the very end of the speech.

For an undecided neutral audience, establish credibility Present new arguments that blend logical and emotional appeals to establish your credibility in this instance. The undecided neutral audience is both interested in and informed about your topic, but these listeners find the arguments for each side equally compelling. Let them know that you understand their ambivalence. Grant the complexity of the issue, and admit that there is truth on both sides. As you present the arguments for your side, stress any recent evidence or new interpretations that might justify a decision. Be sure that you acknowledge and respond respectfully and thoroughly to the main arguments against your position. In short, a well-documented, logical presentation works best for the undecided neutral audience. Appeals to emotions, needs, and values are effective only if used sparingly and clearly interwoven with the logical argument of the speech.

3   Unfavorable audience

An unfavorable audience is by no means a belligerent one—remember that *unfavorable* is defined to encompass anything on the disagree side of neutral, starting with slightly disagree. However, the more intensely the audience disagrees with you, the more members will be predisposed to reject both you and your message. Any idiosyncrasies of appearance and style of delivery will allow them to dismiss you as being on the fringe.

Set realistic goals Do not try to do too much with an unfavorable audience. Attitude change takes place slowly. If most of your audience falls at the strongly disagree end of the continuum, do not expect your 10-minute speech to change them to strong agreement. Even if it means modifying your thesis statement, set a goal that you have a reasonable chance of achieving, such as easing those who strongly disagree over to moderately disagree, or those who moderately disagree over to neutral. Trying to do too much can alienate your audience and lead to a boomerang effect in which the attitude change that occurs is the opposite of what you were seeking. Do not make an express call for action when such action is highly unlikely.

Stress common ground However great the difference between you and your audience on any particular issue, there are bound to be places where your opinions and experiences overlap. When you think about the unfavorable audience you face, ask yourself what goals and values you share. Even the intensity of the disagreement between you and your audience over, say, school busing reveals a common concern for children's education.

Base your speech on sound logic and extensive evidence The unfavorable audience is skeptical of your position and will reject most emotional appeals as manipulative. Your only chance to persuade these listeners is to build an iron-clad case supported by impeccable, unbiased evidence. With this audience, you must clearly indicate every step of your reasoning—nothing can be taken for granted. Discuss and defend even those assumptions that seem obvious to you. Spell out the logical links and connections that hold your argument together. Do not overstate your points; be careful not to claim more than the data allow. Say, "These examples suggest . . . ," rather than "These examples prove . . ."; say, "Smoking is one contributing cause of cancer," rather than "Smoking causes cancer."

Use factual and statistical evidence, and always cite your sources completely. If you mention the results of a survey, for example, tell when, where, and how it was conducted and where it was presented or published. Confront directly the arguments that are foremost in your listeners' minds. Do not be afraid to concede minor points that do not damage your basic case. State the remaining counterarguments fairly and answer them forcefully, but never stoop to ridicule.

Establish a credible image Nowhere is the careful establishment of good character, good sense, and goodwill more important than in a speech to an unfavorable audience. (See **26c**.) Plan every detail of your speech content and delivery to project an image of a calm, reasonable, fair, well-informed, and congenial person. The judicious use of humor can bolster this image while releasing tension and putting the issue in perspective. Direct the humor at yourself, your position, a common enemy, or the ironic aspects of the confrontation. Never direct it at your listeners and their beliefs.

Although you do not want to seem combative, you should remain firm in your position. It is fine to build rapport by stressing common ground and granting minor points, but do not waffle or be overly conciliatory.

23c. Organize your points for optimal persuasive impact

The speech organization patterns discussed in chapter **19**—topical, spatial, and chronological—grow out of analysis of the speech content. Other patterns can form from retracing the reasoning that led you to your conclusion—inductively, deductively, causally, or analogically. (See **21**.) Yet another way to think about ordering points is to consider how your speech unfolds for your listeners. So, if none of the familiar formats seems strategically adequate, here are some suggestions for alternative arrangements.

1 Use the motivated sequence to engage your audience

Developed by Alan Monroe several decades ago, the motivated sequence is one of the most widely used organizers for persuasive speeches.[1] This psychologically based format echoes and anticipates the mental stages through which your listeners progress as they hear your speech.

Attention: The speaker must first motivate the audience to listen to the speech.

Need: Listeners must become aware of a compelling, personalized problem.

Satisfaction: The course of action advocated must be shown to alleviate the problem.

Visualization: Psychologically, it is important that the audience have a vivid picture of the benefits of

[1]Raymie E. McKerrow, Bruce E. Gronbeck, Douglas Ehninger, and Alan H. Monroe, *Principles and Types of Speech Communication*, 14th ed. (Needham Heights, MA: Allyn & Bacon, 2000).

agreeing with the speaker or the evils of
alternatives.

Action: The speech should end with an overt call for
the listeners to act.

Here is an example of a speech that follows the motivated sequence:

Thesis Statement: *We need a light rail system in our county to reduce excessive commuter traffic congestion.*

Attention

Introduction: I was on my way to work, having left home earlier than usual so I could be there in plenty of time for my first important presentation. I heard screeching brakes. It turned out to be only a fender-bender a quarter-mile ahead of me. Nevertheless, I sat in my car, and sat, and sat, while my mood progressed from irritation to outrage to despair. I arrived at work an hour and a half late, just as the meeting was breaking up.

Need

   I. Excessive reliance on automobile transportation to the
county's major employment areas is causing severe
problems.
     A. Major traffic jams
     B. Pollution
     C. Stress to commuters

Satisfaction

   II. A light rail system should be constructed to alleviate these
problems.
     A. (Definition of light rail)
     B. (Proposed route)
     C. (Proposed funding)

Visualization

   III. The new system would be a vast improvement.
     A. Scenario with the light rail system: free parking, time to
relax, drink coffee, read
     B. Scenario without the light rail system: increased traffic,
gridlock, daily stress

Action

Conclusion: Support the county initiative for a light rail system. Urge your friends to vote for it. Write to members of the county board of supervisors on this issue. Ask your employer to commit to providing free shuttle service from the proposed light rail station to your place of business.

This organization is rather similar to a standard problem–solution speech, but the presence of the visualization step makes all the difference. Instead of merely providing a logical need satisfaction in Main Point 2, this speaker has added another psychologically powerful step in Main Point 3. The two narratives should be developed in detail to drive home the case for the listeners.

It is essential that the attention step be engaging and that the action step be concrete.

2   Place your strongest points first or last

Ideally, all of the arguments and support for your thesis statement should be strong. In reality, however, you will find that you must use materials of varying strength. These should not be arranged randomly. Be aware that people will remember best what you say first (the *primacy* principle) and what you say last (the *recency* principle). In light of this, arranging your arguments either from weakest to strongest (climax) or from strongest to weakest (anti-climax) will be more effective than placing your best points in the middle (pyramidal).

The research on which one is stronger—primacy or recency—is far from conclusive. Our best advice regarding what to say first and last is that you consider the importance of your topic to your listeners, their attitude toward it, and your credibility.

3   Consider dealing with opposing arguments

Generally, it is a good idea to address counterarguments in addition to presenting your own viewpoints. On widely debated topics these ideas will already be on listeners' minds, and they expect a response. Even on less familiar subjects on which you may have the first word, you probably won't have the last. At the end of a straightforward "pro" speech, your audience may agree with you. But if, a few hours or a few days later, listeners become aware of powerful opposing arguments, they may discredit your entire position. Speakers often inoculate their audiences by presenting a few counterarguments and answering them. Then, when these points are brought up later, the listeners will say, "Oh, yes, I was warned about this." Inoculation has created "antibodies" to resist the opposing position. In most cases, answer counterarguments after developing your own position. The only exception to this rule is when you know audience members are so preoccupied with an opposing position that they may not listen to you. In that case, respond to the point immediately.

CHAPTER 24

Presenting Your Reasoning

In laying out your speech, you went through a rigorous process of critical thinking to be sure that the evidence is sound (see **16**) and that the links you have drawn are valid (see **32**). Next, you shift your emphasis and recast the arguments into a form that fits speaking to an audience. For example, when you are involved in independent analysis, the final thing you do is draw a conclusion or claim from the evidence. However, in speaking to an audience, stating that claim may well be the first thing you want to do. Then you back up and develop that thesis or main point by retracing your reasoning in an audience friendly manner.

24a. Demonstrate the cost–reward analysis of an inductive argument

A speaker who is using induction (see **21b**) must convince the audience that the conclusion arrived at is probable enough to warrant their acceptance. The issue is one of "enoughness." Are the examples you have examined sufficient in both quantity and quality? The so-called inductive leap is based on an apt image. You lead the listeners to a certain point with your data and then ask them to jump across an imaginary chasm to the conclusion you see.

Suppose you know of a new drug rehabilitation program that has been found to be quite effective in pilot studies in three different communities.

In urging its adoption in your city, your line of reasoning might go like this:

The program worked in Community A.

The program worked in Community B.

The program worked in Community C.

Therefore, it is probable that the program is effective and will work here.

Because there are only three cases in your sample you cannot state your conclusion at a high level of probability, but imagine that both proponents and skeptics of the program agreed that there was about a 75 percent chance of its success. A member of your audience might well ask, "Why should we spend $650,000 for just a three-out-of-four chance we might help a bunch of junkies?" You cannot change the odds, but you can influence your audience's assessment of the costs and rewards. Tell them how the program, if it works, will benefit the whole community: It will decrease crime, put former addicts back into the workforce, and lower the temptations for adolescent drug use. Also minimize the costs: "I know $650,000 sounds like a lot, but it's only 85¢ per citizen." When the listeners reassess the costs and rewards, and see them as you do, the 75 percent odds may look more attractive.

Consider another example, in which the conclusion's probability is very high:

Nuclear power plant A has had no accidents.

Nuclear power plant B has had no accidents.

....

Nuclear power plant n has had no accidents.

Therefore, it is probable that nuclear power plants are safe.

Suppose the conclusion could be granted a 95 percent level of probability. Even so, you might not feel the evidence is sufficient to make the inductive leap. In explaining this to the audience, you would minimize the rewards—most of the energy we would get can be obtained through other sources—and maximize the risks by describing just how awful a nuclear accident would be. Your argument is: "I'm not willing to subject my family to a 5-out-of-100 chance of this sort of destruction just to have a few extra electronic luxuries." In the case of the drug program, a low probability met the test of enoughness for the speaker. In the case of the nuclear power plant, even 95 percent was not enough. The difference lies in the perception of risk and reward. No level of enoughness is too high or too low—no inductive argument is innately logical or illogical. The validity is negotiated between you and your audience.

24b. Explicitly lay out all the premises of a deductive argument

One of the real advantages of structuring ideas deductively (see **21c**) is that you must state the relationships among the concepts with which you are dealing. When you clearly state the major premise on which your argument rests, you call to your listeners' minds certain values and assumptions and even logical truisms. The audience can then apply these concepts when you move on to specific cases in developing your minor premise. In the following logical arguments, notice how the major premise serves in each case to direct the listeners' awareness to a statement that the speaker might otherwise have left implicit.

Anyone who has been elected to high office has had to make a number of political compromises along the way.

Candidate J has served as governor and U.S. senator.

Therefore, Candidate J has made a number of political compromises.

It has always been the goal of our social welfare system to help recipients become self-sufficient.

Certain current programs encourage dependency and discourage initiative.

Therefore, these programs should be changed.

Sometimes, speakers have so internalized a point of view that they leave out parts of their argument they see as obvious. On controversial topics with diverse audiences, neglecting to lay out all parts of the argument is dangerous. In excellent speeches, speakers take the time to articulate and justify their premises.

24c. Explain your causal claims fully and fairly

Pure, simple causal arguments (see **21d**) like those used in some scientific studies are rare. More common are lines of reasoning that lead to probable causal claims, like the following:

X was present in these cases, and Y occurred.

X was absent in these cases, and Y did not occur.

Changes in the amount of X have often led to corresponding changes in the amount of Y.

Therefore, it is probable that X causes Y.

Probable to what degree? To the degree that your examples are sufficient and representative, and that conflicting examples are minimized or explained.

With this sort of causal argument, follow the advice in **16b**. Do not overstate your claim. Say, "This is a major cause," and not "This is *the* cause." Say, "There is strong evidence of a causal link between . . ." and so on.

24d. Show how your reasoning links your evidence to your claim

When speakers present only a cluster of evidence or a cluster of reasons for a claim, they are acting as if communication occurs through the simple act of telling. It is not enough to have a speech that you believe is well reasoned and free of fallacies. The reasoning process must be made transparent, through organization and word choice, to listeners who then decide if it's well conceived and executed.

1 Organize points to show the logical relationships

Controversial claims can be found at all levels of a speech; the thesis statement, main points, and subpoints all require substantiation. How you lay out the speech determines how overall patterns of reasoning come into play. There is no one correct way to display your lines of reasoning in a speech outline, but it is very important that you phrase points to show the connections. Do not simply group "reasons." Show reasoning.

Wrong:

I. Having a longer school day does not improve learning.
  A. They tried it at Riverdale High School, and test scores were unchanged.
  B. They tried it at Glenbrook High School, and test scores actually went down.
  C. At Creekside High School, test scores have gone up even though their school day has not been lengthened.
  D. Braeburn High School shortened their school day, and test scores did not change.

Better:

I. Having a longer school day does not improve learning.
  A. In cases in which the school day was lengthened, test scores did not improve.
    1. Unchanged at Riverdale High
    2. Went down at Glenbrook
  B. In cases in which the school day was not lengthened, test scores were not lower.
    1. Improved at Creekside
    2. No change with shorter day at Braeburn

Summary transitional statement: If there were a causal relationship between the length of the school day and learning as measured by test scores, we would logically expect that scores would be higher where the school day is longer and lower where the school day is shorter. I have just demonstrated that this is not the case. Sometimes, the opposite is true. So you can see why I conclude that having a longer school day does not improve learning.

In order for your audience to accept your reasoning, it is extremely important that you differentiate between points and support for the points. Do not use sources in place of reasoning. In the first example that follows, a speaker attempts to support a causal claim by saying that experts have agreed with the claim. But the listeners do not know *why* these people came to the conclusion they did. In the second example, the reasoning behind the causal claim is explained, with experts used to back up specific points.

Wrong:

I. The use of sexist language perpetuates discrimination against women.
  A. Dr. Deborah Stone says sexist language causes problems.
  B. Professor Lydia Sorenson says sexist language is the root of many social problems.
  C. Linguist Chris Nupriya states that language affects behavior.

Better:

I. The use of sexist language perpetuates discrimination against women.
   A. Language shapes social perception.
   B. Speech that leaves women out can lead to people overlooking them.
      (Cite experts and studies.)
   C. If people subconsciously exclude women from certain roles, they discriminate against women.
      (Cite experts and studies.)

2   Select language that illuminates logical connections

In addition to setting up a speech structure that highlights your reasoning, you should use words, phrases, and transitional sentences that spell out what your evidence means and how the parts of your argument are linked. Never merely jump from one point to the next. Practice adding phrases that are specific cues to the kind of reasoning you are using.

For inductive reasoning Show the strength of your examples:

One case that supports my claim is . . .

Across many levels of income and many parts of the country, the same pattern holds true. For example . . .

Acknowledge the probable nature of your data by using qualifiers:

Many/Most . . .

Virtually every study in the literature . . .

From these cases, I feel quite confident in concluding . . .

Demonstrate costs and rewards:

I'm willing to bet my tax dollars that this program will work . . .

This is a gamble we can't afford to take . . .

The risks, though they do exist, seem minimal compared to the rewards . . .

For deductive reasoning State your premises:

Underlying my position is one of the fundamental tenets of our constitutional form of government.

The argument for my claim rests on one basic assumption that I hope you will agree with. It is . . .

Either . . . or . . .

If . . . then . . .

Spell out your reasoning:

Because I've shown you X and Y, . . .

Therefore . . .

From this it follows that . . .

It seems logical to conclude that . . .

For causal reasoning Show how the cause and effect are related in a predictable way:

In state after state where spending on education went up, crime went down.

This is no coincidence. When X occurs, then Y occurs.

Qualify your causal claims if necessary:

There may be many causes, but the one I have identified is a major causal factor.

It is highly probable that smoking causes these health problems.

Explain the mechanism of the cause:

The reason all these experts have concluded that X causes Y is that . . .

I've shown you all these cases in which being abused as a child seems to lead to being an abusive parent. Let me explain how that happens.

For reasoning by analogy Stress the points of similarity:

In Ecuador, as in neighboring Colombia and Peru, . . .

For 8 of the 10 other universities in our conference, adding women's sports to the athletic program has led to more alumni support.

In a parallel case, . . .

Spell out the link:

If it worked in New Jersey and Idaho and Georgia, it will work in the rest of the country.

Let's not wait too long on planning for earthquake safety. We put off dealing with flood control, and the results have been tragic.

CHAPTER 25

Using Motivational Appeals

This book stresses the role of clear analysis in support of ideas, but it also emphasizes making those ideas meaningful to an audience. Understanding the humanity of your audience means reaching them as total persons—packaging your essentially logical case so that it touches the listeners' feelings, needs, and values.

25a. Consider the emotional impact you want to create or avoid

Keep in mind that everything you say has the potential to trigger some sort of emotional response in your audience. Generally, you can strengthen your speech by selecting main points, supporting material, and language that can engage your listeners' feelings. Positive emotions—hope, joy, pride, love—are surefire motivators. Negative emotions like fear, envy, disgust, and contempt can also motivate; witness the popularity of roller coasters and horror films. The motivational effects of negative emotions are less predictable, however, and can sometimes boomerang. Moderate levels of fear appeal can enhance persuasion, but higher levels may work against the desired effect.

25b. Relate your speech to the needs of your listeners

The best-known way of classifying human needs is the hierarchy devised by Abraham Maslow[1] shown in Figure 25-1.

In this hierarchy, the lower-level needs have to be met or satisfied before an individual can become concerned with the needs on the next-higher level. For instance, on the topic of physical fitness, you could appeal to your audience at any of the following levels:

- The effect of exercise in reducing risk of cardiovascular disease appeals to the survival need.

- Security might be drawn in by mentioning how physically fit people are more likely to be able to resist or evade attackers.

- The need for belonging can be linked to becoming trim and attractive, as well as to making friends through physical activity.

- Esteem needs can be tied into the current popularity of fitness and the social desirability of an active image.

- Fitness can be related to the need for self-actualization—the highs of exercise, and the mental and physical challenge of reaching one's potential.

[1] Abraham Maslow, *Motivation and Personality*, 2nd ed. (New York: Harper & Row, 1970), 35–58.

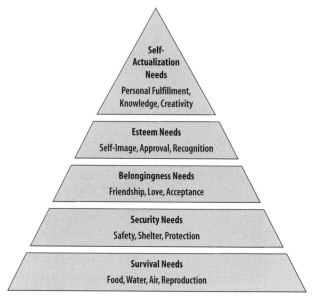

Self-Actualization Needs
Personal Fulfillment, Knowledge, Creativity

Esteem Needs
Self-Image, Approval, Recognition

Belongingness Needs
Friendship, Love, Acceptance

Security Needs
Safety, Shelter, Protection

Survival Needs
Food, Water, Air, Reproduction

F I G U R E   2 5 - 1   Maslow's Hierarchy of Needs

The significance of Maslow's hierarchy to the speaker is apparent. You must analyze your audience well enough to determine which need is most salient. Listeners whose jobs are in danger and who are struggling to feed their families do not want to hear you contrast local economic programs in terms of the implications drawn from Keynesian theory. They want to know which one will create jobs. Being absorbed with their security needs, they are not likely to respond at the self-actualization level. It is counterproductive to aim your emotional appeals too high, and unethical to aim them too low.

25c. Relate your speech to the values of your listeners

We hold a certain value if we believe that a particular thing is either good or bad, in the broadest sense of those terms. Specifically, we *evaluate* concepts, people, objects, events, or ideas every day as we label them just or unjust, wise or foolish, beautiful or ugly, and so on.

1   Incorporate appeals to general values

Although values are individually chosen, the choice is not often a totally conscious and rational one. Culture has a strong influence, shaping values through families, schools, media, and peers. Moreover, values are rarely formed in isolation; rather, they are organized and structured into related clusters. By knowing the culture of your listeners, the influences on them, and perhaps some of the other values they hold, you can make an educated guess as to how much particular values might shape their attitude toward your speech topic.

KEY POINT   **One Popular Classification of Contemporary American Values**[2]

- A comfortable life
- An exciting life
- A sense of accomplishment
- A world at peace
- A world of beauty
- Equality
- Family security
- Freedom
- Happiness

- Inner harmony
- Mature love
- National security
- Pleasure
- Salvation
- Self-respect
- Social recognition
- True friendship
- Wisdom

[2]Sandra J. Ball-Rokeach and Joel W. Grube, *The Great American Values Test: Influencing Behavior and Belief Through Television* (New York: Free Press, 1984), 90.

---

2   Identify and relate to the core values of your audience

If the members of a culture share common values, why do we not see lockstep agreement on every issue? Obviously, not all members of a culture give equal importance to the common values, nor is there a standard ranking of them. Values are very general, and any particular issue can touch on many values, on both the pro side and the con. Examples of this value conflict can become common around election time. Suppose there is a proposed bond issue to build an expensive fine arts complex. A person may be drawn toward approving the bond as a result of holding the values of a world of beauty and a sense of accomplishment. But the individual may also have reservations about taking on a greater tax burden because of a belief in the values of a comfortable, prosperous life and family security. The resolution of this conflict is a function of how this person has prioritized these values.

Because nearly every topic stirs up such value conflicts, a list of audience values will not be useful unless it is supplemented by some estimate of the relative ranking. Each person has a number of deeply held values so central to identity they are called *core values*. Other values, though important, are not as central and therefore can be placed in a rough ranking that approximates their distance from the core. Understanding this, you should try to make reasonable inferences about your listeners' core values and stress them in your speech.

3 Appeal to your listeners' sense of community

Understandably, when people first encounter an issue, they tend to analyze it from a perspective that is close to them in time and space. They ask, "How does this affect me and my immediate circle, now and in the near future?" In contrast to this impulse, a Native American proverb suggests that every decision should be evaluated in terms of its impact on the seventh generation in the future. John Donne's statement that no man is an island has been amended by contemporary thinkers to mean that, today, no person is even a peninsula. One of the most powerful ways that public speakers can use motivational appeals is to draw people outward and refocus their awareness on larger frames of reference.

This broader awareness is there and available to be tapped. When the U.S. public really saw and felt the suffering of Romanian orphans, there was an outpouring of financial support and a series of adoptions. Pictures of fish disfigured by discarded pop-top rings contributed to beverage companies' using a different system for opening soda and beer cans. As a speaker, you can create powerful word pictures to remind listeners of their interdependence with other people and creatures, and to transport them into the past and the future. You can use your words to show people the historical and cultural meanings of endangered objects and places. You can take listeners into the future and reveal the effects of our environmental policies or our national debt on unborn generations. Link your speech topic to your audience's values in ways that tie into the broadest sense of community and situate the present in relation to the past and the future.

25d. Avoid excessive and inappropriate use of motivational appeals

Throughout this chapter, we have promoted the effective use of appeals to the emotions, needs, and values of your listeners. We must end with a caution about the overuse and misuse of these appeals. A speech with too much emphasis on feelings can embarrass and offend the audience. If listeners perceive that the speaker is playing on their emotions to the exclusion of sense and logic, they can become infuriated. It is always a mistake to underestimate the intelligence of an audience. Aside from the issue of effectiveness (advertisers and politicians show us that many times these appeals can be effective), there is the question of ethics. (See **3**.)

CHAPTER 26

Establishing Credibility

Your content and delivery determine, to a great extent, whether your listeners believe what you say. However, beyond what you say and how you say it, your audience is influenced by who you are—or, more accurately, who they think you are. Your *credibility* is that combination of perceived qualities that makes listeners predisposed to believe you. For centuries, scholars have been fascinated by credibility—from classical discussions of *ethos* to contemporary investigations of concepts like *image, personality,* and *charisma.* Aristotle observed that audiences are most inclined to believe a person they see as having good sense, goodwill, and good character. Modern social scientists have tried to isolate the characteristics that distinguish the most credible speakers from others. Their lists include competence, dynamism, intention, personality, intelligence, authoritativeness, extroversion, trustworthiness, composure, and sociability.

You can enhance your credibility, and thus the chances of meeting your speech objective, by projecting these qualities. You can build up your image or reputation prior to the speech, and you can take steps to improve your credibility as you are speaking. The first step, though, is to assess your present image.

26a. Conduct an honest assessment of your speaking image

The perfect speaker is seen as competent, concerned, trustworthy, and dynamic in discussing all topics with all audiences, but most of us fall short of this ideal. One speaker might seem warm, charming, and likable—but somehow have trouble being taken seriously on weighty issues. Another may have a demeanor that immediately inspires confidence—but suffer from seeming dull or distant or not human enough.

Before you can work on improving your credibility, you need to see where you stand now. Is your overall credibility high or low? Do people agree with you because of, or in spite of, your personality? Which components of credibility are strongest for you? Which need to be developed? If possible, have some friends or acquaintances help you with this appraisal. It is very hard to gauge how others see us.

CHECKLIST

Speaking Image

1. Are you perceived as competent?
2. Are you perceived as concerned about your audience's welfare?
3. Are you perceived as trustworthy?
4. Are you perceived as dynamic?

26b. Build your credibility prior to the speech

Provide the contact person with adequate information about your qualifications Do not be overly modest when asked for information for advance publicity. Send a résumé that lists your background and achievements. Include clippings, testimonials about your speaking, a list of your books and articles, and a photograph if appropriate.

Help the person introducing you to set a favorable tone In addition to providing written information, be available to consult by phone or in person with whoever will introduce you. If there are aspects of your background you would like to have stressed for a particular speech, be sure to say so.

Manage your image during all contact with the group prior to the speech In a class, a service organization you belong to, or your own work group, you know that you have a certain image, based on previous interactions. Speaking before an unfamiliar audience is different. Because these people have little to go on to form an impression, virtually all of your interactions with them will affect your credibility. Your friendliness, professionalism, and confidence in negotiating arrangements and even in making small talk prior to the speech will be very influential.

26c. Bolster your credibility through your speech content

As you prepare your speech outline and select your supporting evidence and examples, think about ways to communicate your competence, concern, trustworthiness, and dynamism. The following suggestions are especially relevant in the opening minutes of the speech, when first impressions are being formed (see **31a**). But many credibility boosters can be woven throughout the entire speech as well.

1 Present your credentials

The majority of inexperienced speakers find it difficult to "blow their own horn" and do not do as much credibility building as they should. Do not be reluctant to provide information about your qualifications to speak:

> The most common error I see in the 20 to 30 loan applications I look at each week is . . .

> I've had a special awareness of the barriers the physically handicapped face since 1991, when my brother Dave returned from the Gulf War.

Judgment and tact are important in deciding which qualifications to mention and how to work them into the speech. Our culture frowns on bragging and name-dropping, yet false humility is out of place. You can include many statements of your qualifications without seeming boastful if you present them matter-of-factly and include only relevant qualifications.

2 Demonstrate a thorough understanding of your topic

To communicate a sense of expertise, you must show listeners you have done your homework. Mention the nature of your research when appropriate:

> The seven judges I interviewed all agreed on one major weakness in our court system.

> I read the minutes of all the committee hearings on this bill, and not one expert mentioned . . .

Use concrete examples, statistics, and testimony. Be sure you have your details straight. One obvious error early in the speech can ruin your credibility. The people listening will think, "I wonder what other information is wrong?"

3 Be sure your material is clearly organized

A sense of competence depends on your being in command of the material and seeming to know where you are headed. Listeners will view you as uninformed rather than unorganized if you wander from topic to topic or if you must apologetically insert, "Oh, one thing I forgot to mention when I was discussing. . . ."

4 Present a balanced and objective analysis

To demonstrate that you are fair, trustworthy, and of good character, go out of your way to acknowledge the limitations of your evidence and argument, if appropriate:

> I'm not saying television is the only cause of these problems. I realize that's an oversimplification. But I do think that TV has had a pronounced effect on the imaginative thinking of the last two generations.

Also be sure to acknowledge the existence of opposing evidence and opinions:

> Some studies indicate that an alcoholic can return to social drinking, but . . .

Acknowledge self-interest when it exists to prevent the audience from thinking you are trying to hide something from them.

> It's true I'm a real estate agent and I stand to profit by having folks invest in real estate. But that's not my main reason for urging you to invest.

If they discover later that you are more partisan than you made it sound, your credibility will suffer.

5   Express your concern and goodwill toward the audience

Let them know that your speech is offered to serve their interests:

> I'd do anything to save your families the headaches and heart-aches that go along with having a relative die without a will.

> Taking up cycling has added so much to my life that I'd love to see some of you share in that fun.

26d. Use your speech delivery to increase your credibility

Too many expert and well-prepared speakers lose effectiveness be-cause they cannot *transmit* these qualities to their audience. Drop-ping cards, reading in a shaky voice, fumbling with whatever is at hand—all suggest lack of competence. An unexpressive face and voice might be interpreted as disdainfulness and detract from per-ceived goodwill. Hesitancy and uncertainty are sometimes falsely seen as shiftiness or dishonesty. Listless, monotonous, colorless speaking is the very opposite of dynamism. To be seen as a believ-able source of information and opinion, continue to work on all aspects of delivery covered in chapters **34** and **35**.

CHAPTER 27

Designing Presentation Aids

Depending on circumstances and context, a presentation aid or a series of presentation aids may help you be more effective in com-municating your message. A presentation aid is an object or entity that adds another communicative dimension beyond your vocal content and delivery. Generally, presentation aids are visual, but they can be aural or audiovisual, depending on need.

27a. Determine what aids are appropriate, if any

What items or themes can be represented by presentation aids? And should they be? The first step is to decide whether an aid will help you meet your speaking goal, within its context. Then you can move to deciding what form they will take and what tools you'll use to create and present them.

There are places in a speech where a visual presentation aid can help you make a point more clearly and quickly than if you used your spoken words alone, or where an audio aid can help you make a point more clearly and quickly than your oral description of it. Conversely, aids poorly used or overused can obscure your own ideas and slow the pace of your speech. Keep in mind that the aids are there to support your message, not be your message. Overreliance on presentation aids cuts into speech time better spent on analysis or development of points and ideas. And sometimes a speaker can fall into the trap of spending more time preparing the aids than preparing the speech.

Another consideration is the context. In some settings, perhaps altogether too often in the business world, a speaker is expected to have a projected slide show, regardless of the usefulness of such to the particular subject. To do without would violate the norms of the situation and jeopardize the speaker's credibility. In other settings, like a graduation speech, the expectation is that there be no aids. Finding out this sort of information is an important part of the speech planning process.

1   Ascertain if a presentation aid is appropriate

It's the tail wagging the dog if you decide first on having presentation aids, and then afterward review your content to see what portion(s) would be served by an aid. The need for an aid should arise from an analysis of your material as you weigh the best ways to make your points and pursue your speech goals. Complex data to compare? Well, there's a possible subject for an aid. Need to intensify an emotional point? Another aid possibility. A recurring theme? Yet another aid possibility.

The two most obvious reasons for using presentation aids are to explain an unfamiliar, complex, or technical idea, and to reinforce a particular message. (The approach you use for doing these things will vary to some degree depending on whether you use discrete or continuous aids. See **2** and **3** below.) A geneticist might find it useful to have a wire-frame model of the DNA double helix when talking about how that remarkable molecule duplicates itself. The speaker wishing to impress upon an audience the importance of stiffer drunk-driving penalties may choose to reinforce a recitation of traffic fatality percentages with a "pie" chart graph that demonstrates the overwhelming predominance of drunk driving over other causes of traffic deaths. To help the audience understand the differences between Ragtime, Stride, and Boogie Woogie piano styles, another speaker may choose to play three short audio clips of Jelly Roll Morton, Fats Waller, and Meade "Lux" Lewis to highlight the syncopated scriptedness of Ragtime, the jumping left-hand movements of Stride, and the accelerated bluesiness of Boogie Woogie.

Don't decide which technique or technology you'll use to create your aids before you've determined what you wish to show. Figure out what concepts you want to show first, then decide what symbols or forms you'll need to make those concepts concrete and immediate, and *then* determine the best ways to create and present them.

2   Determine the form and technology that best suit your purpose

If you've concluded that presentation aids of some sort would be useful in your speech, the next questions you ask yourself are: What am I going to use to make them? and How am I going to present them? To answer these questions, you have to investigate the physical environment of your speaking venue, as shown in **27b.1**. Once you know the properties of the venue, you can start choosing what aids would work in the space, primarily related to visibility and volume. You also need to consider how much time you have to prepare your aids; how much time displaying or playing your aids will take; how portable the aids are; what technology is available to you for creating the aids; and what technology is available at your speaking venue for you to exploit.

A multitude of approaches   It may be that, after musing on your needs, you wish to have text highlighting your main points, along with a few graphs and photographs to clarify certain of your points. There are many possible approaches to producing these aids: you can make posters, prepare a flipchart, show slides. Or you may wish to add impact to a particular point. You could choose to handle this with text, or image, or sound. There may be a pithy, evocative quotation that gets to the heart of the matter. Or a photograph that captures the essence of your point. Or an audio clip that brings the point to life. For example, to supplement one point in a speech on hurricanes and hurricane preparedness, you could display the slogan "Run from the water; hide from the wind," or project a photograph of the devastation of Homestead, Florida, by Hurricane Andrew, or play an audio clip of the visceral screech of hurricane-force winds.

K E Y   P O I N T   When to Keep It Simple   Consider how many items or images you want to show. If there are just a few, it would be simpler to create a poster, or model, or equivalent, than to go to the effort of creating a two-slide presentation and introduce a noisy projector, darkened room, and so on, for just a minimal part of your talk.

Presentation software   Microsoft's PowerPoint is but one of many choices. Other presentation software packages available are Corel Presentations, an application included in WordPerfect Office; Freelance Graphics, an application included in Lotus SmartSuite; Keynote from Apple; ProPresentations from Harvard Graphics; and a variety of specialized packages used by religious organizations, law firms, medical providers, and the like. Once you've made the decision to use presentation software, you must decide what physical form the output will take. With the same file you can have the slides blown up, printed, and mounted as posters, or printed on transparency sheets for use with an overhead projector, or not printed at all but projected directly from the software program. Whatever the form of the output, pay particular attention to the design suggestions in **27b** and **27c**.

3   For visual aids, decide on the form of representation

Let's look at three ways of representing something with a *visual* presentation aid. One of them will work best for the information you're imparting.

The object or a physical reproduction of it   While demonstrating the simplicity of a new lens-to-camera attachment system, a speaker can use the actual camera and lens to show the ease of coupling. It would take many more words by themselves to convey the same message. With a large audience, however, this sort of demonstration might not work because of the smallness of the equipment. In this case, the speaker might use larger-than-life-size models to make sure the message is clear. Other objects are obviously too small or large to use, like a nanomanufacturing molecular robot or USS *Carl Vinson*, or the venue might be too small to accommodate the item, so scaled-up or scaled-down reproductions are necessary.

Pictorial reproductions   These can include photographs, sketches, plans, pictures, slides, overhead transparencies, computer animations, film clips, and videotapes. If the mechanical device that makes the lens-to-camera coupling so easy is in itself complex, the speaker might use an exploded three-quarter-view schematic drawing to show the interaction of all the pieces. The speaker wishing to show the musculature might prefer a large photograph of the human heart. Again, object size and audience size are important factors in determining which to use and which technology would best serve to prepare and present them.

Pictorial symbols   Pictorial symbols are used with more abstract concepts and can include graphs, charts, diagrams, maps, and lists of important words and phrases.

When speaking on the declining state of the economy, you may choose to use a line graph showing the buying power of the dollar over the past two decades. An aerial photograph of San Jose will not be as appropriate in a speech on local politics as a map showing city council district boundaries. If a speaker wants to highlight a motto, inspirational phrase, or name of a product, then suitably lettered posters can help. Figures 27-1 and 27-2 show some common pictorial symbols.

Pie Graph

Annotated Map

Slogan or Memorable Phrase

FIGURE 27-1 **Pictorial Symbols**

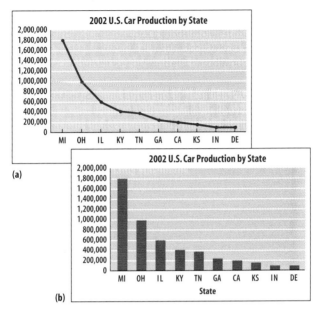

(a)

(b)

FIGURE 27-2 (a) Improper and (b) Proper Choice of Graph to Match Data Type

Each kind of chart or graph is best suited for a particular kind of information. For instance, in general, line graphs are better for showing trends than bar graphs, and pie charts are better for showing relationships of parts to a whole than line graphs. Table 27-1 describes the preferred use of each type, along with some examples, to help you select which might work for the data you wish to present. Be aware that using the wrong type of graph may convey information or implications that are not really present in your data. Figure 27-2 shows U.S. car production data for 2002, using two different graphs. The line graph is the wrong one to use for this information because the connected dots imply some trend or direction among the state totals that does not exist. The bar graph allows the viewer to see the totals and make comparisons without confusion.

27b. Prepare your aids to be clear and manageable

The time spent preparing aids will be wasted if they are mismatched to the situation, or difficult to use.

1   Make aids large enough to be seen, or clear enough to be heard

The nature of the place in which you will be speaking and the size of the audience determine to a great extent the form your aids

TABLE 27-1   Using Charts, Graphs, and Tables

Type	Preferred Use, *with examples*
Bar Graph/Pictogram	To make comparisons, especially differences in quantity or frequency. ■ *Number of users for different computer operating systems* ■ *Sales by region*
Line Graph	To show trends or changes over time, or to show how one thing is affected by another. ■ *New subscribers to a service, per year, over a 5-year period* ■ *Heart rate affected by level of exercise*
Pie Graph	To show relationships between parts and the whole, relative proportions, percentages. ■ *Project costs by department* ■ *World production of heroin, by continent*
Flowchart	To show a process, series of related decisions or actions. ■ *Steps to troubleshoot and fix a problem* ■ *Flow of information through an organization*
Table/Grid	To show large amounts of data in one place (Table) or to juxtapose and compare discrete elements (Grid). ■ *Actuarial table of male and female life expectancy* ■ *Rubella infections by age and location* ■ *Comparison checklist of features among different products*

may take—whether they need to be projected, or the kind and size of your physical visual aids. It helps to look over the facility in advance if possible. Stand at the back of the room and envision the scene. Screens for projected presentations, slides, and filmstrips should be large enough for the size of the room, and projectors should have focal lengths great enough to fill the screen. With a videotape, make sure that the monitor can be mounted high enough to be seen by people in the back row or that there are enough monitors for everyone to get a good view. Check that your sound equipment is adequate for the size of the room and the ambient noise of the environment.

If you already have a rough mock-up or draft of one of your aids, like a poster or a model, place it where you expect it to be when you speak and walk around the space. Obviously, if the aid is too small, you need to enlarge it. Lines on charts should be thick and bold. Captions should be concise and large. Model parts should be large enough to be distinguishable. At some point a room becomes too large for a poster, flipchart, or whiteboard to be effective: consider using an aid that uses a slide projector, overhead projector, or digital projector. Reduce any aid that is too large for the size of the room, or that is so unwieldy you will have to wrestle with it.

2   Keep your visual presentation aids simple and clear

Do not design overelaborate visual aids. They should contain just enough detail to allow your listeners to distinguish easily one part from another. Do not crowd maps, charts, graphs, models, and photographs with so much data that your audience is confused about which part you are referring to. Avoid having so many lines on a line graph that audience members are at risk of taking a "wrong turn" while following one line across. With photographs, try to find one that shows the object in isolation or in sharp focus in relation to other objects.

Keep the wording on any visual aid simple and familiar. Use no more words than strictly necessary to label parts and ideas.

Maintain continuity when you spread your information out. If you use a pie graph for your first aid, any following aids dealing with similar or related information should also be pie graphs. If you are using flipcharts, a white board, or some other hand-lettered means, print in clear block letters.

Use color to delineate different aspects of the object or symbol.

Presentation software packages enable you to create slides that you can either print out and project or project directly using a computer projection system. Keep the following suggestions in mind to ensure that the overheads and slides (and posters) you create are effective:

1. Use simple typefaces. Do not mix more than two typefaces on a sheet. Avoid ornate or showy type, and stay away from drop shadows, outline fonts, and other decorative type modifications that add visual "noise."

2. Use uppercase and lowercase letters in the titles and text. Sentences printed exclusively in capital letters are harder to read.

3. Use a lot of "white space." That is, do not crowd too much information on one sheet. Keep the information simple; use your speech to fill in the details.

4. Maintain continuity throughout the slides. Settle on a design theme and carry it out for each slide. For instance, if you use a border or background, put it on all slides; if you use bullets for a list on one sheet, do not use numbers or dashes for a list on another slide.

27c. Understand the benefits and perils of presentation software

Presentation software can be considered a mixed blessing to the speaker. On the one hand, it is possible to create slides and handouts that are consistent and attractive. On the other, it is possible to be put in a position in which you are narrating your outline rather than giving a speech.

1   Keep your text slides simple

The templates that come with the presentation software application are designed to keep your slides simple. That is, if you use the typefaces in the sizes that come as the default, it will be difficult for you to clutter up a slide with too many words and ideas. This is good; avoid the temptation to finesse your way around the constraints of the type size. Instead, look for better ways to organize your material, and pare down your language to the minimum. (See **18** and **19**.)

You can use animation effects or "builds" to expose certain elements of a slide in a particular order for dramatic effect or to keep the focus on the most immediate point. If you do take advantage of this capability, do so with restraint; the efficacy of the effect will diminish with overuse. Similarly, exercise restraint with the sound effects that come with the package—"zoop"-ing sounds may be fun with 5 slides, but with 30 they will move beyond being irritants.

2   Maintain consistency

Used properly, presentation software can help you maintain a consistent look throughout your slides. While templates work for keeping the type consistent, the program's settings for color schemes, slide backgrounds and patterns, and so on work to keep other elements consistent. Even with this help, though, you need to review your slides to make sure no discrepancies have crept in. Look at the captions. Are they all in burgundy 14-point bold Helvetica? Or has one somehow ended up in green 14-point Arial Narrow? How about the placement of elements? Click through the slide show quickly to see if elements seem to jump from place to place in relation to other instances. Also, check other features, like transition effects and builds, for consistency. Sometimes, especially if a presentation is being created from a number of earlier ones, these may get mixed up, so that you end up with most slides using a "fade through black" transition and a few using a "wipe right."

3   Use clip art with care

Avoid the temptation of using clip art because you feel people expect it or there's "white space" to fill, rather than using it because it adds a dimension to your message or hammers home a point with an apt visual symbol. Because the popular software packages have such wide exposure, the use of a familiar clip art image—for example, of businesspeople standing around a table or the ubiquitous business handshake—makes your message seem less than unique. Additionally, too many images peppered around your text can be distracting. Images in different styles (a line drawing of a person followed by a cartoon image of a person, for instance, or a low-resolution bitmap image followed by a sharp PostScript image) can be distracting as well. (See **27c.2**.)

Figures 27-3 and 27-4 show two text-based slides, the first of which violates many of the design guidelines in **27b** and **c**. In Figure 27-3 the creator has tried to fit too much into the text, making

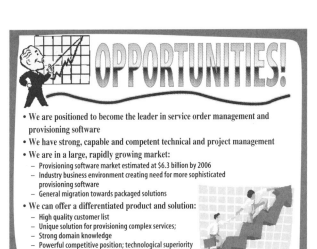

FIGURE 27-3 **Overworked Text Slide**

Opportunities!

- ❈ Positioned to become the leader in service order management and provisioning software
- ❈ Strong, capable and competent management
- ❈ Large, rapidly growing market
- ❈ Differentiated product and solution

FIGURE 27-4 **Effective Text Slide**

it a "read along" slide. Inconsistent clip art fills the empty spaces and does nothing to advance the message. The modification done to the slide title text makes it hard to read. The second slide provides a better approach. Instead of full sentences, it uses key phrases, making the message clear while supporting, rather than supplanting, the speaker. The type is large and readable and is not fighting with extraneous elements for the viewers' attention.

7 Crafting Your Speech

CHAPTER 28. Selecting Your Mode of Delivery

Select a mode of delivery that is appropriate to your topic, audience, and occasion.

CHAPTER 29. Using Language Effectively

Choose words and constructions that make your ideas clear and memorable. Respect the power of language.

CHAPTER 30. Capturing Attention and Interest

Adapt your speech material so that it captures your listeners' attention and retains their interest.

CHAPTER 31. Creating Effective Introductions and Conclusions

Lead your listeners into and out of your topic with a carefully planned introduction and conclusion.

CHAPTER 32. Linking Speech Components

Unify your speech by introducing evidence explicity, and by using transitions between ideas.

CHAPTER 33. Practicing Your Speech

Use practice sessions to help compose and polish your speech.

Selecting Your Mode of Delivery

Decide early if your speech will be *impromptu* (off-the-cuff), *extemporaneous* (given from notes), *manuscript* (written out and read), or *memorized* word for word. Settle on the predominant mode you will use, but be aware that no speech is purely *one* mode.

28a. Use the extemporaneous mode primarily

Extemporaneous speaking is the most common mode of delivery and is the one you should use in all but a few special cases because it makes for a more conversational and flexible presentation. In this mode, you prepare extensively, constructing the progression of ideas with the aid of an outline, planning your content thoroughly, and practicing until you are comfortable and conversational. But you never commit yourself to a rigid, exact sequence of words.

Prepare an extemporaneous speech in four steps:

1. *Begin with a fully developed outline.* Follow the recommendations in chapters **17** through **20** to arrange your material in a logical and effective manner.

2. *If you have used a full-sentence outline, convert it to a keyword or key-phrase outline.* Note that the declarative sentences that characterize a full-sentence outline are written English, not spoken English, and if you follow them too closely as you develop the wording of your speech, the result may be dull and lifeless— you may find your expressiveness being limited by what you see on the page. For this reason, we suggest that you convert the full-sentence outline to a keyword or key-phrase outline that enables you to improvise as you proceed through Step 3.

3. *Word the speech.* Working from this brief outline, practice putting your ideas into words. The second time through, some clumsy phrases will have disappeared as you play with sentence structure, rhythms, and so forth. Third time, fourth time, fifth time through—your topic is becoming more and more familiar, giving you the freedom to relax and to allow yourself to really experiment with construction. You will also discover that one way of expressing a set of thoughts is not necessarily better than another.

4. *Convert your brief outline to speech notes.* See **33b** for directions on how to transfer your content to a format that provides easy visual cues to which you can refer.

28b. Remember these steps when speaking impromptu

No one should give an important speech in the impromptu mode, but sometimes a person is legitimately surprised by the need to give a speech. On these occasions, follow these four simple steps.

1 Keep your composure

Remind yourself that you speak all the time in conversations without extensive preparation. You should have realistic expectations for yourself and not fall apart if you fail to deliver your most polished performance. Do not apologize. Speak slowly and confidently.

2 Select a theme

Very quickly list several possible approaches to the topic. Do it mentally or, if time permits, with pencil and paper. By thinking beyond the most obvious approach, you may discover a way to link your topic to a subject you are conversant with.

3 Select an organizational framework

You will not have time to make an extensive outline, but you can hook your topic to a simple framework like one of the following:

Past–present–future

Pros and cons

Concentric rings, with main points progressing from immediate concerns to universal concerns (e.g., in the home, in the school, in the community; or locally, regionally, nationally, internationally)

Domains, developing the different spheres touched by the topic (e.g., political, social, or economic spheres; or practical, theoretical, or moral implications)

After you have divided your topic along the lines of one of these frameworks, find one means of support or development for each idea, such as an explanation, example, story, fact, or statistic.

If time permits, jot some notes. Even a few keywords on a napkin can reassure you and keep you on track once you have started to speak.

4 Whenever possible, plan your first and last sentences

The beginning and ending are the most difficult parts of any speech, and this is especially true in impromptu speaking. By having introductory and concluding sentences, you avoid the aimless rambling so characteristic of impromptu speaking. When you know your task is to start with Sentence A and work your way to Sentence B, you have a ready reference against which to judge ideas that occur to you as you are speaking.

28c. Speak from a manuscript for precise wording and timing

Limit your use of manuscripts to the following situations:

- The time allotted is specific and inflexible (e.g., the broadcast media)

- The wording is extremely critical (e.g., some sensitive and emotionally charged topics)
- The style is extremely important (e.g., a major speech of tribute)

There is a widespread misconception that speaking from a manuscript is the easiest and safest mode of delivery ("I'm not an experienced speaker, so I'd better write it out"). This is no excuse for avoiding the extemporaneous mode. A bad manuscript speech is much worse than a bad extemporaneous speech. Stilted phrasing, monotonous vocal delivery, and lack of eye contact are all perils facing a novice speaking from a manuscript.

1 Prepare an easily readable manuscript in the oral style.

Work from a full-sentence outline for good organization, but for the actual wording of the speech "talk" the speech out and onto the paper. You need to check your composition against your ear more than your eye. As you write and rewrite, keep saying it aloud, listening for the rhythms of oral style. (See **29**.)

CHECKLIST

Manuscript Production

❏ Print it out on a printer, on heavy paper, triple spaced, with wide margins.

❏ Use capital and lowercase letters in standard sentence format. Make sure the letters are dark and legible.

In some speaking situations, you will not have your manuscript in your hands, but will be reading it from a teleprompter or similar machine.

2 Look and sound as though you are speaking extemporaneously

A poorly delivered manuscript speech is marked by a singsongy cadence, gasping for breath between overlong sentences, and the occasional quick glance up from the page. To avoid these distractions, practice reading and rereading your manuscript out loud until you are comfortable with it. You should neither sight read nor memorize the text, but become familiar with its flow and rhythm.

CHECKLIST

Manuscript Delivery

❏ Retain a conversational style of speaking.

❏ Be familiar enough with your content to sustain eye contact.

❏ Memorize the wording in a few places (e.g., first and last sentences) where audience contact is crucial.

28d. Memorize certain manuscript speeches

By definition, giving a memorized speech entails a manuscript speech—without the manuscript. The only times you should give a memorized speech, therefore, are the same as put forth in **28c**, with the added limitations that the speech should be a short, important one and the situation inappropriate for holding a manuscript. These occasions are most often ceremonial: giving a toast, presenting a plaque, or accepting an honor.

1. *Memorize the structure of the speech before memorizing the speech word for word.* Learn a few keywords that help you internalize the main sequence of ideas.

2. *Read the speech aloud several times and then work on learning it paragraph by paragraph.* Always keep your mind on the meaning. Do not try to learn sentences in isolation, but rather work on whole paragraphs at a time, reinforcing their logical and conceptual unity.

3. *As you practice, visualize giving the speech.* Avoid thinking of your speech as lines of text in a social vacuum. You do not want to be startled and lose your concentration when you realize that you are actually facing a roomful of people.

4. *Do not go into a trance when delivering the speech.* Once again, be comfortably familiar with your material so that you can maintain eye contact and establish a rapport with your audience.

5. *If you go blank, switch to the extemporaneous mode and recall the structure of the speech rather than groping for the next word.* Speaking along the general lines of the point you know you were trying to make, you can collect your thoughts and click back into what you have memorized.

CHAPTER 29
Using Language Effectively

Competent speakers consciously develop their ideas through language to achieve an effective speaking style. In the context of speaking, style is simply your choice of words and the way you string them together. "Good" style involves choosing and combining those words so that your audience can easily understand and assimilate your content. Good style uses clear, appropriate, vivid, and varied language.

29a. Understand how oral and written styles differ

Although oral style and written style use the same components, there are some important ways in which they differ. A speaker is more likely than a writer to use repetition to ensure comprehension. Oral style employs more signposting, internal summaries, and internal previews to make the organization clear. (See **32**.) Shorter sentences and words of fewer syllables are characteristic of oral style as well. And sentence fragments are acceptable, as are contractions. Even in a formal setting, a speech will still be more colloquial than an essay on the same topic. Table 29-1 illustrates some key differences between oral and written style.

29b. Strive for clarity in your language

If you understand the priorities of communication, the first question you will ask yourself is, "Did my listeners get the picture?" When speaker and listeners end up with totally different mental images, something has gone awry.

To construct clear messages, you must do two things. First, invest some effort in clarifying your own thoughts. Know exactly,

TABLE 29-1 Differences Between Written and Oral Style

Written Style	Oral Style
As mentioned above . . .	As I said a few minutes ago . . .
One cannot avoid individuals with this characteristic.	We can't avoid people like that.
A hypothetical case in point might be a situation where government . . .	Imagine this. Suppose Uncle Sam . . .
It is unlikely that such will result.	Well. Maybe.
Subjects were randomly assigned to either a control group or one of three experimental treatment groups, pretested for initial attitudes toward the topic, then posttested after each experimental group had received a persuasive message containing one of three levels of fear appeals.	Here's how we did our research. First, we randomly assigned the subjects to four groups. Next, we gave all four groups a pretest to see what attitudes they held toward the topic. Then, three of the groups heard persuasive messages. One had a high level of fear appeals, one a medium level, and one a low level. Last, we posttested the attitudes of all four groups, including the control group that received no message.

not approximately, what you want to communicate. Second, consider who the receivers of your message are and what the words are likely to mean to them.

1 Be precise

To avoid fuzzy and ambiguous communication, you need to seek out the word that means precisely what you wish to convey and use it in a structure that illuminates, not obscures, its meaning. Many words can denote the same object or idea; however, each may have a slightly different focus. Do not say a person was "indicted" for robbery if in fact you mean "arrested" (much less serious) or "convicted" (much more serious). Learn important distinctions and honor them. Be careful around words that sound similar but have no similarity of meaning. *Allusion* means "a passing mention," and *illusion* means "a false perception." Some other troublesome near-homophones can be found in **Appendix C**.

Remember that oral language is simpler than written language. Avoid using a precise word when it may seem pretentious. Be sure you know what an unfamiliar word means before rushing to use it.

2 Use specific and concrete language

The more specific and concrete your words, the less is left to your listeners' imaginations. Table 29-2 gives examples of specific, concrete language.

3 Be economical in your language

You should express yourself with the fewest, most straightforward words that still effectively convey your meaning. Avoid wordy, euphemistic language. Sometimes, speakers use long words, extra words, and convoluted constructions for the untenable reasons listed in Table 29-3.

Most often, though, wordiness results from lack of discipline. It takes time and effort to find the best wording rather than tossing

TABLE 29-2   **Specific, Concrete Language**

Do Not Say	If You Really Mean	Or Even
We need to attract individuals.	We need to attract customers.	We need to attract grocery shoppers.
This will cause problems.	This will be expensive.	This will cost us $2,500 we don't have.
Our committee has studied it.	Our committee researched and discussed it.	Our committee read documents, heard testimony, and deliberated for several hours.

TABLE 29-3   Motives for Bloated Language

Motive	Uneconomical	Economical
To hide meaning, as with doublespeak	We sustained losses through friendly fire.	We shelled our own troops.
To avoid responsibility, as with the passive voice	It has been determined that your services are no longer needed.	I have decided to fire you.
To soften unpleasant messages, as with euphemism	Jesse has gone on to his reward.	Jesse died.

out a string of redundancies and approximate synonyms. The clear speaker makes every word count.

29c. Use appropriate language

There is no standard style to use in speaking. Different audiences and topics require different approaches. Based on your audience analysis, you must decide how formal to be, which part of your personality to project, and how specialized your language should be. Your age, status, and personality also determine what language is appropriate for you. Listeners have expectations about the vocabulary and stylistic level suitable for, say, a senior executive, that differ from those for a teenager or a poet-in-residence.

Language is not fixed. New words and phrases are always coming into our language, and others fading out. Meanings change, as do standards of appropriateness.

1 Adapt the formality of your language to the occasion

Just as you dress differently for formal and casual events, so should you tailor vocabulary and usage to fit the situation. In general, the more formal the occasion, the more serious the tone, the more subtle the humor, the more elaborate the sentences, the greater the number of figures of speech, the greater the departure from everyday word choice.

More formal occasions include debates, presentations of policy statements, and ceremonial speeches. Less formal occasions include business conferences, roasts, rallies, and after-dinner speeches.

2 Use jargon and slang carefully

Both jargon and slang can be used to create a bond with a specialized audience. At times, jargon can also allow you to get a point across more quickly. Slang, when called into play at opportune moments, can enrich the texture of your language. But the perils they introduce are substantial. You may confuse your audience with technical terms or sacrifice your credibility by using slang expressions that are offensive or out of date.

3   Avoid substandard usage

Remember that the speaker's competence as perceived by the audience has a large bearing on the speaker's credibility. Although acceptable usage varies, there are many words and constructions that are rated substandard by consensus. The speaker who consistently uses double negatives or who gets sloppy with noun–verb agreement will find that a large percentage of the audience does not give serious consideration to the speaker's points. Of course, you can sometimes break the rules for dramatic effect, like capping your opposition to a proposal with "Ain't *no* way!" **Appendix C** gives some examples of standard versus substandard language.

> **KEY POINT**   **Not All Nonstandard Language Is Substandard**
> Sometimes, when people try to "standardize" the language others use, they are actually trying to change the content or mold the identity of the speaker. Women should not have to talk like men. People of color should not have to talk like their compatriots of northern European descent. You will not feel comfortable or seem authentic if you abandon your own idiom. Strive to find a way to maintain your own cultural, ethnic, and individual identity while still speaking in a way that will not lead to social stigma.

4   Use language that is respectful and inclusive

Referring to a group or individuals by the name they prefer is a sign of respect. Make a reasonable effort to learn which reference people prefer. You can make a commitment to flexibility. Acknowledge that it is worth the temporary inconvenience of changing a language habit if that change is highly symbolic and important to the person involved.

Some guidelines for the use of inclusive language can be found on the websites of various universities and publishers; for example:

> **www.hcc.hawaii.edu/intranet/committees/FacDevCom/ guidebk/teachtip/inclusiv.htm**
>
> **www.vic.uh.edu/ac/style/inclusive.html.**

29d. Use vivid, varied language

You can keep your listeners attentive and interested by avoiding dull, stale, and predictable language. Your message may never get past their short-term memory if you do not infuse it with vigor and a sense of newness. Why settle for the common and trite? Energize your language by effective use of various verbal devices.

1 Employ imagery

When you describe something, put the senses and the imaginative capacities of your listeners to work:

Not: The life of the long-haul trucker is rough.

But: The long-haul trucker pulls to the side of the road, and even though the truck is stopped, his arms up to his elbows still throb to the rhythm of hitting four hundred miles of highway expansion joints. The harsh roar of the engine leaves him with an infuriating ringing of the ears.

2 Use stylistic devices

Enliven your language through the planned use of figures of speech and certain arrangements of words and phrases.

Simile and metaphor You can add vigor to your speaking by using language that connects objects or ideas to vivid images. A simile makes a comparison between two things ordinarily dissimilar: "When she came in from shoveling off the walk, her hands were like ice." No one would mistake a hand for some ice, but in this case they share the characteristic of extremely low temperature. A metaphor creates a figurative equation that implies two unlike things are the same: "Her hands were ice cubes."

Personification One way to bring objects or ideas to life is to imbue them with human qualities. We know that no room is really "cheerful," that winds do not actually "whisper," and that, being legless, the economy cannot possibly "limp." Nevertheless, all of these images are potent because we find it easier to identify with reflections of our own behavior.

Hyperbole For emphasis, you may deliberately overstate a point in a way that is clearly fanciful rather than misleading:

This paperwork will be the death of me.

The governor has repeated this same promise to you a million times.

Repetitive language or structure By repeating keywords or phrases, you make your listeners feel that your points are snowballing to a certain conclusion. Use parallel structure to emphasize relationships.

You can use repetition to introduce consecutive ideas. For instance, a speaker can build a sense of urgency or dedication by repeating the phrase "We must act now to . . ." as each problem is presented. Or you might end several sentences with the same words:

What remains? Treaties have gone. The honor of nations has gone. Liberty has gone.

David Lloyd George

Alliteration and assonance Use of these devices involves saying the same sound in a sustained sequence. (Sorry about that silly sentence.) Whether it is with consonants (alliteration) or vowels (assonance), this repetition can make an idea more memorable, or at least charge it with a sense of poetry.

At his brother's grave, Robert Green Ingersoll said the following:

> He who sleeps here, when dying . . . whispered with his latest breath: "I am better now." Let us believe, in spite of doubts and dogmas, and tears and fears, that these dear words are true of all the countless dead.

Antithesis When you want to contrast two ideas, certain sentence structures serve to dramatize the differences. Antithesis uses forms like these:

> Not . . . , but . . .
>
> Not only . . . , but also . . .

Upon the receipt of the 2001 Nobel Peace Prize, Kofi Annan in his Nobel lecture combined antithesis, alliteration and assonance, and repetitive structure:

> Today's real borders are not between nations, but between powerful and powerless, free and fettered, privileged and humiliated.

3 Use fresh language

The power of figurative language lies in the images stimulated in the listener's mind. After too many repetitions, the original psychological impact is lost. "Fresh as a daisy" once summoned a picture of a clean, bright, dew-studded blossom. At the first turn of the phrase "it went in one ear and out the other," its aptness produced pleasant surprise. Now both expressions are likely to be processed as just extra, empty words.

Certain fad words attract a cult following and are used to the exclusion of many good (and fresher) synonyms. Invest the time needed to select original combinations of words and phrases that capture the image, mood, or thought you want to get across.

4 Vary the rhythm of your sentences

Although oral style is characterized by simpler, shorter phrases with less variation in word choice, you are not compelled to homogenize your sentences into dullness. The "singsonginess" associated with doggerel can creep into a speech if you fail to pay attention to how you are stringing your sentences and phrases together. Be sparing in your use of parallelisms and repetition. Consider this plodding passage:

The association's annual convention should be user supported. The convention is attended by a core of regulars. The average association member doesn't benefit from the convention. These average members shouldn't have to bear more than their fair share.

The choppiness of this tedious passage results from the sameness of sentence length and structure. Recasting the sentences will create a more fluid and graceful paragraph:

The association's annual convention should be user supported. Who attends the convention? A core of regulars. The average association members, who don't benefit from the convention, shouldn't have to bear more than their fair share.

CHAPTER 30

Capturing Attention and Interest

When you give a speech or presentation, your words are competing for attention with every other sight and sound in the room and with every daydream or concern in the mind of each listener. The better you understand the psychology of attention, the more likely you will receive the compliment most sought for and appreciated by speakers: a sincere and simple "That was an interesting speech!"

30a. Use techniques that enliven your speech

Be guided by the following principles as you incorporate attention factors into your speech.

1   Use materials that are concrete and close to home

Examples are always more interesting when they are specific and real. Never say "a person" or "one" if you can give a name. Use well-known figures, members of the audience, or hypothetical characters. And give place names, brand names, dates, and details.

2   Link your topic to the listeners' self-interest

Most times, when people say, "So what?" they are really saying, "What's it to me?" Do not assume that the benefits of your particular approach are obvious; motivate your audience to listen by spelling out the rewards. Do careful audience analysis and tap into as many of your listeners' needs and values as possible. (See **25**.)

You don't have to be a vegetarian or a gourmet cook to benefit from these menu ideas. By serving just a few meatless meals a week, you can save 30 to 100 dollars on your monthly grocery bill and also provide a healthier diet for your family.

3   Incorporate storytelling

A well-constructed story commands the interest of nearly everyone. People are fascinated by human interest stories, as well as by hard news of matters that concern them directly. Notice how excellent feature articles and documentary films share many of the qualities of good fiction or drama. A speech, even if it is an annual report, can captivate an audience if it unfolds in a narrative fashion with suspense, conflict, intriguing characterizations, lively bits of dialogue, and a moment of climax leading to the denouement. Your speech need not promise to make your listeners rich or famous if it takes them outside their experience in an engaging way.

4   Use humor in appropriate situations

Of the many factors of attention, humor is so powerful and at the same time so tricky that it deserves a careful look. An infusion of humor into any speech can ease tension, deflate opponents, enhance the speaker's image, and make points memorable. You need not consider yourself a humorous speaker or your speech a humorous talk to benefit from using this attention-getting technique.

What is important is the ability to spot a potentially humorous idea in your speech and to craft it into a genuinely funny moment. Look for the humor in your everyday experience. The boring, frustrating, and mundane aspects of life all have their humorous elements. Take note of the everyday things that make you laugh on your job, in your relationships, on television, and in the paper.

Developing your use of humor is not a matter of collecting jokes and gags. Topically organized books of humor or websites like **www.humorlinks.com** or **www.jokes.com** can sometimes yield just the gem you need to catch people's attention. Be selective, though, when you draw on these resources, choosing only material that is relevant, appropriate, and fresh.

5   Use variety to energize your speech

Change attracts attention. Sameness is dull. One visual aid may add interest to your speech, but a succession of visual aids can drag a speech down if they are not used judiciously. If your content or delivery becomes totally predictable, audience members' interest will start to wane. Vary your forms of support—do not rely on only statistics or only testimony. Draw examples from many domains.

Whenever possible, give the speech a sense of movement. Create images of activity. Use verbs with vivid connotations, and stay in the active voice as much as possible. For instance, instead of saying, "Five new businesses can be seen downtown," say, "Drive down First Street and you will see five new businesses." In your delivery, too, remember the importance of vocal variety and physical movement. Who wants to listen to a deadpan speaker monotonously delivering a presentation while standing on a particularly adhesive spot on the floor? (See **34b** and **35**.)

30b. Keep your audience involved

If you have done a thorough audience analysis, you should have many references to the audience built into the speech, and there are always more opportunities to adapt to your audience once you start your speech. Here are some adaptations you might try.

Use the names of people in the audience "Suppose Ms. Silver's [nodding toward a listener] hardware business is expanding so rapidly that she decides to take out a loan to enlarge her store."

Refer to the person who introduced you and to the other speakers "As Dave was saying . . ."

Refer to details in the immediate setting or from shared experience "And all of that expensive atom-smashing machinery was housed in a room not half the size of this one."

Use audience participation techniques "Can I have a show of hands? How many people here . . ."

Make liberal use of the word *you* "You've probably seen . . ." "Now, I'll bet you're saying to yourself . . ." "You could undoubtedly give me a dozen more examples." "In your city here . . ."

CHAPTER 31

Creating Effective Introductions and Conclusions

Once you have outlined the body of the speech according to the organizational techniques described in part 5, you're ready to compose an introduction and conclusion that present your topic in a way that crystallizes its relationship to your listeners.

31a. Use an introduction to orient your listeners

A speech introduction prepares your listeners to deal with you and your topic. Both speaker and audience need a period of adjustment before getting to the meat of the speech—the audience to get used to a speaker's appearance, mannerisms, and style of talking; you to settle into your role.

1   Project confidence before starting

It is important to realize that your speech really starts before you utter the first word and that that first word is crucial to the success of the speech. The moment the attention shifts to you, you need to begin to develop a rapport and prepare your audience to listen to you. Stand up and, if necessary, move confidently to the position from which you will speak; then pause to engage audience members. Look at them and acknowledge nonverbally the fact that you and they are together.

2   Engage the audience's attention immediately

Because you will be preoccupied with all the things that are going on at the beginning of your speech, you don't want to risk leaving your opening sentences to the inspiration of the moment. You need strong basic material that will carry the speech forward.

Start with a sentence that leaves no doubt that you are beginning. Avoid false starts and apologetic or tentative phrases: "Is the mike on?" or "Well, here goes nothing." Tone is almost as important as content here. Your immediate purpose is to command the attention of your audience. (See **30**.)

You can begin the attention-getting phase of your introduction by telling a joke, relating a story, citing an apt quotation, making a startling statement, or asking a provocative question. Be imaginative, and even a little dramatic; but do not go too far. Avoid contrived and gimmicky openings such as flicking off the room lights and asking, "Are you in the dark about . . . ?" Your attention getter should also be consistent with your personality and the situation. Adopting an unnatural style is doubly troublesome; not only will you be uncomfortable, but your audience will sense that you are not being yourself.

With this in mind, consider the following possible attention getters for the comic book speech in **Appendix A**. A humorous or light introduction of the topic may suit you best:

Did you ever want to leap a tall building in a single bound? I did. Did you ever want to be more powerful than a locomotive? I did. Did you ever want to be faster than a speeding bullet? I did. As you can tell, I was warped early by the influence of comic books.

Or perhaps you are more comfortable with a dramatic attention getter:

> On a May afternoon in Washington, Frank Salacuse and John Snyder wrapped up their negotiations and shook hands. Both were happy with the result. Snyder walked away with $17,500, and Salacuse's syndicate now had a mint copy of *Marvel Comics*, no. 1, a comic book with the 1939 price of 10 cents on its cover.

A straightforward conversational approach to the topic can still get attention:

> In the 10 years I've been collecting comic books, I've learned that they are more than escape or entertainment. As I read the 13,000 comics in my collection, their contribution to popular culture becomes clearer and clearer.

As this third example illustrates, attention getters need not be unduly catchy or clever. However, it is essential that you begin your speech with a few well-planned sentences that say, in effect, "I know where I'm going and I want you to come with me—it will be worth your while."

3   Provide a psychological orientation

Attention, once gained, must be transformed into interest. Before you can ask your audience to concentrate on the substance of your message, you need to orient them psychologically. This orientation has two parts: establishing a good relationship with your listeners and motivating them toward your topic.

Establish a good relationship with your audience   Speakers can seem remote and aloof, cut off from the audience by role and status. Use your introduction to create a personal bond with your listeners. You can do this with, among other things, references to everyday, common occurrences. You want the introduction to set a tone of collaboration with your audience.

CHECKLIST

Connecting With Your Audience
- ❏ Establish credibility.
- ❏ Establish common ground.
- ❏ Refer to the setting or occasion.
- ❏ Flatter your audience.
- ❏ Refer to the person who introduced you or to some other person present.
- ❏ Use humor.

Motivate your audience toward your topic This motivational step is one of those most often overlooked in speech making, but it is the pivotal step of the introduction. Your speech, in spite of your enthusiasm for your topic, can be derailed by your audience's "what's-it-to-me?" attitude. You need to reassure your listeners that there are good reasons for them to be warming seats, that your topic—whether it be of an informative, persuasive, or evocative nature—has a link with their own experiences and is thereby worthy of their attention.

4   Provide a logical orientation

Now that your audience is *motivated* to listen, you must be sure they are *prepared* to listen. In the logical orientation, you show your listeners how you will approach and develop your topic—in effect, giving them an intellectual road map. In this phase of your introduction, you show the larger whole into which your speech fits and the way you have partitioned your topic.

Describing the relationship of your topic to the larger whole is a part of both introductions *and* conclusions. For instance, a speech on the training of teachers may have a format as shown graphically in Figure 31-1.

Establish a context for your speech Give your audience a perspective on your topic by using one or more of the following approaches.

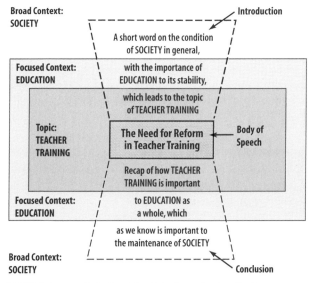

FIGURE 31-1   Relationship of the Introduction, Body, and Conclusion to the Larger Picture

Fit your topic into a familiar framework Consider this statement:

> San Jose is located 50 miles south of Oakland and 54 miles southeast of San Francisco, about 30 miles inland from the Pacific Ocean.

Here, the unknown is linked to the known in a geographical sense. You can also relate your topic to some schema, chart, organizational structure, or process with which your audience is already familiar. In this case, your listeners presumably know where the Pacific Ocean and San Francisco are, so they can start to think about San Jose.

Place your topic historically Another way to provide perspective on your topic is to describe its historical context. It helps listeners to learn about the events that led up to the situation as it stands at the time of your speech. One of the most famous speeches by an American, Abraham Lincoln's "Gettysburg Address," used this simple form of introduction:

> Fourscore and seven years ago our fathers brought forth on this continent a new nation, conceived in liberty and dedicated to the proposition that all men are created equal. Now we are engaged in a great civil war, testing whether that nation or any nation so conceived and so dedicated can long endure. We are met on a great battlefield of that war. We have come to dedicate a portion of that field, as a final resting place for those who here gave their lives that that nation might live. It is altogether fitting and proper that we should do this.

Place your topic conceptually Just as you can place your topic in time or space, so can you locate it in the world of ideas. By showing your listeners how your speech fits in with certain familiar theories, concepts, and definitions, you prepare them to listen. For example:

> You're familiar with the law of supply and demand as it relates to goods and services. Let me review this basic market mechanism with you, because I want to ask you to apply these same essential principles to our system of information exchange.

Provide new definitions and concepts If you use unfamiliar terms and concepts in your speech, or use familiar terms in unfamiliar ways, prepare your audience.

Here is how you might introduce an unfamiliar term:

> *Operations Support Systems* for a telecommunications service provider are software applications that deal with four broad areas: billing and customer care, provisioning, planning and engineering, and network management.

Here is how you might define a familiar term used in an unfamiliar way:

> Often, when people speak of a system of restitution for criminals, they refer to a program in which prisoners contribute wages to a collective pool of some sort. The restitution system I will be talking about involves direct compensation from individual criminals to their victims.

Orient the audience to your approach to the topic The second step in a logical orientation—once you have shown how your speech fits into some larger context—is to preview the structure of your speech. If you give your listeners a framework on which to attach your points as your speech unfolds, you make it easier for them to comprehend your topic and thesis.

In most introductions, you will explicitly state one or more of the following: your topic, thesis, title, or purpose—for example, "I would like to persuade you to change your vote on this bond issue." At times, you also want to tell what you are *not* talking about—essentially explaining to your audience how you have narrowed your topic.

Here is an example, derived from the comic book outline in **Appendix A**, of a speaker spelling out what the speech will not cover:

> I am not going to tell you which comic books are currently the best investment. Nor am I going to explain how to treat and store comic books so that the acid in the paper won't turn them into yellow confetti. I *am*, however, going to tell you some things about comic books that will help you better understand their place in American popular culture.

You must also decide whether to give an exact preview of the points you are going to cover or merely a general overview of your topic. Explicit previews are useful in the majority of speeches and essential for speeches with fairly technical or complex topics. The speaker gives the listeners a reassuring road map to carry through the speech, one that they can refer to if they start to get lost.

5   Make your introduction as compact as possible

Generally, the introduction should take up 10 to 15 percent of your speaking time. To avoid an introduction that is choppy, disjointed, and overlong, organize it in a natural narrative style. Often it is more important to fulfill the *functions* of getting attention and providing psychological and logical orientation than to progress mechanically through the three steps. Whenever possible, select material that fulfills more than one.

In addition to combining parts of the introduction, it is often appropriate to omit steps altogether. A presidential speech can begin, "My fellow Americans, tonight I want to talk about the serious problem of international terrorism." Attention, credibility, and motivation to listen are assumed.

31b. Use a conclusion to provide closure

Many speakers make the mistake of not leaving sufficient time for a proper conclusion. Just as you led your audience into your topic step-by-step in the introduction, so must you lead them out again in a conclusion, tying all the threads together and leaving the audience with a sense of completeness or closure. Like the introduction, the conclusion should be precisely planned, almost to the point of memorization. Social scientists tell us that people are most likely to remember what they hear last, so you should choose your words carefully.

1   Provide logical closure

Although you have already demonstrated the interconnectedness of your points and ideas in the body of the speech by the use of transitions and internal previews and summaries, you still need to tie it all together for your audience at the end.

Summarize the main ideas of the speech In all but the shortest of speeches, you are well advised to include a fairly explicit restatement of your thesis and main ideas. Only in a short, one-point speech can you safely omit a summary. Otherwise, there is no reason not to summarize—you have nothing to lose and only clarity to gain.

Reestablish the connection of your topic to a larger context There can be an integration of the parts of a speech that goes beyond mere summary. In some cases, a conclusion serves to pull together several ideas into a pattern that has been implicit all along. This can be true for either inductive or deductive lines of reasoning, when the final relationship among points needs to be spelled out. (See **21**.)

In the introduction, you drew your speech topic out of some broader context. After developing your ideas, you may want to show how they tie back to the original larger picture. Once again, refer to Figure 31-1.

2   Provide psychological closure

Making your main points fit together logically for your audience is not enough. Members should walk away psychologically satisfied with your speech—you need to have touched them. When you plan your conclusion, think not only about what you want your listeners to understand and agree with but also about how you want them to feel at the end of the speech.

Remind the audience how the topic affects their lives In the introduction, you make the topic personal to your audience. During the speech itself, you implicitly sustain that orientation by making your examples and manner of speaking appropriately personal. At the end, you bring the topic home again and show your listeners why it should be of more than academic interest to them—why they have a stake in what you have described.

> Whether you work for a large organization or have your own small business, whether you keep your own books or deal with a cadre of accountants, these two systems will affect you. Understanding the basic logic of each is necessary if you are to make sound decisions.

Make an appeal Part of the psychological wrap-up of a speech can be a direct appeal to your audience, especially in a speech to persuade. Ask them directly to behave in a certain way, or ask them to change their attitudes.

An appeal can be strengthened by a statement of your own intent: "I plan to give blood tomorrow morning, and I hope to see you down there."

3   End your speech with a clincher

It is as important to plan your last sentence as it is your first. Every speech needs a sentence that leaves no doubt that the speech is finished. Speakers who have not prepared this clincher tend to keep summarizing while trying to devise a good exit line. As a result, many of them taper off in dismay and defeat with such frail endings as

> I guess that's all I wanted to say.

> Oops! My time is up. I'd better stop now.

> Well, I'd like to say more, but I ought to take questions.

Other speakers do not taper off; they simply stop short, leaving the audience to decide whether the blank air is a pause or the real ending.

One type of effective clincher for a speech ties back to the attention getter used in the introduction. This involves answering definitively the provocative question you asked initially or reintroducing your opening joke or story and taking it one step further—or twisting it in the light of your thesis:

> Frank Salacuse's syndicate spent $17,500 for its comic book, but all *you* need is a pocketful of change and transportation to the nearest newsstand or grocery store to rediscover a unique facet of Americana.

Also consider clinching your speech with a proverb, aphorism, quotation, or snatch of poetry. Martin Luther King, Jr., ended his historic "I Have a Dream" speech by evoking the words of an old spiritual: "Free at last, free at last, thank God Almighty, we are free at last." Do not use "thank you" as a substitute for a clincher.

The delivery of your clincher is as important as its content. Do not mumble your final sentence in a throwaway voice or spend the last few speaking moments gathering up your notes and slinking away. Be familiar enough with your clincher that you can deliver it while maintaining eye contact with your listeners.

31c. Avoid common introduction and conclusion pitfalls

1. *Don't* begin with "Before I start, I'd like to say. . . ." You have already started. (See **31a.1**.)

2. *Don't* begin with an apology like "I'm not really prepared" or "I don't know much about this, but. . . ." (See **31a.2**.)

3. *Don't* use an attention getter that has no real link to your topic. Avoid the temptation to stretch a point so you can start with an unrelated joke you think is hilarious. (See **31a.2**.)

4. *Don't* make your introduction seem disproportionately long. (See **31a.5**.)

5. *Don't* use stock phrases like "Unaccustomed as I am to public speaking" or overworked apocryphal stories. Ask a friend to give an honest critique of your trove of expressions and anecdotes. (See **29d**.)

6. *Don't* startle your audience by bursting out of a yogalike trance into an explosion of oral energy. This is a favorite of high school orators. Engage your audience before you start. (See **31a.1**.)

7. *Don't* read your introduction or your conclusion. Or, if you have memorized them, be sure they do not sound mechanical. These are times when you should maximize eye contact and keep your inflection natural and conversational. (See **34b**.)

8. *Don't* end with an apology: "I guess I've rambled on long enough," or "I don't know if I've made this clear," "I'm not usually this hyper; it must be the coffee."

9. *Don't* trail off. Do your audience the courtesy of wrapping things up and using a clincher. (See **31b.3**.)

10. *Don't* introduce a whole new point in your conclusion. The body of your speech is the place for that. (See **18a**.)

11. *Don't* make the conclusion disproportionately long. It is a summary and ending.

12. *Don't* end in a style or mood that is at odds with the tenor of the rest of the speech. You do your listeners a disservice if you have kept them laughing up to the very end only to hit them with a stark recitation of doom.

13. _Don't_ use the phrases "in conclusion" or "in summary" in any part of the speech other than the actual conclusion. You will lose part of your audience while they reorient themselves to the fact that the speech is continuing when they thought it was winding down. (See **32**.)

CHAPTER 32
Linking Speech Components

When you have completed research, selected and organized your points, and added an introduction and conclusion, a final step remains: smoothly and gracefully tying all the components of your speech together. This helps avoid choppiness and provides listeners with a unified presentation more pleasant to listen to and easier to follow. Figure 32-1, at the end of the chapter, illustrates the interconnectedness of speech components and how they flow together.

32a. Weave supporting materials smoothly into the speech

When you have chosen appropriate definitions, facts, examples, statistics, and testimony, you still have to marshal these supporting materials and present them effectively. You want to emphasize the quality of your materials, make them clear and understandable, and organize them appropriately in relation to the points they support.

1   Use a variety of lead-ins

Do not get into the habit of introducing all your illustrations, statistics, and so on with the same phrase: "Some figures about this are . . . some figures about that are. . . ." Be prepared enough that you can employ a number of lead-ins for each kind of supporting material. There are many possibilities:

To support this idea . . .

_____ put it well, I think, when she said . . .

What causes this situation? One answer to that question was offered by _____ when he wrote last year . . .

There are several examples of this. Let me share just two . . .

To introduce a direct quotation (in contrast to a paraphrase), be sure to indicate to your listeners the boundaries of the quoted material. This can be done by saying, "and I quote .`.` ." followed by, "End of quotation," or in some cases a subtle change in your voice or posture is enough.

2 Cite the sources of your supporting materials

By giving credit for your supporting materials, you build your own credibility by showing the range of your research. You are also providing information your listeners are almost certain to want. Very few audiences will settle for "studies show . . ." or "one researcher found . . ." or "a friend once told me . . ." To evaluate these statements, listeners need to know more about where the information came from.

This does not mean that you are required to present regulation footnotes in oral form, citing volume and page numbers. Nor do you need to recite an authority's complete biography or necessarily explain a study's design intricacies. Although you should know the *who, why, when,* and *how* of every bit of data you use, you will probably mention only a couple of these in introducing the evidence.

3 Determine how complete your citations need to be

The form an oral citation takes is, like many choices in speaking, dependent on the context. In some cases there is a rigid and stylized form, in others there is a lot more flexibility available to the speaker. The college debate or speech contest may have a strict form, developed by tradition. Otherwise, you can choose the "density" level of your citation—how much information you need to include about the source as you speak—according to how much you think your audience has to hear to accept the source as legitimate (although they don't have to agree with it).

Here are three examples along the continuum of citation density. The first introduces the information with no citation at all. The second presents the name of the source, which indicates that you are not picking numbers out of the air. The third example is fairly dense, giving your listeners enough information that they can jot down and use to check your source if they so wish.

No citation

> Only 17 percent of all bicycle accidents are car–bike collisions, and in only 10 percent of those collisions was the car overtaking the bike from the rear.

Light citation

> According to transportation engineer John Forester, only 17 percent of all bicycle accidents are car–bike collisions, and in only 10 percent of those collisions was the car overtaking the bike from the rear.

Dense citation

> In his 1993 book, *Effective Cycling*, published by MIT Press, transportation engineer John Forester notes that only 17 percent of all bicycle accidents are car–bike collisions, and in only 10 percent of those collisions was the car overtaking the bike from the rear.

If you must be dense in your citing, make it as conversational as possible. Avoid the "big parenthetical speed bump" that interrupts the flow of a sentence, as in "Transportation engineer John Forester notes (*Effective Cycling*, MIT Press, 1993) that only. . . ." It may take a few more words to come up with a smooth version, but the result will be more natural to the ear.

32b. Use transitions to link points and express relationships

Transitional sentences, phrases, and words serve as bridges between points. They also signal to listeners how two ideas are related. Clear and evocative transitions are more important in speaking than in writing because the spoken message is ephemeral. In this book, for example, we show you the relationships among ideas by indenting, capitalizing, and using different punctuation and typefaces. As a speaker, however, you do not have access to these devices. You need to use verbal signposting techniques to show how your points relate. You can keep your listeners informed about the overall structure of your speech by the generous use of phrases like these:

> My next major point is . . .
>
> To show you what I mean, let me tell you two stories.
>
> What, then, is the solution to this three-part problem I have outlined?

Do not worry about using too many signposts. Your audience will appreciate them.

1 Select transitions that reflect logical relationships

The transitions you choose should illuminate the basic organizational structure of the speech. Without even seeing their content, you can tell what pattern these speeches follow:

Thesis Statement: ....

> I say that for three reasons. First,

I. ....

> This situation is also due to

II. ....

> Last of all, we can attribute the problem to

III. ....

or

Thesis Statement: ....

    Initially,

  I. ....

    Next,

  II. ....

    Finally,

  III. ....

The transitions alone tell you that you are hearing an effect-to-cause speech in the first case and a chronologically arranged speech in the second.

Points can be related in a number of ways. Crystallizing these relationships and expressing them through appropriate transitional phrases will enhance your clarity. Try to use a variety of transitions instead of linking all your ideas with "OK, now let's look at . . ." or "First of all . . . , second of all . . . ," and so on. Table 32-1 lists common transitional words that can be used to tie main points to one another, main points to subpoints, subpoints to one another, supporting evidence to arguments, and introductions and conclusions to the body of the speech. Transitions are needed in all these places.

TABLE 32-1 **Transitional Words That Signal Relationship**

Relationship	Transitional Words
Chronological	First, second, third Next, then Following
Cause–effect	So, since, thus Therefore, hence Consequently, as a result Due to, because
Part-to-whole	One such, another The first (second, third) of these For instance, for example Illustrative of this, a case in point
Equality	Similarly, additionally Another Of equal importance
Opposition	But, though, however On the other hand, conversely In spite of Nonetheless, nevertheless

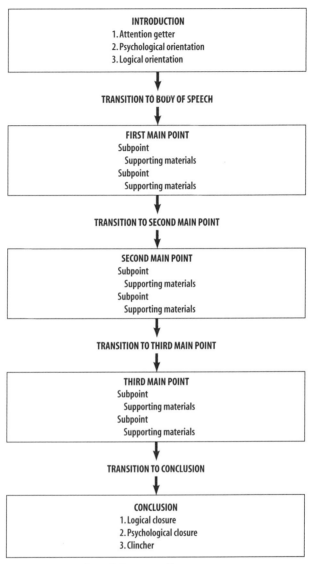

INTRODUCTION
1. Attention getter
2. Psychological orientation
3. Logical orientation

↓

TRANSITION TO BODY OF SPEECH

↓

FIRST MAIN POINT
Subpoint
 Supporting materials
Subpoint
 Supporting materials

↓

TRANSITION TO SECOND MAIN POINT

↓

SECOND MAIN POINT
Subpoint
 Supporting materials
Subpoint
 Supporting materials

↓

TRANSITION TO THIRD MAIN POINT

↓

THIRD MAIN POINT
Subpoint
 Supporting materials
Subpoint
 Supporting materials

↓

TRANSITION TO CONCLUSION

↓

CONCLUSION
1. Logical closure
2. Psychological closure
3. Clincher

FIGURE 32-1   Speech Structure Chart

2   Make use of internal previews and summaries

The importance of previews in speech introductions and of summaries in conclusions is emphasized elsewhere. (See **31**.) Sometimes, transitions between main points should take the form of internal summaries or internal previews that pull together two or three main points.

Internal Preview

Once your résumé is prepared, the next step in job seeking is to prepare a list of specific job openings. The three best sources here are newspaper and web listings, your campus placement service, and word-of-mouth recommendations. We will examine the pros and cons of each of these.

Internal Summary

Because the problems in our department were affecting morale, and because we had found they were caused by poor communication, we instituted an unusual training program. Let me tell you about it.

Internal Summary and Preview

I've told you why we need to reduce our dependence on the automobile, and I hope I've convinced you that a light rail system is the best alternative for our city. Now, you're probably asking two questions: What will it cost? and How will it work? I want to answer both these questions. First, the question of cost.

> **KEY POINT** **Premature Summaries** Do not forecast the end of your speech prematurely by bluntly saying "In summary" anywhere but in the conclusion. (See **31**.) Carefully qualify your internal summaries by using phrases like "So, to summarize this first idea . . ." or "Let me review the points so far."

CHAPTER 33

Practicing Your Speech

Start practicing your speech aloud well before the presentation. Using the three stages of practice sessions enables you to finalize your points, get feedback from others, and polish the delivery. Whenever possible, form a support group of other learners or a network of colleagues and friends. See **2c** for a discussion of constructive feedback.

33a. Allow time for the three stages of practice

Your practice sessions need a timetable: you should plan your practice sessions, write down a schedule of steps and phases, and adhere to it. There is no one, arbitrary timetable to adopt. Table 33-1 shows possible timetables for three speeches in which the

TABLE 33-1   Possible Practice Schedules

Type of Speech	Commitment Made to Speak	Preliminary Analysis, Research, and Outline Completed	Early Practice Sessions (Development)
Major policy address	Several weeks before	1 week before	1–2 weeks before: Discuss ideas with colleagues. 5–6 days before: Talk through speech once a day.
Classroom speech	10 days before	4 days before	4–10 days before: Talk about speech with friends. 4 days before: Read outline several times; practice aloud twice.
Routine oral report in a business meeting	24 hours before	Evening before	Afternoon or evening before: Talk through basic ideas with friends or colleagues. Evening before: Practice aloud one to three times.

advance notice is different for each. This can be used as a guide to help you create a schedule unique to your circumstances.

1   Use early sessions to flesh out your outline

During these early developmental sessions, you transform your outline of ideas into a speech by adding the elements of language and delivery to the logical framework erected by your outline.

Begin by internalizing your outline. Read it over a number of times, becoming familiar with the flow of the logic. Sit at your desk or a table and talk your way through the outline. Try to explain the ideas to yourself.

At this point, pick a quiet spot and start to put together the speech as it will actually be given. Stand up and give the speech out loud in your speaking voice. Visualize the speech situation and mentally put yourself there.

Sometime during this stage, you will have made the first draft of your speech notes. These will evolve. They are mutable according to how things shape up as you tinker with the wording.

2   Use middle sessions to get feedback

After you have become comfortable with your material but before doing the final polishing, you should seek feedback on your speech.

Middle Practice Sessions (Feedback)	Final Practice Sessions (Refinement)
4 days before: Give speech on videotape, review with advisors, repeat.	Beginning 3 days before: Practice aloud once a day; read notes or outline once a day. Day of speech: Practice aloud once; review notes just before speaking.
3 days before: Give speech to friendly critic, receive feedback, practice aloud one other time.	Beginning 2 days before: Practice aloud one to three times a day; read over outlines and notes several times. Day of speech: Practice aloud once; review notes just before speaking.
Morning of meeting: Give report to colleague if possible.	Day of presentation: Practice aloud once; review notes just before leaving for meeting.

This is usually sometime in the middle of your timetable. If you solicit feedback on content, style, and delivery before you have finished shaping your basic speech, you will miss getting help on those parts that have not yet been crystallized. If the feedback comes too late in the schedule, you will not have the time to incorporate comfortably the useful information you have received.

Practice your speech in front of others and ask for their feedback
Just as people are good sounding boards for the development of your ideas, as stated in **10c**, so are they the best source of feedback. Seek a variety of responses from others—colleagues, family members, friends. As you rehearse your speech, imagine that you are in front of your actual audience, and do not leave things out. Do not talk about your speech. Give your speech.

Ask for honest feedback on content and delivery, but do not necessarily take any single person's comments as the last word. He or she has quirks and prejudices just like everyone else. This is why a group of people is preferable, giving you a sampling of responses.

You should not ask, "How'd you like my speech?" Answers like "It was nice" or "I thought it was okay" certainly do not help you much. Lead your critics with a few questions and seek clarification of their answers. Here are some specific questions you can begin with:

- "What did you see as the single most important thing I was trying to say?" If they do not come up with your thesis sentence, then you must look at your structure again.

- "What were the main ideas I was trying to get across?" They should answer with your main points.

It is important to get answers to these first two questions before moving on to finer points of development and delivery. You are speaking for a specific purpose, and everything else is insignificant if your whole reason for speaking is not being understood.

CHECKLIST

Questions to Elicit Useful Feedback

- ❏ "Did my ideas flow in a logical sequence?"
- ❏ "Did the speech hold your attention? What parts were boring? Confusing?"
- ❏ "Did I prove my points?"
- ❏ "Did my introduction show you where I was going?"
- ❏ "Did the conclusion tie the speech together?"
- ❏ "Did I sound natural?"
- ❏ "Did I have any distracting mannerisms?"

Record your practice session and analyze your performance A video is the next best thing to a human critic. When you view your performance on playback, try to get outside yourself and see the image as that of a stranger. In this case, you may temporarily shift your focus from your message and your imagined audience to yourself as a speaker. Become the audience and ask yourself the same questions raised previously. A hazard to avoid here is being too self-critical. Seeing yourself on tape can be devastating if you notice only the aspects that need improvement. Look also for things you are doing right. This is where it can be helpful to watch the video with a friend or coach who can give you a more balanced perspective.

3   Use final sessions for refinements

By this time, you should be committed to a basic version of your speech while maintaining the flexibility of the extemporaneous mode. You should not be making radical changes.

Make the final practice sessions as realistic as possible. If you are going to use presentation aids, they should be ready early enough that you can include them in your final practice sessions. The same holds true for the final draft of your notecards. Check yourself against your time limit. Practice your speech, standing up, at the rate and volume you will be using. Speaking with rudimentary mechanical amplification to a large audience, for example, will use more breath than will the conversational volume used in early practice. You need to unabashedly boom out your speech in the final practice sessions if that is what it will take to be heard when you actually give the speech.

Continue reading through your notes and outline, but do not think of these activities as a substitute for the formal practice sessions. Save the hours just before the speech for one final runthrough and for getting into the proper, relaxed frame of mind.

33b. Prepare speech notes

You should not confuse speech notes with your outline; they serve different functions. An outline is used to ensure that the speech has a logical organization. Speech notes, in contrast, are used as a guide and a safety net while you are actually speaking.

Like your outline and wording, your notes should go through several drafts. Do not feel committed to the first thing you write.

1 Include keywords, key phrases, and material that is to be cited directly

Unlike your outline—in which your points must be parallel, mutually exclusive, and in full sentences—your speech notes do not have a rigid, regulation form. A point can be represented by a word, a sentence fragment, or an actual sentence or two. See Figure 33-1. What goes into your notes depends on what you find you need during practice.

While practicing, you may also find that you want more than just a keyword reminder to get through an important but tongue-twisting sentence or to ensure that you remember an especially eloquent turn of phrase that has a delicate rhythm. Your notes

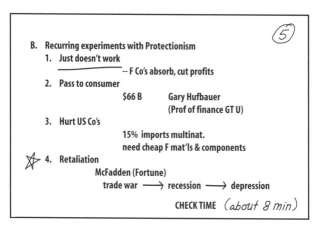

FIGURE 33-1   Speech Notes

may also contain material that you will be citing exactly as written out, such as long quotations or complicated statistics.

Keep in mind, however, that your notes should remain *notes*. If you make them too extensive and detailed, you risk moving out of the extemporaneous mode and into the realm of the manuscript speech. Your notes should be referred to, not read from.

2   Prepare your speech notes in a format that aids your delivery

There are many contexts in which your speaking can occur (see **part 2**), and these will dictate to some degree the format your notes take. The invited speaker at a world affairs forum may use 4″ × 6″ cards. An attorney in court does not look out of place referring to a legal pad while speaking. A project manager can glance at the PowerPoint note page on her laptop screen covering the content of her slides. For all of these instances, however, the advice in **33b.1** still applies.

CHECKLIST

Formatting Suggestions for Speech Notes

❏ Words and phrases should be large, well spaced, and uncluttered.

❏ Include visual cues (large card numbers, underlining, indenting, stars, highlighting, different colors) to make it easy for you to find what you want at a glance.

❏ Add time notations to keep on track (writing, "If more than 8 minutes, skip to [card 6/point 4/slide 10]").

❏ Mark optional sections of the speech, if appropriate (highlighting in yellow to mean: "Include this if the audience seems uncertain about my point. Otherwise, omit it").

If you choose to go the notecard route, a few medium-sized cards can easily become an extension of your hand as you gesture and move about. They will not be distracting to your listeners if you seem comfortable with them. Whatever medium you choose for your notes, do not be coy about using them—refer to them honestly. A surreptitious peek will not fool your listeners into believing that you are speaking without aids.

Do not go to the other extreme and get lost in your notes. You should be able to look down, see what is next, and then talk about it. If you find yourself burying your nose in your notes, you have not prepared them correctly.

Preparing speech notes with presentation software   Presentation software gives you the option of entering notes to accompany the slides you create. Here is where you can put the tongue twister, the precise data, or the quotation mentioned in **33b.1**, but don't be constrained by the default font settings to make everything too small to read easily. Also, feel free to mark up the output with the other visual cues as illustrated in Figure 33-1 and noted previously. If you don't want to have to deal with 8½″ × 11″ sheets, use a paper cutter to lop off the top part of the printer output with the image of the slide—assuming you have prepared your notes with adequate keywords to cover the content.

33c. Fit your speech into the time limit

In a speech class, there may be penalties for not reaching a minimum time limit. In most other settings, no one is going to be awfully upset if you take only 15 out of the 20 minutes you have been given. However, taking 40 minutes when you have been allotted 20 can disrupt the schedules of countless other people.

Often, you cannot tell for sure how much time your speech will take until you have gotten well into the practice sessions. In extemporaneous practice, you will experience variations in length as you work with the form of your ideas and the style and rhythm of your speaking. Most first-time speakers practice at a speaking rate faster than the one they find necessary for clarity during the speech itself. The more realistic your practice, the less likely you are to incorrectly estimate your time.

To clock your speech, do not glue your eyes to the sweep hand of your watch. Merely note the time when you begin and when you finish. A sweep hand can induce unnatural behavior, such as speaking at twice your normal rate for the last minute if you think you are running long, or, in the opposite case, slowing your delivery to a tired shuffle. There are more sensible ways to address problems of length. The first step is to time the parts of your speech. Two possible ways of doing this are to have a helper jot down the times of your main points on your outline as you practice or to do it yourself with a tape recorder.

Look at the relative proportions of the parts of your speech: introduction, body, conclusion. Generally, the body should make up 75 percent of your speech. Does an extended story make the introduction too long? Look, too, at the relative proportions of your main points. Are you spending half your time on only the first main point? Is it worth it?

When your delivery time becomes consistent, mark the cumulative times of the parts in your notes. For example, you might print "2 min" at the bottom right of your notes on the introduction, "5 min" after the first main point, "8 min" after the second, and so on. (See Figure 33-1.)

Some people have internal clocks that are accurate enough that they do not need external cues. If yours is not that well developed (and most of ours are not), feel free to take off your watch and lay it where you can see it, or have a colleague in the audience give you prearranged time signals. Avoid excessive reliance on the clock, though. Become comfortable with your presentation by practicing and timing your speech.

KEY POINT **Avoid "Mental" Rather Than Oral Practice** Sitting and thinking about your speech, or reading over your outline or notes, is no substitute for rehearsing the speech aloud. Oral practice is essential to get comfortable with phrasing and to check your timing. Do not let "speaker's" block make you put off working orally until the last moment.

8 Presenting Your Speech

CHAPTER 34. Achieving Effective Vocal Delivery

Speak clearly, correctly, and conversationally. Vary your vocal delivery for interest and emphasis.

CHAPTER 35. Achieving Effective Physical Delivery

Use your physical delivery to create a visual effect that complements the content of your speech.

CHAPTER 36. Using Your Presentation Aids

Introduce your presentation aids so that they blend smoothly into the speech.

CHAPTER 37. Answering Questions

Use the question-and-answer period to ensure that your message was understood by as many people as possible.

CHAPTER 34

Achieving Effective Vocal Delivery

As important as preparation, organization, content, and style are, the essence of the speech is still your spoken words. What a waste of time and brainpower if what you have to say cannot be heard or understood at the critical moment of speaking. You must be aware of the mechanics of transmitting sound: articulation, breath control, projection, and so on. At the same time, your most important goal is to develop a style of vocal delivery that sounds natural and conversational.

34a. Speak to be heard and understood

1 Speak loud enough to be heard by the entire audience

For the inexperienced speaker, just about *any* volume level will sound too loud. This is understandable, for there are few occasions where we speak above a conversational level.

The only thing that will make loud speaking more comfortable and natural is, of course, practice. In the early stages, you have to ignore the feedback on volume that you receive from your own ears and rely on a friend or perhaps a tape recorder set some distance away. What you are aiming for is a louder voice that retains the rhythms and inflections of your normal conversation. You want to be loud, but not to yell like a drill instructor. As you practice, you will discover that this requires more air for each phrase and that you need to develop breath control to permit you to keep your breathing pauses in normal patterns.

Maintain a mental image of broadcasting or propelling your voice to the far corners of the room. You will then find yourself doing those things that naturally aid projection, such as keeping your head up and opening your mouth wide.

2 Speak at a rate your audience can follow

In general, plan to speak more slowly than you do in daily conversation. The need to speak a little louder and a little more distinctly will require extra breath. It will be more natural to pause to breathe between phrases than to rush through the last few words of a sentence and gasp for air. To be sure you have timed the speech realistically, practice at the rate and volume you will actually use. An average rate of speaking is around 125 words per minute.

3 Enunciate words distinctly and naturally

In public speaking settings, much information can be lost due to distance from the speaker and to distracting noise. Thus it is important to work on crisp, precise articulation. Use your tongue, teeth, and lips to pronounce every sound. Be sure you say "gover*n*ment" rather than "goverment" and "hundred" rather than "hunnerd." Do not mumble, run words together, or swallow whole phrases. (See **34d.2** for a discussion of chronic articulation problems.)

You can enunciate properly and still sound natural. It merely takes some practice incorporating precision into your normal conversation instead of creating a separate "speaking persona."

4 Consider making some adjustments if you have an accent

If you have a regional accent or if you are not a native speaker of American English, you may be concerned about being understood. Do not try to eliminate or hide your accent. Your manner of speaking is part of your unique personality. The differences can add interest and charm to your presentation. To ensure comprehension, follow these suggestions:

1. Do not start out with the most important material. Use your introduction to let the audience adjust to the pronunciations and patterns of emphasis that differ from their own. Usually, this will take just a few minutes.

2. Speak more slowly and distinctly than you do in conversation.

3. Be very alert to feedback. If you see confused faces, repeat ideas slowly. Unclear vocabulary or mispronunciation of one keyword may mystify your listeners. Try several synonyms for important words.

4. Consider using more presentation aids with key phrases.

If you are a nonnative speaker of English, you may find these two simple tips useful in increasing your intelligibility:

1. Prolong your vowel sounds. In contrast to many other languages, spoken American English carries more meaning in vowels than consonants. It will sound odd to you, but make a conscious effort to extend your vowels. Maaaaake eeeeeach laaaaaast a loooooong tiiiiiime.

2. Also blend the end of one word into the beginning of the next so that each phrase sounds like one long word. This reduces the perceived choppiness of much accented English.

For more detailed suggestions, refer to

Porter, Patricia A., and Margaret Grant. *Communicating Effectively in English: Oral Communication for Non-Native Speakers,* 2nd ed. Belmont, CA: Wadsworth, 1992.

Raifsnider, Barbara. *American English Pronunciation Program for Speakers of English as a Second Language and Native Speakers with Strong Regional Accents.* New York: Living Language, 1999.

34b. Use vocal variety

Your voice should not simply transmit words; you can use it to underscore and reinforce your message. The speaker who has a clear speaking voice devoid of vocal tics wastes these good qualities if the person speaks hypnotically, with no variation in pitch, rate, or volume. Change and movement are intrinsically more interesting than the static or predictable. Vocal variety is equally important, and the need for it goes beyond a mere desire for novelty. Suppose your speech on air pollution contained these two sentences:

> When the pollution levels are high, my hair feels gritty, and I have to wash it more often.

> Every time pollution reaches the Alert level in our city, more people with chronic respiratory problems die.

Delivering these sentences in the same tone of voice could imply that they are of equal importance. Changes in emphasis through pace, volume, and pitch show your audience what is significant and can signal humor, seriousness, irony, and a range of emotions.

34c. Use standard, acceptable pronunciation

Some regional differences in the ways people pronounce words are inevitable and cause no problem for public speakers. If, however, a person says "warsh" instead of "wash" or "ax" instead of "ask," many listeners will consider this substandard and draw conscious or unconscious conclusions about the speaker's educational level, competence, and intelligence. This sort of linguistic snobbery can be unfair, but it is easier to change some pronunciations than to change everyone else's attitudes.

1 Identify words that you habitually mispronounce

Look over the list in **Appendix C** and see if you are guilty of any of the identified pronunciation errors. If you find one or two words that you mispronounce, you can easily work on correcting them. If you find five or more, you may need more extensive help in the form of coaching or coursework. Due to factors in your background or perhaps a lazy ear for the finer distinctions of speech, you probably are also mispronouncing several other words and impairing your effectiveness in communicating with certain groups of people. Here, too, feedback from your practice audience can alert you to errors of which you were unaware.

2 Check the preferred pronunciation of unfamiliar words

Your reading vocabulary and your speaking vocabulary are different. There can be words you frequently see and understand yet rarely speak or hear spoken. Without exposure and feedback, you might develop your own way of mentally pronouncing such a word that involves a mistake like adding a sound or reversing sounds. The incorrect pronunciation will feel right to you because you have said it to yourself so often as you read and did research. If you give a whole speech about the Electorial College (instead of Electoral), your listeners might wonder just how knowledgeable you really are. Or they may be confused or amused if you constantly refer to the need for a counselor to listen "emphatically" when you think you are saying "empathically," a word that means something entirely different. Check words you encounter in research, but do not use regularly, to be sure you have them right.

Refer to these sources for questions of pronunciation:

Dauer, Rebecca M. *Accurate English: A Complete Course in Pronunciation.* Englewood Cliffs, NJ: Prentice-Hall/Regents, 1994.

Prator, Clifford H., Jr., and Betty Wallace Robinett. *Manual of American English Pronunciation,* 4th ed. New York: Holt, 1985.

Silverstein, Bernard. *NTC's Dictionary of American English Pronunciation.* New York: McGraw-Hill, 1994.

Yates, Jean. *Pronounce It Perfectly in English* (with 3 cassettes). Hauppauge, NY: Barrons Educational Audio, 1995.

34d. Eliminate distracting vocal characteristics

Your reason for speaking is undermined when your listeners begin to pay less attention to what you are saying and more to how you are saying it: "That's the fifteenth time she's said 'quite frankly'" or "Why doesn't he clear his throat?" or "That repetitious inflection is really irritating." Your voice and speech style should be unobtrusive vehicles for your ideas.

Distracting speech habits are difficult to identify and even more difficult to change. Vocal mannerisms become so familiar to you and your closest associates that they are overlooked and cease to distract, but to a new audience they are blatant. Follow the suggestions in chapter **33** for receiving feedback. Use video, audiotape, and critics to get some objective perspective on your performance.

1 Identify problems of voice quality

The resonant, musical voice you view as an ideal may be beyond your reach, but there is, of course, no one perfect voice for effective speaking. Although the quality and timbre of one's voice are determined to a great extent by the larynx and by the size and shape of the nasal cavities, you can still find yourself within a range of pleasing voices unless you are hampered by one or more of the following problems.

- Harshness, hoarseness, or stridency, giving an impression of anger or gruffness.

- Breathiness, thinness, or weakness, resulting in a soft, childish-sounding voice that lacks authority and power.
- Nasality and denasality, producing either whiny or listless qualities.

2 Identify problems of articulation

Many people have speech problems that are not severe enough to be considered disabling but that are still sufficiently distracting to impede good communication. Stutterers will certainly be aware of their condition, whereas people with lesser problems are usually not conscious of their misarticulations.

Listen closely to your speech for irregularities in the way you produce consonant sounds or blends of consonants. Many articulation errors take the form of *substitutions*, such as "*th*olution" for "*s*olution" or "*d*ese" for "*the*se." Also common are sound *distortions*: the slushing, hissing, or whistling *s*, or the lazy *l* or *r*. Less frequently encountered articulation errors are *additions* ("ath*a*lete" for "athlete," "real*a*tor" for "realtor"), and *omissions* ("doin'" for "doing," "reg*lar*" for "regular").

3 Identify irrelevant sounds and phrases

Do not be afraid to pause between sentences or thoughts when you speak. But avoid filling those pauses with distracting and meaningless sounds and phrases. When a speaker is nervous, a 1-second pause can seem like a 10-second stretch of dead air, and the temptation to fill it with something can be great. Consider these questions:

- Do you use vocalized pauses: "uh," "um," "err"?
- Do you fill pauses with other nonspeech sounds: lip smacking, tongue clicking, throat clearing, snuffling?
- Do you unconsciously insert a giggle after every sentence?
- Do you repeat to excess certain words or phrases in nonsensical places?

Here is a list of words and phrases that lose their original meanings when allowed to spread cancerlike throughout a speech:

okay?

y'know

see

like

I mean

or whatever

and so on and so forth

et cetera

in other words

you might say

4 Identify repetitious patterns of inflection

While growing up and listening to other people, you learn very early that there are logical and natural places in sentences to vary the pitch of your voice. For instance, in English, your voice usually goes higher in pitch at the end of a question or deepens for an emphatic statement. In normal conversation, we use a variety of inflections without having to think about it. In public speaking, however, there can be a tendency to deliver every sentence with the same inflectional pattern regardless of the sentence's meaning or grammatical structure. This happens when the speaker is not thinking about the content of the speech, is nervous, or is reading from a manuscript or recalling a memorized text. A singsongy, hypnotic pattern of inflection can easily lead to drooping eyelids in the audience.

5 Employ a systematic self-improvement program or get professional help

Self-improvement When you identify a problem and your motivation to correct it is strong, you may devise a simple plan of action. Books and recordings are available to provide exercises in breathing and projection. These also have exercises, like tongue twisters, that make apparent the muscle groups used to produce certain sounds properly. You can start with such books as these:

Hahner, Jeffrey C., Martin A. Sokoloff, and Sandra L. Salisch. *Speaking Clearly: Improving Voice and Diction*, 6th ed. (with pronunciation CD-ROM). New York: McGraw-Hill, 2002.

Modisett, Noah F., and James G. Luter, Jr. *Speaking Clearly: The Basics of Voice and Articulation*, 4th ed. Minneapolis: Burgess, 1996.

Wells, Lynn K. *The Articulate Voice*, 4th ed. Boston: Allyn & Bacon, 2004.

For a deeply ingrained habit, you may choose to map out a program of behavior modification. This approach, which has been quite successful in helping people to lose weight or quit smoking, is based on the premise that habits that develop gradually are best eliminated gradually. New behaviors are substituted for old ones, and the new behaviors are rewarded.

CHECKLIST

Steps to Behavior Modification

1. Assess your present behavior. Quantify the exact frequency of the distracting habit.

2. Set a specific, realistic goal. If you say "okay?" after nearly every sentence, perhaps 20 times in a 10-minute speech, resolve to cut down to 10 times in a 10-minute speech.

Steps to Behavior Modification

3. Monitor your behavior. Do not simply estimate your progress. Have a friend tally the occurrences, or tape each speech yourself. Keep a written chart of your progress.

Professional help Some problems of vocal delivery are difficult to diagnose or solve without professional help. In seeking help, consider the nature and seriousness of your vocal problem, as well as the time and money you are able to commit. Then consult the appropriate professional person, such as a speech therapist, a voice coach, or a public speaking consultant.

CHAPTER 35

Achieving Effective Physical Delivery

Much of how your listeners respond to you is a result of what they see rather than what they hear. Do people dismiss you because you look 10 years younger than you are? Or, your words may be confident, but do shaking knees and fidgeting fingers tell another story? Poor posture and a grim expression can reveal the lie in "I'm so happy to be here!" When practicing and delivering your speech, be aware of the visual image you are creating. Correct false impressions. As with vocal delivery, the goal is to be natural and to avoid any actions that will distract your audience from your message.

35a. Be conscious of your appearance

As you get ready for a particular speech, consider what your hairstyle, grooming, and clothing might communicate to your audience. You should show that you took care in preparing, that you consider the event important enough to expend some energy in trying to look good.

Ideally, your clothes should provide a tasteful and unobtrusive frame for your personality and your remarks. Be aware of regional, cultural, and occupational norms. There is no need to be drab, but remember that your audience could be distracted by gaudy colors, busy patterns, eye-catching jewelry, unorthodox combinations of apparel, and any clothing they associate with seduction or courtship.

35b. Eliminate distracting mannerisms

Distracting mannerisms fall into two categories: those you have all the time (tucking your hair behind your ear, cracking your knuckles), and those you have only when giving a speech (noisily fanning and squaring up your notecards, rocking back and forth on your heels). Few acts are inherently distracting—it is the repetition of some act that becomes distracting. As with vocal mannerisms, you are probably unaware of the frequency of the act until someone points it out. Thus, the biggest step toward eliminating the problem is becoming aware of it. Sometimes this awareness is sufficient to resolve it, or you may want to adapt the behavior modification techniques described in **34d.5**.

35c. Stand or sit with a relaxed but alert posture

As a general rule, you should stand when speaking. This focuses audience attention on you and gives you a better view of your listeners.

There are exceptions, of course—as a member of a panel discussion, you may be constrained to follow the sedentary lead of the moderator. If, however, you can learn to be comfortable speaking without a lectern—with your weight evenly distributed, your notes grasped casually in one hand at waist level, and no props of any kind for support—then you can easily adapt to any setting. Appropriate variations might include leaning across the lectern to show deep involvement or sitting on the edge of a desk or table to signal the shift to an informal mood. Draping yourself across the lectern, lounging at the side with one elbow extended, or standing in an off-center posture are incompatible with the energetic and controlled image of a polished public speaker.

35d. Make only purposeful and relevant movements

You can give a perfectly good and proper speech standing behind a lectern. However, most speeches can be aided by movement at appropriate times. Taking a few steps to the left or right or moving closer to your listeners can add variety and emphasis to your speech. You also establish contact with the segment of the audience that you move toward. Moreover, physical movement during a speech is a constructive way to release tension.

Make your movements purposeful. Pacing nervously around the room is distracting. If you are going to move at all, be decisive. Take at least two or three normal paces diagonally or directly forward.

The timing of your movement can reinforce your ideas. Generally, it is not effective to move around when explaining complex material or when delivering your most emotional examples or powerful arguments. Physical movement works best at transitional points, where it signals a change in mood, content, or form.

35e. Keep your hands free for natural gestures

What you should do with your hands in a speech is exactly what you do with them in normal conversation. For some people, using their hands in this manner means hardly using them at all. For others, it means gesturing a great deal. Whether you gesture a little or a lot, you do it to describe, to point out, to enumerate, to emphasize, to entreat, and so on.

There is no need to plan what gestures go with your speech. If you are absorbed with your topic and with communicating it to your listeners, your gestures will emerge spontaneously at the appropriate points. But this will happen only if your hands are free to move. Too many speakers immobilize their hands completely, out of both the panicky need to cling to something and the desire to prevent uncontrolled movement. Do not lock yourself into any of these gesture-inhibiting stances:

The bear hug:	Arms across the chest—one of the most common ways of getting a grip on yourself
The flesh wound:	One arm hanging useless at the side, the other hand serving as a tourniquet above or below the elbow
The choirboy/girl:	Hands clasped at waist level, with fingers entwined
The fig leaf:	Demurely crossed hands, strategically placed

Actually, all of these are perfectly acceptable *transitory* postures. The problem with them lies not in the position of the limbs, but in the temptation to remain in one stance, statuelike, while concentrating on what is coming out of your mouth.

So, what *do* you do with your hands? First, do nothing distracting such as nervously shredding notecards, drumming on the table, or making other kinds of unproductive hand movements:

The Lady Macbeth:	Hands wrung compulsively and continuously to wash out the "stain" of having to speak
Happy pockets:	Keys, change, and other pocket articles set to jingling by restless hands, the sound competing with the speaker's voice

Second, do nothing contrived—no rehearsed gestures. What matters most is that your arms, wrists, and fingers are relaxed so that your hands can move if you find a need for that movement arising naturally.

35f. Maintain eye contact

In any speech, even a manuscript speech, you should have eye contact 85 percent of the time, looking down only to read technical material or to refer briefly to your notes. Most important, be sure to maintain eye contact throughout your introduction and conclusion and during the most telling points and pivotal arguments.

Be familiar enough with your material that you can look at as many members of your audience as possible, as often as possible. Maintaining eye contact allows you to read your listeners' faces to get feedback on how your message is being received. Advice to fake eye contact by looking between heads or just over the heads of the people in the back row misses the whole point.

Actually look into the eyes of the individual audience members and hold that contact for at least three seconds. Do not skim across rows of faces. Move your eye contact randomly throughout the room. Do not fall into a head-bobbing pattern: left, center, right, center, left . . .

> **KEY POINT**   **The Smile**   The *one* expression that has the same meaning in every culture is the smile. Most public speakers underuse or misuse this powerful tool. A constant, fixed, jaw-aching grin is as bad as a deadpan expression. A smile at a sad or serious moment is inappropriate. However, remind yourself to smile genuinely whenever it can reinforce your message. It is one of the easiest ways to establish rapport, show your goodwill, and put you and your audience at ease.

CHAPTER 36

Using Your Presentation Aids

Whether discrete or continuous, hand-held or projected, seen or heard, your presentation aids should be a seamless part of your speech, not an interruption. Choosing appropriate aids that supplement and augment your points will go a long way toward easing this blending (see **27**). Beyond the structural appropriateness of the aid or aids you select, there are a few simple things you can do to smooth your aids' introduction.

36a. Practice with your aids

Your aids should be prepared early enough that you can practice with them several times. (See **33b.3**.) This will alert you to any changes that might be necessary. Become comfortable with them so that you do not fumble around during the presentation.

36b. Have your aid ready to go

For audio aids, have the tape or CD cued to the spot so you have only to press a button. If you are projecting off a computer, have the program launched and the file(s) open. Don't subject your audience to a navigation exhibition through your folder structure.

36c. Maintain eye contact

Be so familiar with your material that you can look at your listeners while explaining a visual aid. Often, a speaker will turn away from the audience and talk directly at the visual aid. This deprives the speaker of feedback and strains the listeners' hearing.

36d. Keep talking while using visual aids

Avoid long pauses when demonstrating a process. If there is some complexity, or if many steps are needed to produce your desired result, you might take a hint from television cooking shows and prepare a series of aids to demonstrate the various phases. Doing so will eliminate those periods when both you and the audience are waiting for something to happen. For example, a speaker could say, "Then you apply glue to the two blocks, press them together like this, and let the bond dry. Here are some that have already dried. Now, I'll show you the next step. . . ." When you cannot avoid a time lag introduced by some process, have a planned digression—some bit of history related to the process, perhaps—to fill the gap.

36e. Do not become secondary to your slides

It is a common scene in conference and convention settings: One or two large screens dominate a room holding dozens or hundreds of people; dwarfed by the screens, a speaker is partially hidden behind a bank of computer monitors, hunched over in the dim light, clicking away at the mouse while talking into the body mike, and often commenting on some glitch with the system. Obvious problems here are lack of connection with the audience because of the darkened room and the focus on the machine, confinement of the speaker to the space in front of the computer, and the "aid" becoming an impediment.

  If you are in a situation in which this sort of projection will be used, take steps to counteract the potential difficulties. Enlist a colleague or friend to operate the computer so that you are free to move around and make eye contact with the audience. If you cannot avoid operating the equipment, or if you must compensate for dim lighting, use vocal variety to counterbalance immobility and lack of visibility. (See **34b**.) If possible, use the slides for key illustrations and points, but leave the screen blank the rest of the time.

36f. Do not let your aids become a distraction

Keep your visual aids out of sight, turned off, covered, or turned away from your audience until you are ready to use them. Remove or recover them immediately after they have served their purpose. If you are using an overhead projector or similar device, turn it off whenever you can to eliminate the cooling fan noise. For a continuous visual aid like a PowerPoint presentation of charts and graphs that support particular points, introduce a blank slide between each content slide. When you have finished addressing the point related to one of the content slides, move to the blank slide until it is time to reveal the next content slide as you get to the point it illustrates. If you use a flip chart, use every other sheet when you are preparing it—this gives you the same effect as the blank slide, and you should use it in the same way.

Refrain from passing objects around the room; it will cause a ripple of inattention. This rule is flexible, especially when you are dealing with an unusual object and a small audience, but still it is probably best to share the item *after* the speech—say, during the discussion period. By the same token, handouts should be distributed after a speech. You want the audience to listen now and read later. (Of course, there are some contexts, primarily business, where this is not necessarily the norm. See **7**.)

Finally, presentation aids are most distracting when you are clumsy with them. Be sure that your charts are in the right order, your models are set up, and your equipment is in perfect working order.

KEY POINT   **Avoiding Presentation Aid Fiascoes** Practice carefully, arrive in plenty of time for setup, and bring interface cables, pins, tape, extension cords, extra projector bulbs, CD-ROM backups, and the like to ensure that what you envision comes to pass.

If you are using electronic aids, find the outlets in the room and actually test both your aids and the outlets for proper functioning. If you are being provided with equipment, insist that it come with spare bulbs, batteries, and so on. If you are using a computer, make sure it is compatible with the projection system.

CHAPTER 37

Answering Questions

The question-and-answer period is a great opportunity to further the goals of your speech. While you spoke, you attempted to address the needs of your audience, and now you can see how close you came. From your listeners' questions, you can learn what points are unclear or what arguments and objections they have. Communicate an eagerness to interact with your listeners and to hear their ideas on your topic.

Do not lose your delivery skills just because the speech is over. Maintain eye contact, and avoid fidgeting or mumbling.

37a. Come prepared for a question-and-answer period

Keep in mind the importance of the question-and-answer period throughout the stages of preparing your speech. Anticipate the questions that will arise naturally from each of your points. One aid to this is to have the friends who listen to your practice sessions ask you questions afterward. Although you can never predict the exact questions that will come up, certain ones are more probable than others. Rehearse aloud possible answers to the most complicated and difficult ones. This is how public figures prepare for news conferences.

Ideally, your research has been so extensive that you have much more material than you were able to use, and you have reviewed this extra material so you are familiar enough with the content to use it in response to questions.

37b. Invite questions and be direct in your answers

Do not worry if there are not any questions immediately, or if at first there are long pauses between questions. It usually takes your listeners a moment to collect their thoughts. In some cases, you can start the ball rolling yourself by asking a question of the audience.

Call on questioners in the order they sought recognition, and maintain eye contact while the question is being asked. If you are not sure you understand the question, paraphrase it according to your own interpretation and ask the questioner if it is accurate. When both of you are satisfied, restate or paraphrase it for the entire audience and direct the answer to them.

Be sure you *answer* the question. To avoid oversimplification, you want to elaborate, expand, or qualify your answer, but if your discussion becomes too diffuse, you will appear to be avoiding the issue. Consequently, always include a one-sentence, direct answer in your response to a question. For emphasis, place this sentence first or last, as in these examples:

First: *Yes, I do oppose building nuclear power plants*, at least until several safety questions are answered satisfactorily. My reasons include . . .

Last: . . . so, because of all these serious problems I see, my answer to your question would be *Yes, I do oppose building new nuclear power plants at this time.*

37c. Manage self-indulgent questioners

The purpose of a question-and-answer period is to clarify issues for the entire audience. When individual audience members attempt to use this time for detailed consultation on a specialized problem or to get on their favorite soapbox, you have an obligation as speaker to bring the interaction back on its true course. Be prepared to keep control of the situation by dealing in a firm and tactful manner with several types of distracting questioners.

- *The person who wants to give a speech.* This person may agree or disagree with you, or may have a favorite ax to grind that is only tangentially related to your topic. It becomes obvious that, rather than asking a real question, the person is taking advantage of an assembled audience to hold forth. It is rarely effective to ask, "What is your question?" The person will just say, "Don't you agree that . . ." or "What do you think of the position that . . ." and take off for another five minutes. You have to jump in at the end of a sentence, manufacture a question somewhat related to the person's ramblings, answer it, and recognize another questioner on the opposite side of the room.

- *The person who wants to have an extended dialogue.* This person might begin with a genuine question but, after you respond, may refuse to relinquish the floor by countering with follow-up questions, commenting on your answer, or opening new lines of discussion. The best way to deal with this sort of person is to end the exchange firmly but with a compliment: "Thank you, you've given me quite a number of interesting insights here."

- *The person who wants to pick a fight.* Intellectual confrontation and probing, penetrating questions are to be expected, and even welcomed, from audience members who disagree with you. But sometimes questioners become inappropriately argumentative and mount hostile, personal attacks against a speaker. Rather than seeking an answer to a question they are trying to destroy your credibility. Do not let them succeed by becoming angry or by defending yourself against generalized name-calling. Pick out the part of such a person's diatribe that contains the kernel of a question, paraphrase it, and answer it calmly and reasonably.

Q: What about all this poisonous junk that you greed-crazed despoilers dump into our rivers to kill our children and whole species of animals?

A: The questioner has brought up the valid and difficult subject of toxic waste disposal. What is our company doing about it? Well . . .

In short, respond to these disruptive people diplomatically. Do not take cheap shots or direct humor at them to shut them off.

Likewise, when you are taken aback by incomprehensible questions or questions that demonstrate gross ignorance or misinformation, you should react positively. Avoid language that embarrasses the questioner or points out errors:

Not: You've totally confused fission and fusion!

But: Many of those problems relate to nuclear *fission*. The *fusion* reaction is quite different. It works like this. . . .

Try to find ways to dignify bad questions and turn them into good ones. Your listeners' empathy is with the questioner, who may be nervous or confused. Your efforts to put others at ease will earn you an audience's goodwill.

APPENDIX A

A Sample Speech and Outlines

This appendix contains a sample persuasive speech and the outline used in creating it, as well as a sample outline for an informative speech—the "comic book outline" referred to in various chapters of this compact handbook. Annotated versions of these materials are available on the *The Speaker's Compact Handbook* website.

A. Sample persuasive speech transcript

In a persuasive speaking course, students were required to develop a 10-minute persuasive message that was adapted to the specific audience in the class. The speaker had given previous speeches on environmental topics to this class. Based on that experience and through an audience survey she concluded that her listeners were generally favorably disposed to these issues but were not extremely well informed.

Rainforests Are in Need of Defense

by Karen McNeil

"Save the Rainforest!" But for what and from whom? The rainforest issue has had great media coverage, and we are all too familiar with this slogan. I'm not sure, though, that we're actually aware of what is at stake. I know I wasn't, even being really concerned about the environmental issues that face this planet, until I came across the orangutan. I'm an anthropology minor, and this semester I'm taking a class that details the habitats of primates. This is where I got to know more about orangutans, the threats they face, and what it means to the rest of us.

Do you know where orangutans live? In the wild, these great apes live on two Indonesian islands: Borneo and Sumatra. Their habitat is exclusively tropical rainforest. They are frugivorous, which means that they rely on fruit as their source of nutrition. Because of this, they need a wide range of habitat to provide them with fruit year-round. Orangutans used to free-range in Southeast Asia, but development has pushed them out of these areas. The primary threat to these animals is habitat destruction—destruction of the tropical rainforests. I was alarmed to see that almost all of the primates live exclusively in tropical rainforests. Suddenly I had a new perspective on what we stand to lose as we continue to destroy these tropical zones.

These, then, are the questions that I want to address today: What are we saving when we save the rainforests? Who are we saving them from? What can we do that can actually make a difference?

First, I'll briefly outline the threats to the ecology of the rainforest and then detail some of the investment policies of the World Bank, which is the institution that contributes to major destruction of the tropical rainforests. And then finally I have some suggestions for what you can do to ensure the well-being of our planet.

To understand the seriousness of the current threat to the rainforests, we need to recognize what they represent ecologically, culturally, and economically. These elaborate ecosystems are a kaleidoscope of biological diversity. The vegetation in these towering forests is divided into dozens of layers, each of which provides a distinct habitat for different plants and animals, literally thousands of species. Within the tropical belt that circles the equator there exist more plant and animal species than in the rest of the world combined! The rainforests are also home to millions of indigenous people. Thousands of tribal groups exist in rainforests throughout the world. Most of these peoples live as hunters and gatherers or they conduct small agricultural projects that fit the cycle of the land. Their centuries-old cultural practices have grown up in harmony with their environment. Another value of the rainforests is the important role they play in our weather patterns, both locally and globally. In fact, they are often referred to as the lungs of our planet. Economically, these regions are a bountiful source of rubber, hardwood, food products, and essential medicines for heart disease and cancer.

Although lush, these ecosystems are really quite fragile. Similar to the old-growth forests that run from the northern part of our state up through the Pacific Northwest, these interdependent biological systems took centuries to develop. Without the constant renewal of the protective overgrowth and dense canopies the inhabitants of the lower levels—plants, animals, birds—die from exposure to the sun. The laterite soil on which the forests are built turns to clay and erodes quickly when cleared, as many farmers and ranchers are beginning to discover. Topsoil is swept away by floods. Sediment flows into the rivers and affects fishing. Most of the damage is irreversible. You can see why deforestation for farming, ranching, and logging has such a devastating effect.

Yet it goes on, and worsens, even as we speak. To give you some sense of the scope and urgency of the situation, let me cite some statistics from *The Rainforest Book* by Scott Lewis. Half of the earth's rainforests have already been destroyed. Thirty-five million acres a year are eliminated. That's an area the size of New York State gone forever. The rates of deforestation have doubled in the last decade and they are continuing to rise. In the name of progress, the industrialized Western world destroys these irreplaceable plants and animals. It alters the environment of the region and the climate of the world. It wipes out indigenous cultures of rainforest peoples without even realizing the rich traditions that they have to offer us. These tribal people are not in a position to resist change that others define as progress. Imagine what it would be like if you had to defend your own home against lawyers of a multinational logging firm. Would you have any chance of winning? If it would be an uphill fight for someone like you, think what it would be like for someone from a community that has no grounding in Western-style law and that has no connection to the Western economic system.

Profits are the major factor that lead to rainforest destruction. My next point highlights the destructive investment practices that lead to environmental ruin. One investment institution that can be credited with funding a majority of the environmental devastation is the World Bank. After World War II the world community assembled the World Bank to help war-torn countries rebuild. After they completed that work, they turned to the Third World. The Rainforest Action Network of San Francisco argues that the World Bank has turned the Third World into a resource colony for the Western industrialized nations. The World Bank has become a power that dictates what's developed and created by countries, and also even at times how governments treat their own people. The World Bank is an organization that is funded by money that is borrowed on international markets and also money contributed by 148 member nations. The United States is the most influential of these members. We have 20 percent of the overall vote. The president of the World Bank, Barber C. Conable, is a United States citizen. U.S. members of the World Bank are given direction by the United States Department of Treasury and the Congress. The money the United States supplies to the World Bank comes from the taxpayers. The World Bank prefers to finance huge megaprojects: hydroelectric dams, massive relocations and resettlements, agricultural and industrial projects that involve building roads into areas that have previously been inaccessible. Bruce Rich of the Environmental Defense Fund states that over half of the loans given by the World Bank and its three regional counterparts in recent years have gone to support projects in sectors that can seriously affect tropical forests. Survival International, an organization that advocates the rights of tribal people and serves as a watchdog of the World Bank, makes these recommendations for the bank's reform. First, they want public access to all information regarding the bank's projects. They want the World Bank's staff to include people that are trained in ecology as well as in socioeconomic analysis. Systematic involvement of organizations representing the environment and indigenous people should be a part of all projects. The bank should increase its proportion of ecologically beneficial programs. These Survival International recommendations reflect their analysis that the World Bank has been developing projects solely on economic criteria without regarding or understanding the environmental effects of their actions. If you're shocked that these practices continue, and with our country's support, I'm glad. I want you to see how important it is that we understand these issues. I have some recommendations that I want you to consider adopting in your own lives.

My suggestions begin with learning more about this complex problem and then taking action both individually and collectively. Education is the key to bringing about change. Read some of the books that discuss the rainforest. Here is one concise (and inexpensive) one: *The Rainforest Book* by Scott Lewis, published in 1990. Share your knowledge about environmental subjects with children and support them as they try to make sense of these issues. Take some classes that are offered here at San Jose State that promote a global perspective on environmental issues. For instance, I know that many of you are communication studies majors or minors. You might be especially interested in a course that Dr. Dennis Jaehne will be offering next fall called Communication and the Environment. I took it the first time it was offered and it was excellent! Whenever you possibly can, travel to other countries and see for yourself what's going on. I've traveled four times around the world, and I wouldn't trade those experiences for anything. It's one thing to understand intellectually that our industrially advanced lifestyle and Western values are not universal. But it becomes meaningful in a different way when you have the chance to experience firsthand the incredible diversity of this planet. You realize how privileged we are in terms of material goods and political freedom. Yet you also see that there are places in this world of unbelievable physical beauty and cultures of such depth and richness that they must be preserved and cherished. Travel, especially off the beaten path of the usual tourist spots, really dramatizes the choices before those of us who live in rich and powerful societies. We can either expand our consumerism more and more by exploiting other parts of the world or we can start evaluating the impact of our economic policies on the rest of the world. Through education, as you continue to learn about how we are all complicit in the problems of the rainforest, you will want to take some direct action. There are several ways to do this.

First, you can boycott products that are known to cause destruction of the rainforest. A typical four-ounce fastfood hamburger that's been made from "rainforest beef" took 55 square feet of rainforest to produce. Is one hamburger worth that destruction? We can insist on clearer labeling of meat so that we know where it comes from. Disposable chopsticks are oftentimes made from tropical timber, or in some cases whole stands of rainforest are cleared to plant trees that produce a color of wood more popular for chopsticks. In 1979 Japan used enough disposable chopsticks to build 11,000 timber-frame family dwellings. You can imagine what those statistics would be today. You may not use many chopsticks, but you can be aware of the exotic wood products that are being stripped from these regions. I've included a list of these woods on a handout that I'll give you in a few minutes.

Next, you can support organizations that are involved with saving the rainforest. I've listed several of them on the same handout. It is only through collective action in organized groups like these that we have any chance of influencing the policies of government and of the World Bank. The decision makers will continue to listen to business interests unless we show them how many of us there are that value long-term social and environmental goals over short-term material gains.

Finally, I encourage you all to stop by the Art Quad before three o'clock today and buy a scoop of Rainforest Crunch ice cream. Representatives of Ben & Jerry's Ice Cream are going to be here today, and they are going to donate the proceeds of the ice cream sales to SAFER, Students Affiliated for Environmental Respect, the campus environmental group. Rainforest Crunch is made from Brazil nuts, thus making it advantageous for the trees in at least one rainforest to be left standing. You'll find the address of the Rainforest Action Network printed on every carton of Rainforest Crunch they sell. This is just one example of how business organizations can take steps to be socially responsible while still making a profit and offering a quality product.

Since I began this presentation, 1,000 acres of rainforest have been destroyed or degraded severely. These fragile ecosystems need to be protected; once they're destroyed they're gone forever. My studies about the primates intensified my interest in the rainforest because I realized how fragile they are and that these precious creatures have become very close to extinction. It isn't the Brazilian or Malaysian or Indonesian farmers who pose the real threat to these areas. It is the governments of the developed countries in cooperation with multinational development banks that initiate large projects and create real havoc in these areas. As Americans we contribute to the problem in a number of ways. As we drive the world market through our obsessive consumption, we entangle developing nations in outrageous debts. As American taxpayers we're helping to fund the World Bank's destructive policies through the taxes we pay. There are other organizations worldwide that we could support, groups that are committed to grassroots development. These smaller projects often are far more beneficial to the local people in other countries. The only way that we can hope to get a realistic picture of this problem is through education and involvement. We can no longer afford to think merely on a local or national level. We must learn to think on a global level and feel that the well-being of humanity and this planet is a responsibility we all share. Although the problem is a huge one, we as individuals should not feel powerless. By taking even a small step, you can begin to make a difference. Please, don't wait. Take a step now.

B. Sample persuasive speech outline

Here is a sample speech outline for the preceding speech. This is just one illustration of the sort of speech outline that helps a speaker get organized. Some outlines are more spare and compact, and others are more like argumentative briefs containing full citations of all evidence.

Notice that the main points listed here are never stated in precisely those words in the speech transcription. The outline is a logical plan, a place to set down your main points in propositional form, to fit the subpoints beneath the main points, and fit your support beneath the subpoints. Uncluttered with transitions and extra words, and properly indented, the outline allows the reader to see the basic speech development at a glance.

Along with the outline of the body of the speech, we include the thesis sentence and identify the text that delineates the parts of the introduction (attention getter, psychological orientation, logical orientation) and conclusion (logical closure, psychological closure, clincher).

Thesis The continuing and accelerating destruction of the tropical rainforests, due largely to the policies of industrialized nations, poses a serious threat to the global environment and community—a threat that must be met by immediate action from concerned individuals.

Introduction

Attention Getter "Save the Rainforest!" But for what and from whom? . . . what is at stake.

Psychological Orientation I know I wasn't, even being really concerned about the environmental issues . . . we continue to destroy these tropical zones.

Logical Orientation These, then, are the questions that I want to address today . . . well-being of our planet.

Body

    I. Tropical rainforests, important to the well-being of the planet, are being subjected to rampant destruction, with irreversible effects.

        A. Rainforests are an important component of the planet.

            1. Ecologically complex systems

                a. Towering forests divided into layers

                b. More plant and animal species than rest of world

            2. Thousands of tribal groups live there.

                a. Hunters and gatherers/small agriculture

                b. Irreplaceable ancient cultures

            3. Rainforests affect weather patterns.

4. Economically important
    a. Rubber, hardwood, food products
    b. Medicines for heart disease and cancer

B. Rainforests are in serious danger.
  1. They are fragile.
    a. Need dense canopies to protect inhabitants of lower layers
    b. When exposed, laterite soil turns to clay, erodes
    c. Topsoil swept away, affects rivers
    d. Damage is irreversible
  2. Rainforests are being destroyed.
    a. By farming, logging, ranching
    b. Half of world's rainforests already gone
    c. 35 million acres a year, size of New York
    d. Rate of destruction is doubling
    e. Tribal people powerless to resist

II. Short-sighted economic policies of the industrially advanced countries, carried out through multilateral development agencies like the World Bank, are responsible for the destruction.

A. The World Bank's policies tend to serve the industrialized nations.
  1. History
    a. Formed to rebuild after WWII
    b. Later took on Third World development
  2. U.S. plays major role in the World Bank's policies
    a. Of the 148 member nations, U.S. funds 20 percent
    b. President, Barber C. Conable, is U.S. citizen
    c. Directed by U.S. Department of Treasury and Congress

B. World Bank policies are destructive to the rainforests.
  1. Tends to fund huge projects such as hydroelectric dams
  2. Half of its loans have gone to projects that endanger rainforests

C. Reforms of World Bank have been suggested.
  1. Public access to records
  2. Staff should include ecologists
  3. Should collaborate with environmental organizations and representatives of indigenous peoples
  4. Should consider more than economic criteria in selecting projects

III. Concerned individuals can help save the rainforests through education and collective action.

A. Education is a key to saving the rainforests.
  1. Read books
  2. Educate children

      3. Take courses

      4. Travel

    B. Boycott products that cause destruction to rainforests.

      1. Need to label meat so we can tell if it is "rainforest beef"

      2. Wood from tropical lumber

        a. Chopsticks from light wood could have built 11,000 houses

        b. List of exotic woods to avoid will be on handout

    C. Support organizations to save the rainforests.

      1. Several national and international groups listed on handout

      2. Campus organization SAFER

        a. Ice cream social today until three at Art Quad

        b. Ben & Jerry's Rainforest Crunch saves nut trees

Conclusion

Logical Closure Since I began this presentation, . . . education and involvement.

Psychological Closure We can no longer afford to think merely . . . not feel powerless.

Clincher By taking even a small step, you can begin to make a difference. Please, don't wait. Take a step now.

C. Sample informative speech outline

Thesis Statement With their scope, history, and influence, comic books are an interesting component of American popular culture.

  I. Comic books are not merely "comic," but rather explore a range of subject matter.

    A. Funny animal comics and kid comics are parables and parodies of the human condition.

      1. Elmer Fudd and Bugs: Tradition versus the pioneering spirit.

      2. Barks's ducks: Epic adventure and human foibles.

      3. Harvey's rich kids: Capitalism with a human face.

    B. True-love and teen comics present a hackneyed, boring, and sometimes disturbing picture of male/female relationships.

      1. True-love girl meets, loses, gets, marries boy (and vows never to be so stupid as to put her needs above his again).

      2. Teen comic girl fights other girls for the favors of a jerk male like Archie, who her father thinks is a twerp.

3. True-love and teen comics foster the "us versus them" view of the male/female world.

C. Western and adventure comics concentrate on the triumph of good over evil.

1. Western cattle barons learn that six-gun-slinging saviors arise naturally from oppressed common folk.

2. Adventure stories pit virtuous types against the blind malice of uncaring nature.

D. Horror and mystery comics investigate ethics and morality while titillating and scaring readers.

1. Eternal punishment for an unethical choice is a recurring theme of horror comics.

2. The tempting hedonism of wrongdoers is graphically displayed in mystery comics—until the ironic twist of fate on the last page.

E. Superhero comics manifest the unspoken and sometimes frightening fantasies and aspirations of the American people.

1. Superman is the supremely powerful spokesman and policeman for the American definition of the "right way."

2. The jackbooted hero, Blackhawk, was created in World War II to fight totalitarian fire with fire.

3. Mar-Vell personifies the desire for total knowledge and the wisdom needed to use it.

4. Spider-Man is the embodiment of the perennial underdog triumphant.

II. Comic books started as anthologies of another medium but soon grew into a separate art form developing along a path of its own.

A. Early comic books were mostly reprints of Sunday newspaper comic strip sections.

1. "Foxy Granpa" was reprinted in a number of comic books just after the turn of the century.

2. The following decades saw strips like "Mutt & Jeff," "Little Orphan Annie," and "Moon Mullins" reprinted.

3. Reprint books in the thirties included such titles as "Tarzan" in Tip Top Comics and "Terry and the Pirates" in Popular Comics.

B. By 1938, the majority of comic books contained original work, and, with the appearance of Superman, the golden age of comics began.

1. Detective Comics was the first single-theme, all-original comic.

2. Superman, the first costumed superhero, was featured in Action no. 1.

3. More than 150 titles were in print by the end of 1941.

C. During the decade after the war, comic books for the most part went into a slump.
   1. With the Axis powers defeated and the Cold War not yet focused, the perceived need for superheroes lessened, and the sales of their books slacked off.
   2. Many horror, mystery, superhero, adventure, true-love, and teen comics fell before the wave of censorship following the publication of *Seduction of the Innocent.*
   3. Funny animal comics and kid comics retrenched behind the strongest series.
D. By the late fifties, comic books had started to recover, overcoming their tarnished image.
   1. In creating the Comics Code Authority, publishers hoped to reassure worried parents and legislators.
   2. The silver age of comics began with the reintroduction of long-idle golden age characters.
E. In the early sixties the trend toward emphasizing characterization, motivation, and involvement with issues initiated a new and still-developing era in superhero comics, the effects of which were eventually felt in the other comic genres.
   1. The Fantastic Four, Spider-Man, and the Hulk were the first fallible and self-questioning superheroes.
   2. Comic books became accepted by a wider, more literate audience.
   3. Concern with ethical and even political questions became more evident, even in kid comics and funny animal comics.
III. Comic books have an effect beyond their entertainment value.
   A. Comic books are a unique and vigorous art form.
      1. Comic books have developed exciting and innovative methods for transcending the static nature of the panel format (series of distinct pictures across and down the page) to produce a sense of motion and drama.
      2. The art of comics is not confined to the work within a single panel, but also touches the arrangement of panels on a page.
      [as a result]
   B. Comic books can be seen to influence other media.
      1. Many filmmakers' use of split screens and quick cuts demonstrates a stylistic adaptation of the comic panel format.
      2. Camp and pop art drew heavily on comic book themes and styles.
      [and as a result]

C. Comic books are in demand with collectors.
   1. Some issues of rare comics can bring prices in the thousands of dollars.
   2. Every year there are many large conventions around the United States where comics can be bought, sold, and traded.

APPENDIX B
Citation Guidelines

Two standard formats for citing references in reference lists or other collateral materials are "APA style" as set out in the *Publication Manual of the American Psychological Association,* and "MLA style" as set out in the *MLA Handbook for Writers of Research Papers.* See **16d.** The following table shows a sampling of 13 types of reference citation for both print and nonprint sources done in both styles.

TABLE 8-2
Selected Reference List Entries in APA and MLA Styles

Print Sources

Publication Manual of the APA	*MLA Handbook*
Book, single author	
Lastname, A. A. (date). *Title of work.* City: Publisher.	Lastname, Firstname. Title of Work. City: Publisher, date.
Pagels, E. (1995). *The origin of Satan.* New York: Random House.	Pagels, Elaine. The Origin of Satan. New York: Random House, 1995.
Book, two authors	
Lastname, A. A., & Lastname, B. B. (date). *Title of work.* City: Publisher.	Lastname, Firstname, and Firstname Lastname. Title of Work. City: Publisher, date.
Crossan, J. D., & Reed, J. L. (2001). *Excavating Jesus: Beneath the stones, behind the texts.* San Francisco: HarperSanFrancisco.	Crossan, John Dominic, and Jonathan L. Reed. Excavating Jesus: Beneath the Stones, Behind the Texts. San Francisco: Harper, 2001.
Book, edited	
Lastname, A. A. (Ed.). (Date). *Title of work.* City: Publisher.	Lastname, Firstname, ed. Title of Work. City: Publisher, date.
Smiley, J., & Kenison, K. (Eds.). (1995). *The best American short stories 1995.* Boston: Houghton.	Smiley, Jane, ed., and Katrina Kenison, series ed. The Best American Short Stories 1995. Boston: Houghton, 1995.
Book, no author or editor (anonymous)	
Title. (Edition.). (date). City: Publisher.	Title. Edition [if any]. City: Publisher, date.
The New York City Public Library Desk Reference. (3rd ed.). (1998). New York: Macmillan.	The New York City Public Library Desk Reference. 3rd ed. New York: Macmillan, 1998.
Periodical, journal	
Lastname, A. A. (date). Title of article. Periodical, volume, pages.	Lastname, Firstname. "Title of Article." Periodical volume (date): pages.
Hughes, M. (2002). Moving from information transfer to knowledge creation: A new value proposition for technical communicators. *Technical Communication, 49,* 257–285.	Hughes, Michael. "Moving from Information Transfer to Knowledge Creation: A New Value Proposition for Technical Communicators." Technical Communication 49 (2002): 257–285.

Publication Manual of the APA	MLA Handbook

Periodical, magazine

Lastname, A. A. (date). Title of article. *Periodical,* volume, pages.

Lastname, Firstname. "Title of Article." *Periodical* date: pages.

Schoenfeld, S. (1997, May/June). An experience in culture. *Timeline, 33,* 3–4.

Schoenfeld, Samantha. "An Experience in Culture." *Timeline* May–June 1997: 3–4.

Newspaper

Lastname, A. A. (date). Title of article. *Newspaper* [add city in brackets if necessary], pages.

Lastname, Firstname. "Title of Article." *Newspaper* date [edition, if named]: pages.

Guido, M. (2003, September 11). Lawmakers seek to plug loophole: Chipmakers got refunds but paid no tax to state. *San Jose Mercury News*, pp. C1–2.

Guido, Michelle. "Lawmakers Seek to Plug Loophole: Chipmakers Got Refunds but Paid No Tax to State." *San Jose Mercury News* 11 Sep. 2003, Peninsula/SF ed., C1–2.

Nonprint Sources

Television series (single episode)

Writername, A. A. & Directorname, A. A. (date). Title of episode. In Producername, A. A. *Series title*. City: Station/Network.

"Episode." *Series*. Narrator/Producer. Director. Network, Station, City. Date.

Ward, G. C. (Writer) & Burns, K. (Director). (2001). Gumbo [Television series episode]. In K. Burns & L. Novick (Producers). *Jazz*. Washington, DC: WETA.

"Gumbo." *Jazz*. Narr. Keith David. Dir. Ken Burns. PBS, WETA, Washington DC. 8 Jan. 2001.

Internet document (nonperiodical, no author)

Organization publishing website. (date). Document title in *Section*. Retrieved date from address

"Document Title." *Site*. Date. Organization publishing site. Date of retrieval <address>

League of American Bicyclists. (n.d.). How to commute by bicycle. *Better bicycling fact sheets*. Retrieved September 10, 2003 from http://www.bikeleague.org/educenter/factsheets/commuteemployee.htm

"How to Commute by Bicycle." *League of American Bicyclists*. 2003. League of American Bicyclists. 10 Sep. 2003 <http://www.bikeleague.org/educenter/factsheets/commuteemployee.htm>

Internet periodical (newsletter)

Lastname, A. (date). Title of article. *Publication*. Retrieved date from address

Lastname, Firstname. "Title of Article." *Publication* Date. Date of retrieval <address>

Hansen, S. (2003, June 4). For poorer or for poorer: For young couples trying to start a new life together, the dismal economy means more fighting, postponed weddings—and less sex. *Salon*. Retrieved September 10, 2003 from http://www.salon.com/mwt/feature/2003/06/04/couples/index.html

Hansen, Suzy. "For Poorer Or For Poorer: For Young Couples Trying To Start a New Life Together, The Dismal Economy Means More Fighting, Postponed Weddings—And Less Sex." *Salon* 4 June 2003. 10 Sep. 2003 <http://www.salon.com/mwt/feature/2003/06/04/couples/index.html>

Publication Manual of the APA	*MLA Handbook*

Message posted to online forum

[Only if forum threads are archived, otherwise considered personal communication not included in reference list.]

Lastname, A. A./Screenname (date). Subject line/Thread. Message posted to address.	Lastname, Firstname. "Thread/Subject Line." Online posting. date. Forum Name. date of retrieval <address>
Randya (2003, Aug. 28). Taking the lane, and not quiet about it [Msg 18]. Message posted to http://www.bikeforums.net/showthread.php?threadid=35868	Randya. "Taking the Lane, and Not Quiet About It." Online posting. 28 Aug 2003. BikeForums.net. 10 Sep. 2003 <http://www.bikeforums.net/showthread.php?threadid=35868>
E-mail (Personal communication not included in reference list.)	Lastname, Firstname. "Subject Line/Description." E-mail to Firstname Lastname. date.
	Thor, Leifur. "Info on the Design Science Initiative Project." E-mail to Doug Stuart. 2 May 2003.
Interview conducted by the speaker (Personal communication not included in reference list.)	Lastname, Firstname. Personal/Telephone/E-mail interview. Date.
	Thor, Leifur. Telephone interview. 5 May 2003.

Common Pronunciation and Usage Errors

For a speaker, pronunciation and usage errors are impediments to intelligibility and credibility. Well-reasoned points and lively descriptions can lose their impact if a mispronounced or misused word lands with a clunk to interrupt the concentration and attention of your listeners. In this appendix we list just a few of the common errors that can crop up; references at the end describe many more usage and word choice snares to which you should be alert. You can find pronunciation references in **34c2**.

Problems in Pronunciation

Word	Proper	Improper
get	get	git
just	just	jist
across	a cross	a crost
nuclear	nu clee ar	nu cyou lar
perspiration	pers pir a tion	press pir a tion
strict	strict	strick
escape	es cape	ex cape
compulsory	com pul sory	com pul so rary
recognize	rec og nize	reck a nize
library	li brar y	li berry
mischievous	mis che vous	mis chee vious
theater	THEE a ter	thee A ter
picture	pic tchure	pit chure
surprise	sur prise	sup prise
comparable	COM per able	com PARE able
larynx	lar inks	lar nix
relevant	rel a vant	rev a lant
drowned	drowned	drown ded
et cetera	et cet era	ek cet era
February	feb roo ary	feb you ary
temperature	temp per achure	temp achure
athlete	ath leet	a thuh leet
err	ur	air

Word Choice Errors

Wrong Use	Comments
adverse/averse	
"I would be adverse to adopting this plan."	Because the speaker is talking about an aversion to something, the proper adjective is "averse." When describing feelings, use averse; when describing things, use adverse, e.g., "Without restructuring, we shall end up working in adverse conditions."
alternative/alternate	
"Or, we could adopt an alternate plan."	"Alternate" means to switch back and forth between two things. In this case, the speaker should have said "alternative," meaning a second choice.
affect/effect	
"The affect of the plan could be very beneficial."	Usually "affect" is a verb. Properly, this sentence should use "effect" in its definition of "result."
bi/semi	
"Under this plan, paychecks will be distributed bimonthly on the 1st and 15th."	One should use bi for "every two" and semi for "twice a," so in this case it should be "distributed semimonthly on the 1st and 15th."
disinterested/uninterested	
"Some of you may be disinterested in the workings of this plan."	"Disinterested" means having no stake in the outcome, or neutral, as in "a disinterested third party will judge the results." If you mean "lack of interest," use "uninterested."
nonplussed/nonchalant	
"The opponents of this plan seem remarkably nonplussed in their calm acceptance of the status quo."	When one is nonplussed, one is bewildered or perplexed, not "nonchalant" or "calm."
tortuous/torturous	
"The torturous logic of the opponents of this plan is hard to fathom."	Because the speaker means "twisted or complex"—not "painful"—in this context, "tortuous" would have been the better choice.
imply/infer	
"I'm not inferring this plan will solve everything."	Imply means to suggest something that has not been stated explicitly and infer means to draw a conclusion from something not

stated explicitly. So, correct use would be either "I'm not implying this plan will solve everything," or something like, "You may have inferred that I think this plan will solve everything; that is not the case."

less/fewer

"There are less opponents to this plan than supporters."

If something can be counted in discrete units, it should be modified by "fewer" rather than "less." So, "there are fewer opponents" is correct. Note that changing to "there is less opposition than support" makes the usage correct, too.

ironic/coincidental

"It's ironic that, after working on this plan, Alexis and I discovered we both changed our original positions."

Irony is more than mere coincidence. There has to be some incongruity rising from a result that was different from the one expected. So, unless the speaker and Alexis had both vowed repeatedly that they were going to be steadfast in their original positions, a better sentence would have been, "Coincidentally, Alexis and I discovered we both changed our original positions after working on this plan."

comprise/compose

"Let's look at the three actions that comprise this plan."

A whole comprises its parts, so this sentence is backward with "comprise" in it. *Compose* or *constitute* would be correct. For "comprise" to be correct, the sentence might look like, "The plan comprises three actions; let's look at them now." Also, using "is comprised of" is not correct.

flaunt/flout

"One thing about this plan is that it makes it less easy for users to flaunt our guidelines."

"Flaunt" means to show off; "flout" means to treat with disregard or scorn. They are not interchangeable.

i.e./e.g.

"Some parts of this plan, i.e., restructuring, won't take place immediately."

This is wrong at two levels. First, i.e. is an abbreviation of the Latin *id est*, meaning "that is." It does *not* mean "for example"— that role is taken by e.g., from Latin *exempli gratia*. Second, a speaker should not use these abbreviations orally, but should use plain English "that is" and "for example" instead.

Some Grammar and Usage Problems

Wrong Use	Comments
Dangling/Misplaced Modifier	
"Having failed twice before, I wouldn't support any more attempts by the Baker committee to come up with a plan."	As constructed, this sentence makes the speaker the one who has failed twice. To be grammatically correct, and certainly less confusing, the sentence could be, "Having failed twice before, the Baker committee won't get my support for any more attempts to come up with a plan," or "I wouldn't support any more attempts by the Baker committee to come up with a plan because they have failed twice before."
Subject-Verb Agreement	
"The source of these failures are to be found in the incomplete research done."	"Of these failures" is a phrase that modifies the singular subject of the sentence, "source," and the fact that the noun in the phrase is plural has no impact on the verb. Because the subject is singular, the verb should be singular as well: "The source of these failures is to be found in . . ."
Misuse of Reflexive Pronoun	
"The people who looked over the plan were David, Carla, and myself."	"Myself" is the reflexive form of the pronoun, and the reflexive ordinarily is used only where the object of a sentence is the same as the subject ("I overworked myself on this project"), an object of a preposition that refers to the subject ("I worked on this project by myself"), or to emphasize the subject ("Although others helped with the research, I wrote the plan myself.") The sentence in this case should use the objective case for the pronoun: "The people who looked over the plan were David, Carla, and me." Be alert to the misuse of other reflexive pronouns like himself, herself, yourself, themselves.
Misuse of Pronouns in the Subjective Case	
"The composition of the Baker committee came as a surprise to Alexis and I."	"I" is reserved, as a pronoun in the subjective case, for use as the subject of a sentence, such as, "Alexis and I were surprised by the composition of the Baker committee." For a sentence in which the speaker is the object

of the verb, the objective case is appropriate: "The composition of the Baker committee came as a surprise to Alexis and me." A preposition (to, by, from, etc.) is usually a dead giveaway to use the objective case of a pronoun.

Here are two good resources for information on correct usage and word choice:

The American Heritage Book of English Usage. Boston: Houghton Mifflin, 1996.

Website: www.bartleby.com/64/

Brians, Paul. *Common Errors in English Usage.* Wilsonville, OR: William, James & Co., 2003.

Website: www.wsu.edu/~brians/errors/index.html

INDEX

References to sections of this book are printed in boldface type.

A

absolute statements, **21c(1):**105

accents, compensating for, **34a(4):**185

accuracy, of statistics, **16b(1):**79

acquaintances, as information sources, **15a(1):**75

acronyms, **22b(1):**114

action
  calling for, **23b(1):**118
  motivated sequence and, **23c(1):**121–123

adapting to speech situation
  distractions and, **2a(1):**10
  involvement techniques, **30b:**161

ad hominem fallacy, **21f(1):**110

adverse/averse, 216

affect/effect, 216

age of audience, **12b(1):**60–61

alliteration, **29d(2):**158

alternative/alternate, 216

analogies
  in informative speeches, **22b(4):**115–116
  language to illuminate, **24d(2):**128–129
  reasoning by, **21e:**108–109

anticlimax arrangement of arguments, **23c(2):**123

antithesis, **29d(2):**158

APA style, **16d:**82–83, 211–213

appeals. *See* emotional appeals

appearance, **35a:**190

appropriate language, **29c:**155–156

arguments. *See* reasoning

articulation problems, **34d(2):**188

assonance, **29d(2):**158

attention, getting and keeping
  audience involvement, **30b:**161
  energy level and, **30a(5):**160–161
  humor, **30a(4):**160
  motivated sequence and, **23c(1):**121–123
  neutral audiences and, **23b(2):**119
  with openings, **31a(2):**162–163
  self-interest of listeners and, **30a(2):**159–160
  storytelling, **30a(3):**160
  techniques for engaging, **30a:**159–161

attention getter, for sample persuasive speech, 204

attitudes, persuasive goals and, **23a:**117

audience analysis, **12:**58
  attitude toward topic, **11b(2):**52, **12c:**63–64, **13d:**68–69
  demographic characteristics, **12b:**59–63
  expectations, **12d:**64–65
  psychological closure for, **31b(2):**167–168
  sources of information for, **12a:**58–59
  topic appropriateness, **11a(2):**50

audiences. *See also* favorable audiences; neutral audiences; unfavorable audiences
  attitudes toward topic, **23b:**117–121
  as carriers of message, **23b(1):**118–119
  for ceremonial speeches, **9a:**42
  concern for, **26c(5):**137
  core values of, **25c(2):**132
  engaging, **30b:**161, **31a(2):**162–163
  establishing relationship with, **31a(3):**163
  fear of speaking and, **4a:**20
  identification with, ethical issues and, **3b:**18
  immediate or extended, **5c:**27–28
  for job interviews, **7a(1):**31
  question-and-answer period and, **37b:**196–197, **37c:**197–198
  respect for, 16

audio aids, **36b:**194. *See also* presentation aids

audiotaping practice sessions, **33a(2):**178

authorities. *See also* experts
  evaluating credibility of, **16c(1):**81
  testimony of, **16c:**81–82

averages, fallacy of, **16b(2):**79–80

averse/adverse, 216

awards
  acceptance of, **9b:**43
  presentations of, **9b:**42

B

balance
credibility and, **26c(4):**136
in ethical decisions, 18
of resources, **1d:**6–7
ballooning, **17b(2):**88
bandwagon approach, **3b:**18–19
bar graphs, **27a(3):**142, 143
behavior modification,
34d(5):189–190
bi/semi, 216
book catalogues, searching,
14b:69–70
brainstorming, **17a:**87
organizing ideas from,
17b:87–89
branching, **17b(2):**88
breathiness, in vocal delivery,
34d(1):188
business settings, **1a:**2–3
context of speech and, **7:**30–37
job interviews, **7a:**30–34
team presentations, **7b:**34–37

C

card stacking, ethical issues and,
3b:18
catchwords, **22b(1):**114–115
causal reasoning, **21d:**106–108
language to illuminate,
24d(2):128–129
organization of speech and,
24c:126
oversimplification of,
21d(2):107–108
testing validity of relationships,
21d(1):107
cause–effect patterns,
19a(3):93–94
transitional words for,
32b(1):173
central idea, **11d(1):**55. See also
main points
ceremonial settings, **9:**41–43
change
as persuasive goal, **23a:**117
unfavorable audiences and,
23b(3):120
charts, **10b:**46, **27a(3):**141, 142, 143
Chicago Manual of Style, The (CMS),
16d:82–83
Chicago style, **16d:**82–83
chronological patterns, **19a(1):**92
transitional words for,
32b(1):173
citations
density of, **32a(3):**171–172
guidelines for, 211–213
for List of References,
16d:82–83
notecards for, **16e:**83–84
record keeping, **16d:**82–83
during speech, **16f:**84–85
speech notes for,
33b(1):179–180
for supporting materials,
32a(2):171
civic settings, **8:**37–38
debates, **8b:**39–40
group formats, **8a:**38–39
claims. *See also* causal reasoning
linking evidence to, **21a(1):**102,
24d:126–128
clarification
language use for, **29b:**153–155
for neutral audiences,
23b(2):119
statistical evidence for,
16b(3):80–81
classroom participation, **1a:**2
climax arrangement of arguments,
23c(2):123
clinchers, ending with,
31b(3):168–169
sample, 206
clip art, **27c(3):**145–147
clustering, **17b(2):**88
cognitive restructuring technique,
4d(2):22
coincidental/ironic, 217
collaborative planning and preparation, **10c:**48
commitment, calling for,
23b(1):118
common ground, unfavorable
audiences and,
23b(3):120
communication. *See also* fear of
speaking
joint creation of, **1c(2):**4–5
meaning-centered, **1c:**4–5
communities, existing, **5c:**27
comparison, in causal reasoning,
21d(1):107
competence, conscious and unconscious, **1e:**7
composure, for impromptu speaking, **28b(1):**150
concept mapping, **17b(2):**88, 89
conceptual context, **31a(4):**165
concern, sense of, **26c(5):**137
conclusions, **31b:**167
clinchers for, **31b(3):**168–169
linking evidence to, **21a(1):**102
logical closure, **31b(1):**167
pitfalls, **31c:**169–170

conclusions (*cont.*)
  psychological closure,
    31b(2):167–168
  in team presentations,
    7b(2):35–36
concrete language, **29b(2):**154
concurrent presence and absence,
  21d(1):107
confidence, projecting, **31a(1):**162
conscious competence or incompetence, **1e:**7
consciousness, skill-learning stages
  of, **1e:**7
consistency
  in outline symbols, **20a(1):**95
  in presentation software slides,
    27c(2):145
consultants, public speaking,
  2c:12–13, **34d(5):**189
contact person
  advance information for,
    26b:135
  audience analysis by, **12a:**59
context
  ethics and, **3a(2):**16
  meaning and, **1c(2):**4
context of speech. *See also* topic of
    speech
  civic and political, **8:**37–40
  connecting conclusion to,
    31b(1):167
  dimensions of, **5c:**26–28
  educational, **6:**28–30
  establishing, **31a(4):**164
  fundamentals, **5a:**24–25
  relevant formats for, **5b:**25
  social and ceremonial, **9:**41–43
  workplace, **7:**30–37
contingent meaning, **1c(2):**4–5
conversation skills
  citations and, **16f:**85
  drawing on, **1d(1):**5, **1d(4):**6–7
  reading from manuscript and,
    28c(2):151
coordinate points, **18d:**91
Corel Presentations (WordPerfect
    Office), **27a(2):**139
core values, of audience,
  25c(2):132
cost–benefit (or reward) analysis,
  21b(2):104, **24a:**124–125
counterarguments, dealing with,
  23c(3):123
counterfactual statements,
  3b(2):17
coworkers, as information sources,
  15a(1):75
creativity process, four phases of,
  10a:45

credentials, presenting,
  26c(1):135–136
credibility, **26:**134
  building prior to speech,
    26b:135
  delivery and, **26d:**137
  image assessment, **26a:**134
  neutral audiences and,
    23b(2):119
  speech content and,
    26c:135–137
  unfavorable audiences and,
    23b(3):121
cross references, **7b(3):**36
culture, values and, **25c(1):**131–132

D

dangling/misplaced modifiers, 218
databases, searches of, **14b:**70
data collection for audience analysis, **12a:**58
daydreaming, listening and,
  2e(1):14
deadlines, for speech planning,
  10b(3):47–48
debates. *See also* group presentations
  guidelines for, **8b:**39–40
  participation in, **8a(1):**38–39
debriefing, after team presentations, **7b(5):**37
declarative sentences, **11d(1):**55,
  20b:96–97
deductive reasoning, **21c:**104–106
  absolute statements and,
    21c(1):105
  language to illuminate,
    24d(2):128–129
  organization of speech and,
    24b:125–126
definitions
  in introduction, **31a(4):**165–166
  personal lexicon of, **13c:**68
delivery. *See also* nonverbal behaviors; physical delivery;
    vocal delivery
  credibility and, **26d:**137
  extemporaneous mode for,
    28a:149
  impromptu mode for,
    28b:149–150
  from manuscript, **28c:**150–152
  of memorized manuscripts,
    28d:152
  speech notes and, **33b(2):**180
  use of multiple modes for,
    22b(5):116
demographics, audience,
  12b:59–63

denasality, in vocal delivery, **34d(1):**188

descriptors, searches using, **14b:**70

details, appropriate number for examples, **16a:**78–79

diagrams, **27a(3):**140–142

dialogic situations, **5c:**26

dictionaries, research searches of, **14b:**70

discourse communities, meaning negotiated by, **1c(2):**5

disengaging, listening and, **2e(1):**14

disinterested/uninterested, 216

distractions
  presentation aids as, **36f:**195
  preventing and managing, **2a(1):**10

domain for speech, **5c:**26

doodling, listening and, **2e(1):**14

E

economy of language, **29b(3):**154–155

educational settings, **6:**28
  oral assignments for skill development, **6a:**28
  oral assignments for specific professional contexts, **6b:**29
  oral assignments to facilitate learning, **6c:**29–30

educators, as information sources, **15a(2):**75

effect/affect, 216

e.g./i.e., 217

electronic information
  record keeping, **16e(1):**83
  retrieval, **14c:**70–74

emotional appeals
  audience motivation and, **25c(3):**133, **31a(3):**164
  as closures, **31b(1):**168
  excessive or inappropriate use of, **25d:**133
  to favorable audiences, **23b(1):**117–118
  impact of, **25a:**130
  listener's needs and, **25b:**130–131
  listener's values and, **25c:**131–133
  to neutral audiences, **23b(2):**119

emphasis cues, **22b(2):**115

employment interviews. *See* job interviews

encyclopedias, research searches of, **14b:**70

energy level of speech, **30a(5):**160–161

enumeration, **22b(1):**114

enunciation, **34a(3):**184–185

equal relationships, transition words for, **32b(1):**173

ethical issues
  awareness of, **3a:**15–16
  context of, **3a(2):**16
  human choices and, **3a(1):**15
  integrity of ideas and, **3b:**16–18
  lies *versus* truthful statements, **3b(2):**17
  in listening, **2e(3):**14
  oversimplification, **3b(3):**17–18
  plagiarism, **3b(1):**16–17
  speaking and, 15

ethnic characteristics of audience, **12b(3):**62–63

eulogies, **9b:**42–43

evidence
  arrangement of, **23c(2):**123
  linking to claims, **21a(1):**102, **24d:**126–128
  for neutral audiences, **23b(2):**119
  statistical, **16b:**79–80
  unfavorable audiences and, **23b(3):**120–121

evocative speeches, **11c(1):**53

examples
  appropriate detail for, **16a:**78–79
  factual, **16a(1):**77–78
  hypothetical, **16a(2):**78
  in informative speeches, **22b(3):**115
  use of, **16a:**77–79, **30a(1):**159

expectations, audience, **12d:**64–65

experience, personal, **11a(1):**49

expertise, personal, **11a(1):**49

experts, **15a(2):**75. *See also* authorities

explanation principles, informative speeches and, **22b:**114–116

extemporaneous speeches, **28a:**149
  manuscript reading and, **28c:**151, **28d:**152

eye contact, **35f:**192–193
  for job interviews, **7b:**34
  presentation aids and, **36c:**194, **36e:**194–195
  for reading from manuscript, **28c:**151

F

fact, propositions of, **11d(3):** 56–57

factual examples, **16a(1):**77–78

fallacies
  in reasoning, **21f:**109–111
  statistical, **16b(2):**79–80
false dichotomies, **21f(4):**111
familiar to unfamiliar subjects, in informative speeches, **22a(4):**114
family members, as information sources, **15a(1):**75
favorable audiences, **12c:**64, **23b(1):**117–119
fear of speaking
  analysis of, **4a(2):**19–20
  as normal response, **4a(1):**19
  perspective for, **4a:**19–20
  positive self-suggestion techniques, **4d:**21–22
  preparation, practice and, **4b:**20–21
  professional assistance for, **4e:**22
  reconceptualizing audience role and, **4a:**20
  relaxation techniques, **4c:**21
  "speaker's" block and, **33c:**182
feedback
  constructive, **2c:**12–13
  in practice sessions, **33a(2):**176–178
  for team presentations, **7b(5):**37
fewer/less, 217
figurative analogies, literal analogies *versus,* **21e:**109
flaunt/flout, 217
flowcharts, **27a(3):**143
focus groups, **12a:**59
formality of language, **29c(1):**155
formality of speech setting, **5c:**26
format of speech, speech context and, **5b:**25
forums, **8a(1):**38–39. *See also* group presentations
framework for speech, **22a(2):**113, **31a(4):**165, 166. *See also* context
Freelance Graphics (Lotus SmartSuite), **27a(2):**139
free text search, **14b:**70
fresh language, **29d(3):**158
full-sentence outlines, **20b:**96–100
  topic outlines *versus,* **20b:**99–100

G
Gantt charts, **10b:**46
gender
  audience composition and, **12b(2):**61–62
  inclusive language issues and, **29c(4):**156
generalizations
  audience demographics and, **12b:**60
  hasty, **21f(5):**111
generations, in audience, **12b(1):**60–61
gestures, hand, **35e:**192
glittering generalities approach, **3b:**18
grammar and usage problems, 218–219
graphs, **27a(3):**140–142, 143
grids/tables, **27a(3):**143
grooming, **35a:**190
group presentations, **7b:**34–37, **8a(1):**38–39

H
hand gestures, **35e:**192
hierarchy of needs (Maslow's), **25b:**130–131
historical context, **31a(4):**165
hoarseness, **34d(1):**187
honors, presentations of, **9b:**42
human resources, for research, **15a:**74–75
humor, use of
  attention-getting and, **30a(4):**160
  unfavorable audiences and, **23b(3):**121
hyperbole, **29d(2):**157
hypothetical examples, **16a(2):**78

I
ideas for topics
  assembling, **17a:**87
  concept mapping, **17b(2):**88, 89
  manipulation of, **17b(3):**88–89
  narrowing topic and, **11b:**51–52
  outlines of, **17b(1):**87–88
  thesis statement and, **18a:**89–90
i.e./e.g., 217
illumination phase, creativity and, **10a:**45
image assessment, **26a:**134, **26b:**135
imagery, **29d(1):**157
impact
  emotional, **25a:**130
  phrasing for, **20c:**101
imply/infer, 216–217
impromptu speeches, **28b:**149–150
inclusive language, **29c(4):**156

incubation phase, planning time for, **10a:**45

independent agencies, as information sources, **15a(2):**75

inductive reasoning, **21b:**103–104, **24a:**124–125, **24d(2):**128

inference, audience analysis using intelligent, **12a:**59

infer/imply, 216–217

inflection pattern, repetitious, **34d(4):**189

informality of speech setting, **5c:**26

information, communication *versus* transmission of, **1c(1):**4

information gathering
    for audience analysis, **12a:**58–59
    electronic, **14c:**70–74
    library research for, **14a:**69, **14b:**69–70
    listening to optimize learning in, **2d:**13–14

information overload, **22a(1):**113

informative speeches, **11c(1):**53
    explanation principles and, **22b:**114–116
    listener information processing and, **22a:**113–114
    sample outline for, 206–209
    thesis statements for, **11d(2):**55

InfoTrac College Edition, search using, **14c:**70–71

Internet
    effective searching, **14c(1):**72
    evaluation of sources on, **14c(2):**73–74
    information gathering using, **14c:**70–72
    useful reference sites, **14c(1):**73

interruptions. *See* distractions

interviews
    for audience analysis, **12a:**59
    employment/job, **1a:**2–3, **7a:**30–34
    follow-up tasks, **15b(2):**76–77
    preparation for, **15b(1):**76
    recording information from, **16e(2):**83–84
    for research, **15a:**74–75
    techniques for, **2d:**13–14, **15b(2):**76

introductions, **31:**161
    advance information for, **26b:**135
    attention-getting openings, **31a(2):**162–163
    confidence and preparedness during, **31a(1):**162
    length of, **31a(5):**166–167
    for listener orientation, **31a:**162–167
    logical orientation, **31a(4):**164–166
    pitfalls, **31c:**169–170
    psychological orientation, **31a(3):**163–164
    for team presentations, **7b(2):**35

ironic/coincidental, 217

J

jargon, **29c(2):**155–156

job interviews, **1a:**2–3
    answering questions, **7a(3):**31
    audience analysis, **7a(1):**31
    delivery skills, **7a(5):**34
    group, **7a:**30–34
    opening statements, **7a(2):**31
    problem–solution–result statements, **7a(4):**31–33

K

Keynote (Apple presentation software), **27a(2):**139

keywords or key phrases, **33b(1):**179–180

L

language. *See also* style
    appropriateness of, **29c:**155–156
    clarity in, **29b:**153–155
    formality of, **29c(1):**155
    fresh, **29d(3):**158
    imagery in, **29d(1):**157
    inclusive, **29c(4):**156
    jargon, **29c(2):**155–156
    oral *versus* written, **29a:**153
    respectful, **29c(4):**156
    rhythm of, **29d(4):**158–159
    slang, **29c(2):**155–156
    substandard, **29c(3):**156
    variation in, **29d:**156–159

leadership roles, **1a:**2–3

less/fewer, 217

librarians, **14a:**69

Librarian's Index to the Internet, **14(1):**72

library research, **14a:**69, **14b:**69–70

lies *versus* truthful statements, **3b(2):**17

line graphs, **27a(3):**142, 143

listening
    as audience member, **2b:**11–12
    curious and critical, **2b:**12–13
    in information gathering, **2d:**13–14

listening (*cont.*)
  pitfalls, **2d:**14
  preparation for, **2a:**10–11
  purpose of, **2a(3):**11
  questions following, **2c(5):**12
  speaking, relationship with, **2:**10
lists of important words or phrases, **27a(3):**140–142
literal analogies, figurative analogies *versus,* **21e:**109
logical closures, **31b(1):**167, 206
logical relationships
  deductive reasoning and, **21c:**104–105
  indentation in outlines and, **20a(2):**95–96
  introductory orientation to, **31a(4):**164–166
  language to illuminate, **24d(2):**128–129
  organizing points to show, **24d(1):**126–128
  in sample persuasive speech, 204–206
  transitions and, **32b(1):**172–174

M
main points
  arranging, **19a:**92–94
  in debates, **8b(4):**40
  mutually exclusive, **18b:**90–91
  narrowing topic and, **11b(2):**52
  number of, **18c:**91
  subpoint forecasting and, **20c:**100–101
  in team presentations, **7b(2):**35
  thesis statements and, **18a:**89–90
major premise, **21c:**105
mannerisms, distracting, **35b:**191
manuscript, reading from, **28c:**150–152
maps, annotated, **27a(3):**140–141
Maslow's hierarchy of needs, **25b:**130–131
meaning, construction of
  by audience, **12b(3):**63
  statistical evidence for, **16b(3):**80–81
meaning-centered communication, **1c:**4–5
memorable phrases, **22b(1):**114–115, **27a(3):**140–141
memorial addresses, **9b:**42–43
memorized speeches, **28d:**152
metaphors, **29d(2):**157
mindmapping, **17b(2):**88

minor premise, **21c(2):**106, **21c:**105
misconceptions about public speaking, **1f:**8
mispronounced words. *See also* pronunciation
  identification of, **34c(1):**186
MLA Handbook for Writers of Research Papers, **16d:**82–83, 211–213
MLA style, **16d:**82–83, 211–213
modifiers, dangling/misplaced, 218
monologic situations, **5c:**26
Monroe, Alan, **23c(1):**121
motivated sequence, **23c(1):**121–123
motivation. *See* emotional appeals
movements during speeches, **35d:**191

N
name-calling approach, **3b:**18
narrowing a topic, **11b(1):**51–52
nasality, in vocal delivery, **34d(1):**188
National Communication Association, code of ethics, 15
needs hierarchy (Maslow's), **25b:**130–131
negotiated meaning, **1c(2):**5
neutral audiences, **12c:**64, **23b(2):**119
90/10 principle, **2c:**13
nonnative English speakers, **34a(4):**185
  respect for, **2c(1):**12
nonplussed/nonchalant, 216
nonstandard language, **29c(3):**156
nonverbal behaviors
  in group presentations, **8a(3):**39
  listening and, **2e(6):**14
notecards
  grouping, **16e(3):**84
  research from interviews and surveys, **16e(2):**83–84
  research from print and electronic sources, **16e(1):**83
  for speech notes, **33b(2):**179–180
notes, speech, **33b:**179–181
note-taking, listening and, **2d:**14

O
objectivity, **1d(2):**5–6, **26c(4):**136
observation
  for audience analysis, **12a:**58
  inductive reasoning and, **21b:**103–104
one-time assemblies, **5c:**27

opening statements
    for debates, **8b(3):**40
    for job interviews, **7a(2):**31
opinions. *See also* core values; per-
        suasive speeches
    personal, **11a(1):**50
opposing arguments
    consideration of, **8b(1):**40
    dealing with, **23c(3):**123
opposition, transition words for,
        32b(1):173
oral planning and preparation,
        10c:48, **33c:**182
oral style. *See also* conversation
        skills
    reading from manuscript and,
        28c(1):150–152
    written style *versus*, **29a:**153
organization of speech. *See also*
        main points; outlines; team
        presentations
    assembling ideas and informa-
        tion, **17a:**87
    audience awareness of,
        31a(4):166
    concept mapping, **17b(2):**88,
        89
    counterarguments, placement
        of, **23c(3):**123
    credibility and, **26c(3):**136
    for debates, **8b(2):**40
    flowchart, 174
    for impromptu speaking,
        28b(3):150
    for informative speeches,
        22a(2):113, **22b:**114–115
    listening for, **2c(3):**12
    manipulation of movable com-
        ponents, **17b(3):**88–89
    motivated sequence,
        23c(1):121–123
    notecard groups, **16e(3):**84
    patterns for, **19a:**92–94
    for persuasive speeches,
        23c:121–123
    using causal reasoning, **24c:**126
    using deductive reasoning,
        24b:125–126
    using inductive reasoning,
        24a:124–125
    working outline, **17b(1):**87–88
    writing as aid to, **1d(2):**5–6
orientation
    logical, **31a(4):**164–166, 204
    psychological, **31a(3):**163–164
outlines, **20:**95–101
    conventional format for,
        20a:95–96
    full-sentence, **20b:**96–100

practice sessions and,
        33a(1):176
    subpoint forecasting using,
        20c:100–101
    for team presentations,
        7b(2):34–36
    of topics, **17b(1):**87–88
overload, information, **22a(1):**113
oversimplification. *See also* simple
        to complex; simplicity
    causal reasoning and,
        21d(2):107–108
    ethical issues and, **3b(3):**17–18

P

panels, **8a(1):**38–39. *See also* group
        presentations
parallelism, in team presentations,
        7b(3):36
paraphrasing, listening and, **2d:**13
partially truthful statements,
        3b(2):17
part-to-whole relationship, transi-
        tion words for, **32b(1):**173
past–present–future pattern,
        19a(1):92
patterns
    deductive reasoning and,
        21c:104–106
    inductive reasoning and,
        21b(1):103–104
    linking evidence to claims,
        21a(2):102–103
    organizational, **19a:**92–94
    for subpoints, **19b:**94
pauses
    discrete visual aids and,
        36d:194
    vocalized, **34d(3):**188
performance skills, drawing on,
        1d(3):6, **1d(4):**6–7
periodical indexes, searches of,
        14b:70
personal attacks, **21f(1):**110
personification, **29d(2):**157
persuasive speeches, **11c(1):**53
    for favorable audiences,
        23b(1):117–119
    goals clarification for,
        23a:116–117
    for neutral audiences,
        23b(2):119
    opposing arguments and,
        23c(3):123
    organization of, **23c:**121–123
    sample, 199–204
    sample outline for, 205–206
    strongest points for, **23c(3):**123
    thesis statements for, **11d(2):**55

persuasive speeches (*cont.*)
for unfavorable audiences, **23b(3):**120–121
PERT systems, **10b:**46
phrases
common, **7b(3):**36
memorable, **22b(1):**114
physical delivery, **35:**190. *See also* eye contact
appearance, **35a:**190
eye contact, **35f:**192–193
hand gestures, **35e:**192
mannerisms, **35b:**191
movements during speech, **35d:**191
performance qualities, **1d(3):**6
posture, **35c:**191
smile, use of, **35f:**193
pictograms, **27a(3):**143
pictorial symbols, **27a(3):**140–142
pictures, **27a(3):**140
pie charts (graphs), **27a(3):**141, 142, 143
pitfalls. *See also* fallacies
introductions and conclusions, **31c:**169–170
listening, **2d:**14
plagiarism, **3b(1):**16–17
planning. *See also* outlines; practice; preparation
audience analysis, **12:**58–65
conclusions, **31b:**167
for impromptu speaking, **28b(4):**150
oral and collaborative, **10c:**48
preparation timetable, **10:**45–48
research strategy, **13:**67–69
response or rebuttal, listening and, **2e(5):**14
topic selection and analysis, **11:**49–58
points in a speech. *See also* organization of speech; outlines
arranging main points, **19a:**92–94
coordinate and subordinate, **18d:**91
mutually exclusive, **18b:**90–91
number of main points, **18c:**91
for persuasive speeches, **23c(2):**123
presentation of, **24:**124–129
thesis statement and, **18a:**89–90
policy, propositions of, **11d(3):**56, 57
political settings, **8:**37–38
debates, **8b:**39–40
group formats, **8a:**38–39

posture, **35c:**191
power
in speaker, **3b(2):**17
in speaker or listeners, **5c:**27
PowerPoint (Microsoft), **27a(2):**139, **33b(2):**180, **36f:**195
practice
early sessions, **33a(1):**176
fear of speaking and, **4b:**20–21
feedback and, **33a(2):**176–178
final sessions, **33a(3):**178–179
middle sessions, **33a(2):**176–178
with presentation aids, **36a:**193, **36f:**195
stages of, **33a:**175–179
taping yourself, **33a(2):**178
for team presentations, **7b(4):**37
time limit adjustments, **33c:**181–182
timetables for, **33a:**175–177
precision in language, **29b(1):**154
premature summaries, **32b(2):**175
premises. *See* deductive reasoning
preparation. *See also* planning; practice
for debates, **8b(3):**40
fear of speaking and, **4b:**20–21
for interviews, **15b(1):**76
for manuscript delivery, **28c(1):**151
oral and collaborative, **10c:**48
of presentation aids, **36b:**194, **36f:**195
projection during introductions of, **31a(1):**162
for question-and-answer period, **37a:**196
of speech notes, **33b:**179–181
for team presentations, **7b(1):**34, **8a(2):**39
time allotted for creativity and, **10a:**45
prescriptions for speeches, **1f:**8
presentation aids, **27:**137
appropriate use of, **27a(1):**138–139
considerations in using, **27a:**137–139
design and construction of, **27b:**142–144
as distractions, **36f:**195
eye contact and, **36c:**194
form and technology for, **27a(2):**139–140
practice with, **36a:**193
preparation of, **36b:**194, **36f:**195

simplicity and clarity of,
27b(2):143
size of, **27b(1):**142–144
speaker dominated by,
36e:194–195
speaking while using, **36d:**194
presentation software,
27a(2):139–140,
27c:145–147
as possible distraction,
36e:194–195
preparation of, **36b:**194
speech notes preparation in,
33b(2):180–181
prevarications, **3b(2):**17
previews, internal, **32b(2):**174–175
primacy principle, **23c(2):**123
print sources
locating, **14b:**69–70
record keeping, **16e(1):**83
priorities for speech planning,
10b(2):46
private spheres, speaking in, **5c:**26
probability statements
demographic generalizations,
12b:60
inductive reasoning and,
21b(2):104
problem–solution pattern,
19a(3):94
problem–solution–result (PSR)
statements, **7a(4):**31–33
professionalism, in debates,
8b(6):40
professional settings, **1a:**2–3, **6b:**29
pronouns
misuse of reflexive, 218
misuse of subjective case,
218–219
pronunciation
common problems in, 215
of unfamiliar words,
34c:186–187
propaganda, **3b:**18–19
propositions of fact, value, or policy,
11d(3):56–57
ProPresentations (Harvard Graphics), **27a(2):**139
PSR statements, **7a(4):**31–33
psychological closure,
31b(2):167–168
sample, 206
psychological orientation,
31a(3):163–164, 204
*Publication Manual of the American
Psychological Association,*
16d:82–83, 211–213
public officials, as information
sources, **15a(2):**75

public speaking
communicative resources and,
1d:5–7
consciousness in skill-learning
and, **1e:**7
five-step preparation for,
1g:9–10
meaning-centered communication and, **1c:**4–5
misconceptions, **1f:**8
oral assignments to develop
skills for, **6a:**28
reasons for, **1a:**2–3
role of, **1b:**3
understanding, **1:**2–10
public spheres, speaking in, **1a:**2–3,
5c:26
purpose of listening, **2a(3):**11
purpose of speech
audience outcomes desired,
11c(3):53–54
general, **11c(1):**52–53
in persuasion, **23a:**116–117
specific, **11c(2):**53
pyramidal arrangement of arguments, **23c(2):**123

Q
question-and-answer period
managing self-indulgent questioners, **37c:**197–198
preparation for, **37a:**196
for team presentations,
7b(2):36
technique for, **37b:**196–197
questions
for feedback, **2c(5):**12,
33a(2):177–178
follow-up, for clarification,
2d:13–14
in job interviews, **7a(3):**31
in research process, **13d:**68
thesis statements as list of,
11d(2):55–56
quotations
editing, **16c(2):**82
finding, **16c:**82

R
race
audience composition and,
12b(3):62–63
inclusive language issues and,
29c(4):156
rate of speaking, **34a(2):**184
reasoning, **21:**101
by analogy, **21e:**108–109
causal, **21d:**106–108
credibility and, **26c(2):**136

reasoning (*cont.*)
  deductive, **21c:**104–106
  fallacies in, **21f:**109–111
  inductive, **21b:**103–104
  linking evidence to conclusions,
    21a:101–103
  for neutral audiences,
    23b(2):119
  presentation of, **24:**124–129
  propaganda *versus*, **3b:**18–19
  testing validity, as listener,
    2c(4):11–12
recency principle, **23c(2):**123
record keeping, of sources,
    16d:82–83
  discrete units for, **16e:**83–84
redundancy, in informative
    speeches, **22b(6):**116
references. *See also* citations
  List of, **16d:**82–83
refinement phase, in creativity,
    10a:45
reflexive pronouns, misuse of, 218
refutation techniques, **8b(4):**40
rejecting message, listening and,
    2e(4):14
relaxation techniques, **4c:**21
repetition
  inflection pattern, **34d(4):**189
  in informative speeches,
    22b(6):116
  of meaningless sounds or
    phrases, **34d(3):**188
  as stylistic device, **29d(2):**157
reproductions, as visual aids,
    27a(3):140
research
  effective Internet searching,
    14c(1):72
  electronic information retrieval,
    14c:70–74
  evaluation of Internet sources,
    14c(2):73–74
  general to specific, **13b:**67–68
  interviews for, **15a:**74–75
  library, **14a:**69, **14b:**69–70
  on personal interests, **11a(1):**50
  questions to direct, **13d:**68–69
  record keeping of, **16e:**83–84
  strategy for, **13:**67–69
  terminology lexicon creation
    and, **13c:**68
  time allotted for, **13a:**67
resources, communicative, **1d:**5–7
respect
  for integrity of ideas,
    3b:16–18
  for speakers, **2e(4):**14
respectful language, **29c(4):**156

reticence. *See* fear of speaking
rhythm of language,
    29d(4):158–159
rules of speaking. *See also* grammar
    and usage problems; pro-
    nunciation
  highly prescribed *versus* more
    open, **5c:**26–27

S

samples
  outline for informative speech,
    206–209
  outline for persuasive speech,
    205–206
  persuasive speech, 199–204
schedule. *See* timetables
self-improvement, **34d(5):**189
self-respect, 16
semantic fallacy, **21f(3):**110
semi/bi, 216
sequence
  confusing with cause,
    21f(6):111
  motivated, **23c(1):**121–123
sex of audience, **12b(2):**61–62
shyness. *See* fear of speaking
signposts, **22b(1):**114
similes, **29d(2):**157
simple to complex subjects, in in-
    formative speeches,
    22a(3):113
simplicity. *See also* oversimplifica-
    tion
  in presentation aids, **27b(2):**143
  in presentation software slides,
    27c(1):145
skill learning, stages of, **1e:**7
slang, **29c(2):**155–156
slides, **27c(1):**145, **27c(3):**145–147,
    36e:194–195
slippery slope fallacy, **21f(2):**110
slogans, **22b(1):**114–115,
    27a(3):140–141
smile, use of, **35f:**193
snob appeal approach, **3b:**19
social meaning of communication,
    1c(2):4
social settings, **1a:**2–3, **9:**41–43
  common guidelines for,
    9b:42–43
  identify needs of people in-
    volved, **9a:**42
sounds, meaningless, **34d(3):**188
sources. *See* authorities; citations;
    experts
spatial patterns, **19a(2):**92–93
speakers
  point of view of, **2c(2):**12